TRUMP

How to Get Rich

and

Think Like a Billionaire

TRUMP

How to Get Rich

and

Think Like a Billionaire

Business wisdom from
the star of *The Apprentice*

Donald J. Trump

with Meredith McIver

RANDOM HOUSE
NEW YORK

To my parents,
Mary and Fred Trump

The Mother and Father of All Advice

*"Know everything you can
about what you're doing."*
—MY FATHER, FRED TRUMP

"Trust in God and be true to yourself."
—MY MOTHER, MARY TRUMP

*"When I look back, that was great advice, concise and wise at
once. I didn't really get it at first, but because it sounded good,
I stuck to it. Later I realized how comprehensive this is—how to
keep your bases covered while thinking about the big picture. It's
good advice no matter what your business or lifestyle."*
—DJT

*"In business everyone is out to grab, to fight,
to win. Either you are the under or the over dog.
It is up to you to be on top."*
—ALICE FOOTE MACDOUGALL

*"Being good in business is the most fascinating kind of art. . . .
Making money is art and working is art and
good business is the best art."*
—ANDY WARHOL

Contents

Book I: How to Get Rich

Introduction
Five Billion Reasons Why You Should Read This Book
3

PART I
The Donald J. Trump School of Business and Management
5

PART II
Your Personal Apprenticeship (Career Advice from The Donald)
41

PART III
Money, Money, Money, Money
101

PART IV
The Secrets of Negotiation
117

PART V
The Trump Lifestyle
153

PART VI
Inside *The Apprentice*
215

Acknowledgments
233
Appendix
235

Book II: Think Like a Billionaire

Introduction
Thinking Like a Billionaire
257

PART I
Real Estate
269

PART II
Money
313

PART III
The Business of Life
345

PART IV
Slices of the Billionaire's Life
393

PART V
Inside *The Apprentice*
461

Acknowledgments
499

TRUMP

How to Get Rich

Introduction
Five Billion Reasons Why
You Should Read This Book

A lot has happened to us all since 1987. That's the year *The Art of the Deal* was published and became the bestselling business book of the decade, with over three million copies in print.

(Business Rule #1: If you don't tell people about your success, they probably won't know about it.)

A few months ago, I picked up *The Art of the Deal*, skimmed a bit, and then read the first and last paragraphs. I realized that after seventeen years they still rang true. I could have written these words yesterday:

First paragraph: *I don't do it for the money. I've got enough, much more than I'll ever need. I do it to do it. Deals are my art form. Other people paint beautifully on canvas or write wonderful poetry. I like making deals, preferably big deals. That's how I get my kicks.*

Last paragraph: *Don't get me wrong. I also plan to keep making deals, big deals, and right around the clock.*

It's now 2004, I'm still making deals around the clock, and I still don't do it for the money.

I don't think you should do it for the money, either. Money is not an end in itself, but it's sometimes the most effective way to help us realize our dreams. So if you've got big dreams and you're looking for a way to make them happen, this book is for you.

How to Get Rich. That's what I decided to call it, because whenever I meet people, that's usually what they want to know from me. You ask a baker how he makes bread. You ask a billionaire how he makes money.

Sure, there have been countless how-to-get-rich books written by millionaires. Billionaire authors are harder to find. Billionaire authors with interests in real estate, gaming, sports, and entertainment are rarer still.

And billionaire authors with their own Manhattan skyscrapers and hit prime-time TV series are the rarest of all. I'm pretty sure I'm the only one, though Oprah could give me a run for the money if she ever decides to write another book and get into real estate.

Business Rule #2: Keep it short, fast, and direct. The following pages will be straightforward and succinct, but don't let the brevity of these passages prevent you from savoring the profundity of the advice you are about to receive. These stories and words of wisdom have been distilled from almost thirty years at the top.

So here it comes: The Scoop from The Donald. After you make your first billion, don't forget to send me a thank-you note. You know the address.

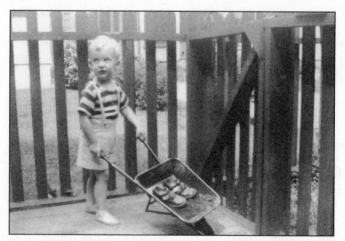

Business Rule #3: Begin working at a young age. I did.

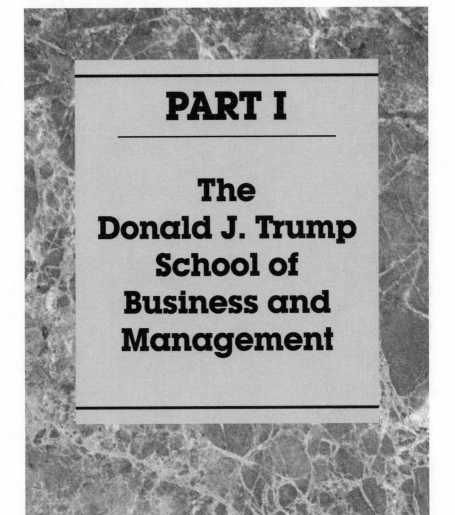

PART I

The Donald J. Trump School of Business and Management

In The Art of the Deal, *I mentioned my nemesis and mentor at New York Military Academy, Theodore Dobias, here on my left. Major General James Lyle is on my right.*

Be a General

I am the chairman and president of The Trump Organization. I like saying that because it means a great deal to me. There are almost twenty thousand members of this organization at this point. I did a print ad once in which I declared, "I only work with the best." That statement still stands.

More and more, I see that running a business is like being a general. Calling the shots carries a great deal of responsibility, not only for yourself, but for your troops. Your employees' lives, to a large extent, are dependent on you and your decisions. Bad strategy can end up affecting a lot of people. This is where being a leader takes on a new dimension. Every decision you make is an important one, whether there are twenty thousand people working for you or just one.

If you are careful when finding employees, management becomes a lot easier. I rely on a few key people to keep me informed. They know I trust them, and they do their best to keep that trust intact.

For example, when I need to know something about my casinos and hotels in Atlantic City, I know I can call up Mark Brown, my CEO, and get a fast and informed answer. If I call Laura Cordovano over at

Trump Park Avenue and ask about sales, she'll give it to me exactly as it is. If I call Allen Weisselberg, my CFO, he'll tell me what I need to know in twenty words or less. My senior counsel and *Apprentice* adviser, George Ross, can do it in ten words or less. Find people who suit your business style and you'll have fewer problems to deal with as time goes on.

Good people equals good management and good management equals good people. They have to work together or they won't work together for very long. I've seen good management get by with mediocre people, and I've also seen excellent people get stuck in the mires of bad management. The good managers will eventually leave, followed by the good workers, and you will be left with a team that gets along because they're all mediocre. Save yourself time by getting the best people you can. Sometimes this can mean choosing attitude over experience and credentials. Use your creativity to come up with a good mix.

Creative people rarely need to be motivated—they have their own inner drive that refuses to be bored. They refuse to be complacent. They live on the edge, which is precisely what is needed to be successful and remain successful.

One of my former employees was in charge of a new project. He had done a thorough and acceptable job, but I felt that something was missing. It wasn't *fantastic*, which, knowing his capabilities, it should have been. I decided to challenge his creative ego by mentioning that it was fine but seemed to lack inspiration. I politely asked him whether he was genuinely interested in the project and suggested that perhaps that might be the problem.

Well, the guy went ballistic on me. He was deeply insulted.

And, as you can probably guess, the revision he turned in was terrific. The difference between the first draft and the final version was incredible. I didn't slam the guy because he was usually demanding of himself and had never let me down. But I had to give him a jolt.

Generals motivate their soldiers; they inspire them when it is necessary. They do the same for their highest-ranking officers. We all need a boost now and then. Learn how to tailor your method to the personalities you are managing.

Keep the big picture in mind while attending to the daily details. This can seem like a balancing act, but it is absolutely necessary for success in running a company.

Stay Focused

In the 1980s, I was riding high. After learning the essentials of real estate development from my father, Fred, a builder in Queens and Brooklyn, I'd become a major player in Manhattan, developing Trump Tower, the Grand Hyatt Hotel, and many other top-tier properties. I had a yacht, a plane, a bestselling book.

One magazine headline said, EVERYTHING HE TOUCHES TURNS TO GOLD, and I believed it. I'd never known adversity. I went straight from Wharton to wealth. Even in down markets, I bought properties inexpensively and made a lot of money. I began to think it was easy.

In the late eighties, I lost focus. I'd fly off to Europe to attend fashion shows, and I wasn't looking at the clothing. My lack of attention was killing my business.

Then, the real estate market crashed. I owed billions upon billions of dollars—$9.2 billion, to be exact. That's nine billion, two hundred million dollars. I've told this story many times before, but it bears repeating: In the midst of the crash, I passed a beggar on the street and realized he was worth $9.2 billion more than I was. I saw a lot of my friends go bankrupt, never to be heard from again.

The media had me for lunch. *Forbes, BusinessWeek, Fortune, The Wall Street Journal, The New York Times*—they all published major stories about my crisis, and a lot of people seemed to be happy about it.

I'll never forget the worst moment. It was 3 A.M. Citibank phoned me at my home in Trump Tower. They wanted me to come over to their office immediately to negotiate new terms with some foreign banks—three of the ninety-nine banks to whom I owed billions.

It's tough when you have to tell a banker that you can't pay interest. They tend not to like those words. An ally at Citibank suggested that the best way for me to handle this difficult situation was to call the banks myself, and that's exactly what they wanted me to do, at three o'clock on a cold January morning, in the freezing rain. There were no cabs, so I walked fifteen blocks to Citibank. By the time I got there, I was drenched.

That was the low point. There were thirty bankers sitting around a big table. I phoned one Japanese banker, then an Austrian banker, and then a third banker from a country I can no longer remember.

In *The Art of the Deal*, I had warned readers never to personally guarantee anything. Well, I hadn't followed my own advice. Of the $9.2 billion I owed, I'd personally guaranteed a billion dollars. I was a schmuck, but I was a lucky schmuck, and I wound up dealing with some understanding bankers who worked out a fair deal. After being the king of the eighties, I survived the early nineties, and by the mid-to-late nineties, I was thriving again.

But I learned my lesson. I work as hard today as I did when I was a young developer in the 1970s.

Don't make the mistake I did. Stay focused.

Maintain Your Momentum

William Levitt, the master builder of Levittown, taught me the true meaning of "momentum."

In the 1950s, he was the king. No detail was too small for his attention. He would personally collect stray nails and extra chips of wood from building sites to make sure his construction crews used all available materials.

He sold his company in 1956 to ITT for $100 million, which is equivalent to billions today. Then he made some terrible mistakes.

He retired.

He married the wrong woman.

He moved to the south of France and lived on the Riviera with his new boat and his new wife.

One day, ITT called. The executives in charge of the conglomerate had no aptitude for home building. They had bought huge tracts of land but didn't know how to get them zoned. So they sold it back to Levitt, who thought he'd gotten a great deal.

He went back into business. And he proceeded to go bankrupt.

I saw William Levitt at a cocktail party in 1994, two weeks before he died. He was standing by himself in a corner, looking defeated. I didn't know him well, but I approached him, hoping to acquire some wisdom from the master. "Mr. Levitt," I said, "how are you doing?"

"Not good, Donald, not good." Then he said the words I'll never forget. "I lost my momentum. I was out of the world for twenty years, I came back, and I wasn't the same."

No matter how accomplished you are, no matter how well you think you know your business, you have to remain vigilant about the details of your field. You can't get by on experience or smarts. Even the best surgeons need to be retrained regularly, to stay current on the latest research and procedures.

No matter what you're managing, don't assume you can glide by. Momentum is something you have to work at to maintain.

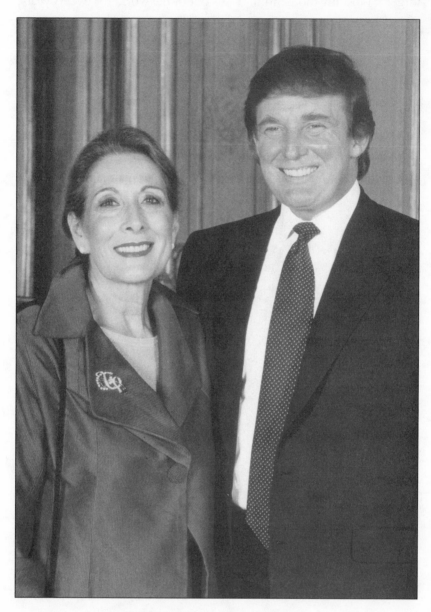

My loyal assistant, Norma Foerderer.

Get a
Great Assistant

Surround yourself with people you can trust. I often say it's good to be paranoid, but not when it comes to your home team.

Ask God for a great assistant. No joke. A great one can make your life a whole lot easier—or, in my case, almost manageable. Norma Foerderer has been with me for twenty-three years. If you want to know what a great guy I am, just ask her. But not on a Friday.

Handling me, the office, and several hundred calls a week isn't easy. She's as tough and smart as she is gracious. She's also indefatigable, which helps a lot if you work for me.

My phones are so busy that I require two executive assistants, and they never stop. They alone handle, on the average, more than 1,250 calls a week. They are not only efficient and fast, but also very pleasant and beautiful young women.

You don't have to be beautiful to work for me—just be good at your job. I've been accused of admiring beautiful women. I plead guilty. But when it comes to the workplace, anyone who is beautiful had better have brains, too. You need competent people with an inherent work ethic. I'm not a complacent person and I can't have a complacent staff. I move forward quickly and so must they.

Once, I wanted to know how fast a new employee could work, so I told him I was leaving in fifteen minutes and needed something done within that time. I wasn't actually going anywhere, but, sure enough, I had what I needed in fifteen minutes. Machiavellian? Maybe, but both of us learned something that day.

One final piece of advice on assistants, which I learned from experience and which, I admit, may not be as relevant to your career as it's been to mine: Find a receptionist who can speak English. We had a breathtaking European beauty out front who could easily rival Ingrid Bergman in her heyday, but I discovered that her ability to recognize well-known people in the United States was limited to myself and maybe President Bush. She wasn't so familiar with the likes of Hugh Grant, Reggie Jackson, George Steinbrenner, Jack Welch, Paul Anka, Mohamed Al Fayed, Regis Philbin, or Tony Bennett. Their calls never got through to me and their names were placed on her "psycho list."

But you should have seen her. What a knockout. She's since moved on to better career opportunities, but we'll never forget her. Neither will anyone who ever called in. Or tried to.

Remember:
The Buck Starts Here

Set the standard. Don't expect your employees to work harder than you do. In my case, I don't have to worry about that, because I work seven days a week and love almost every minute of it. But also realize that your company will sometimes function as an extended and dysfunctional family. It's only natural, considering that people often spend more waking hours with coworkers than they do with their families.

A visitor in my office once mentioned that the goings-on there reminded him of a family fight in progress. I will admit that the volume level gets high now and then, and he wasn't far off in his assessment. But if you want smooth sailing every day, move to the Mediterranean.

Winners see problems as just another way to prove themselves. Problems are never truly hardships to them, and if you haven't got any problems, then you must not have a business to run.

Regard your company as a living, breathing organism, because that's what it is. Those figures you see on your spreadsheets will reflect the health of that organism. Watch out for bad cells while allowing good cells to flourish.

Growth is an indication of life, so keep your organization moving forward at all times. Having a passion for what you do is crucial. If you can't get excited about what you are doing, how can you expect anyone else to? If your employees can see and feel your energy, it is bound to affect them.

Don't intimidate people. If you do, you'll never get a straight answer from anyone, and you'll be defeating your own purpose. I keep my door open, and my people know I'm available as well as approachable. We don't have chat-fests, but whatever needs to be done gets accomplished, and quickly.

Remember that your organization is *your* organization. That sounds simplistic, but, bottom line, it's your ball game. The strategy is up to you, and so are the results. Remember Harry Truman's famous words, which he kept on his desk in the Oval Office? THE BUCK STOPS HERE. I keep a similar quote on my desk. It reads: THE BUCK STARTS HERE.

Don't Equivocate

If you equivocate, it's an indication that you're unsure of yourself and what you're doing. It's also what politicians do all the time, and I find it inappropriate, insulting, and condescending.

I try not to do it. Fortunately, I don't have to try too hard at this one, because I've been known to be on the blunt (and fast) side at times, which is good.

I once asked an executive in my organization to give me a synopsis of a new development we were considering. He'd been to the city in question, had spent some time there, and had done some careful investigating. He went on to describe the merits of the site, the pitfalls, the good things, the bad things, the pros, the cons—on and on in great detail. He must've talked for ten minutes straight. Judging from what he was telling me, there were just as many reasons to drop the project as there were reasons to jump right in and get going. It was like a tied game with no overtime.

I asked him more questions, and we ended up exactly where we were before. He was on both sides of the fence at once and didn't seem to want to take a stand either way. This guy had a lot of experience and a good track record, so finally I asked him what he thought of the project in ten words or less.

"It stinks," he said.

He had eight words left, but he didn't need them.

Ask Yourself Two Questions

1. Is there anyone else who can do this better than I can?
That's just another way of saying: Know yourself, and know your competition. If your competition is better than you are, you need to offer some quality they lack.

2. What am I pretending not to see?
We can all get swept up in the euphoria of a creative moment, or what former president Richard Nixon's speechwriters used to call "the lift of a dream." Before the dream lifts you into the clouds, make sure you've looked hard at the facts on the ground.

Bullshit Will
Only Get You So Far

I think it's funny that the phrase most closely associated with me these days is "You're fired," because, the truth is, although I've had to fire people from time to time, it's not a big part of my job. I much prefer keeping loyal and hardworking people around for as long as they'd like to be here. There's a wonderful lady in her nineties, Amy Luerssen, who worked for my father and still reports to work every day at our Brooklyn office. Here at The Trump Organization, Helen Rakotz has worked for me from the day I moved to Manhattan, and she still puts in long hours every week. She is eighty-two.

Once I delayed firing someone for two years because this guy always had such a great line of bullshit every time I came close to the topic. No matter what was going on, he had some huge deal lined up that was just about to come through.

He managed to string me along for two solid years, and I believed him every time—or wanted to. Finally, I was forced to realize that his claims were bogus, but I gave him every chance before finally axing him.

Unless your boss is a total sadist, he (or she) doesn't want to fire you or cause hardship to your family. If you think you're in danger of being fired, take control of the situation and ask your boss for a meeting.

Make sure you ask for the meeting at the right time. Tell your boss you want to make sure you are communicating and doing your job to everyone's satisfaction.

Of course, if your boss is a sadist, or just a lousy communicator, you've still got a problem. In that case, fire your boss and get a better job. There's no sense in trying to cope with a bad situation that will never improve.

I never try to dissuade people from quitting. If they don't want to be here, I don't want them to be here, either. No one has ever come to me with an ultimatum. People see how it works here, and if it doesn't suit them, they move on. Sometimes it happens quickly. A qualified and experienced receptionist worked here for a grand total of six hours. She realized right away that the pace just wasn't suited to her, and she very politely told us so and left. I appreciated her quick thinking and efficient decision-making skills. She'll have a successful career some-where else.

Every New Hire Is a Gamble

Some people give such great interviews that you're ready to make them vice presidents on the spot, until you realize that their true talent is simply giving a great interview. That's why, in a sense, every new hire is a gamble.

Impressive credentials don't always add up to a great performance or a good fit. Nonexistent credentials don't necessarily mean a no-talent. Being circumspect helps a lot and keeps you from being surprised. People can offer an interesting mix of pros and cons. Time will do the weeding out for you. All you have to do is pay attention.

What I look for in employees is a sense of responsibility that goes beyond what is merely sufficient. Some people do the bare minimum, and some people will actually be concerned about the organization as a whole. They see themselves as having a direct relationship to the success or failure of the company they work for. They believe they are important, and their work shows it. If you can instill this sense of worth in your employees, you will have a tip-top team working for you. People who take pride in their work are the kind you want to have around—and the kind I like to keep around.

I especially like employees who spend—and, more important, save—the company's money as if it were their own. Companies suffer when employees don't make enough of an effort to control costs. The employees who feel a personal responsibility for their budgets, who view the company's bottom line as an extension of their own personal savings account, are often the ones who get the best results. If you let your boss know that you're watching out for his or her bottom line, you'll always be appreciated.

I respect employees who can think on their feet. So does George Ross, my senior counsel. His assistant, Carole Berkowitz, was helping out at the front desk one day when she received a call from a stranger who said she was about to commit suicide. Carole deemed the call credible and took a few moments to listen to the distressed woman.

Carole asked her where she was from, and the woman replied that she lived in Southern California, not far from the beach. Carole responded, "You live in California? Near the beach? Do you know how cold it is in New York today? It's eight degrees outside! And that's without the windchill. I almost froze just getting to work. If I were you, I'd go out right now, take a long walk on the beach, and sit in the sun for a while. That's what I'd do if I were you." The woman instantly calmed down and thanked Carole for being so nice to her.

That's the kind of person we like to have around.

A certain amount of personal ambition is necessary, but not to the point where it undermines the common goal of the company. If your group can't work together, you won't accomplish much. I don't like backstabbing. It's not necessary, and it's insulting to me. I have eyes and ears and instincts, too. I can assess people and situations for myself. If people have time to be petty, it's an indication they're not busy enough with their work.

You can't expect to be a valuable employee if you don't make yourself valuable. Think about it: What do you contribute to the welfare of the organization? Are you instrumental in keeping it humming and moving forward? Do you work wholeheartedly or halfheartedly? Are you just going through the motions and hoping no one will notice?

The only person you ever fool is yourself. You can't fool others, even though you might *think* you can.

A lot of people say they're going through the motions because their position isn't challenging or rewarding and there's no room to grow. It's a dead-end situation. That might very well be. If so, look elsewhere for a company that could offer you a promotion in your particular area of interest or expertise. There are times when you should move on, and situations in which the only way up is out.

Ideas Are Welcome, but Make Sure You Have the Right One

If you run a company, make yourself accessible to your employees. If they feel they can bring ideas to you, they will. If they feel they can't, they won't. You might miss out on a lot of good ideas, and pretty soon you might be missing a lot of employees.

I allow people to run their ideas by me. I don't have a lot of time, so they have to be prepared and succinct. I'm sure that's the protocol of any busy CEO. So if you're going to be bold enough to present your idea, make it as clear as possible, and don't take it casually. Think of it as a presentation that could cost you a lot of money if you were to lose the client. Your boss's time is important, and you won't win any points by wasting it.

Learn to recognize the fine line between being pushy and being intelligently assertive. It can be an issue of timing—pay attention to what's happening around you and pace yourself according to that rhythm. I try to develop a tempo when I'm working. Someone who interrupts it is not going to receive a warm welcome.

Also, remember this: The boss has the big picture; you don't. So if your idea doesn't meet with hurrahs, it could very well be that a similar idea is already in development or that your idea is not in step with plans that have already been made. This shouldn't discourage you, because your initiative will always be noticed. But recognize when *not* to press an issue, and don't expect a lengthy explanation of why.

I like people who don't give up, but merely being a pest is detrimental to everyone. Once again, fine-tune your discernment. Know when to ease up. Keep your antennae up for another idea and a more appropriate opportunity. Sometimes we hesitate with good reason.

There was one former employee who I liked a lot, but he reminded me of a jumping bean. He couldn't keep still for more than three seconds at a time. Even riding in the car with him became an ordeal, because being in an enclosed space seemed to warm him up even more and then he'd really get going. I finally learned to avoid him as much as possible, and that's too bad, because he was a great guy. But enough is enough. Too much will cause people to tune you out—or wish that you would move to another state. Last I heard, the jumping bean was living in Montana. I only hope they have enough space there to contain him, and every time I hear about UFO sightings in Montana, I have to laugh. I know who it is.

One last thing: If your boss says no to an idea, pay attention. Most likely, there's a good reason. No one disregards a terrific idea. It just might not be the *right* terrific idea for the company you're with. Maybe you're meant to go off on your own as an entrepreneur. Let that be an indication to you. It could be the beginning of your career, rather than the end of it.

Focus on the Talent Instead of the Title

People who work for me know there's a lot more to me than my public persona. I'm not one-dimensional, and if you realize that the people around you aren't either, you'll be utilizing the hidden potential that just about everyone has. Whether they want to use it or not is up to them to a certain extent, but it's also up to a leader to recognize it or at least to give it a chance to unfold. Most people don't like to stagnate, and if you want to keep your company moving forward, look around you now and then for fresh possibilities within your organization. Never let someone's job title be the sole indication of their worth.

People at The Trump Organization have transcended their positions on many occasions. Matthew Calamari, the executive vice president of operations, started as a security guard. After getting to know Matthew, I realized he had a lot more to offer than his job title warranted, and he has proven me right. He's a dedicated and trustworthy worker, and any CEO in his right mind would want to have him around. As an executive VP, he is in charge of building operations and runs my entire security organization. He is in charge of major building projects, with his brother Michael and Andy Weiss. Their most notable

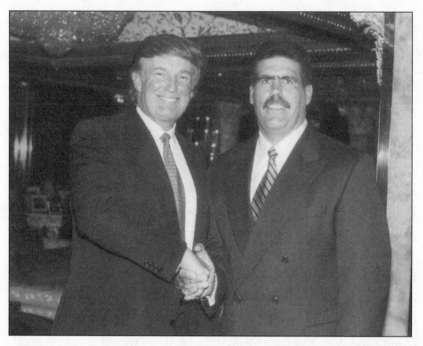
With Matthew Calamari, an executive vice president at The Trump Organization.

recent accomplishment is the new building on the site of the former Delmonico Hotel at Park Avenue and Fifty-ninth Street. I'm calling it Trump Park Avenue. Catchy, right?

Vinnie Stellio, who was hired by Matthew Calamari, started as my bodyguard and is now a vice president. He has just what it takes to be an effective executive, which was clear to me, if not immediately to him. Vinnie would often drive executives, architects, and contractors up to Westchester to look at developments I was building. Now they report to him. I am perhaps the largest owner of land in Westchester County, and now it's Vinnie who keeps his eye on it all.

John Tutolo, president of Trump Model Management, our modeling agency, started as a booker and now has what many guys would consider a dream job.

Meredith McIver, who made the writing of this book a pleasure instead of a headache, started out as a media assistant. I recognized that her talents encompassed much more. Of course, it takes talent to deal with me and everyone else every day (but especially me). I could have hired an outside collaborator to help me with this book, but why spend time looking outside the organization when you have all the people you need right beside you?

Very often, your resources are greater than you might think. I don't like it when people underestimate me, and I try not to underestimate anyone else, either. People are multifaceted, and it's important to let them function in a way that will allow them to shine. Most people would rather succeed than fail, but sometimes the leader has to be the catalyst for putting "success" into their personal vocabulary.

In other words, try to see beyond a person's title. You can find talent in unlikely places.

Meredith McIver, Rhona Graff, and Norma Foerderer of The Trump Organization.

Manage the Person,
Not the Job

I once heard a story about a guy who owned an advertising agency. There was one writer who drove the other writers crazy because he would appear to be doing nothing in his office. He made no attempt to look busy.

Finally, his colleagues complained to his boss about his laziness. The boss suddenly perked up and asked, "How long has he been this way?"

One of the other writers answered, "For weeks and weeks! He sits there and does zip. It's like he's in a coma."

The boss said, "I want all of you to be quiet and not to disturb him, and every now and then ask if you can get him some coffee or some lunch or run some errands for him."

Needless to say, the employees were deflated and started grumbling. Then the boss explained his rationale: "Listen, the last time he was acting this way, and the time before that, he came up with ideas worth many millions of dollars. So when I tell you not to disturb him, I have a reason for it."

People have different ways of achieving results. I enjoy figuring out how each of my key employees excels. If people are your resource, you'd better try to learn something useful about them. Being able to do so is what makes a good manager a great one.

Some people respond well to the fear factor. Ever hear this exchange?

> *Question:* "How long have you been working here?"
> *Answer:* "Ever since they threatened to fire me."

Well, it applies to some employees. Fortunately, I seem to attract people who enjoy working, but now and then a few slugs will show up, and the loss of face (or job) can be a good motivator for many.

That said, it will always work against you to demoralize your employees in any way. I can be tough, but most people will admit I'm fair. You can crush people if you don't weigh your words carefully. Your power as a leader should be used in the most positive way, which sometimes calls for a great deal of restraint as well as patience. I have to laugh when I hear people say, "I can't wait until I'm the big shot so I can order everyone around." It doesn't quite work that way.

Abraham Lincoln made an appropriate remark that is pertinent to management: "Nearly all men can stand adversity, but if you want to test a man's character, give him power."

Keep Your Door Open

I'm always taken aback when people say, "Oh, he's got it made," as if that's the end of the conversation about a person. They seem to be saying that the person can just check out and coast because he's already arrived.

To me, arriving means something is about to begin. Graduation from college is a beginning, not an ending. Each success is the beginning of the next one.

Learning is a new beginning we can give ourselves every day.

A know-it-all is like a closed door. Everyone who knows me knows I keep the door to my office open. It's symbolic of the way I choose to think, and it's the way I operate. My father was much the same. He once said to me, "You know, the more I learn, the more I realize I don't know. I think that has kept me young at heart more than anything else." It was an offhand comment, a quiet realization he mentioned to me one day while he was reading, but it has stuck with me for decades.

Every day is a reminder to me of how much I don't know. Everything I learn leads me to something else I didn't know. Fortunately, I don't pride myself on being a know-it-all, so every day becomes a new

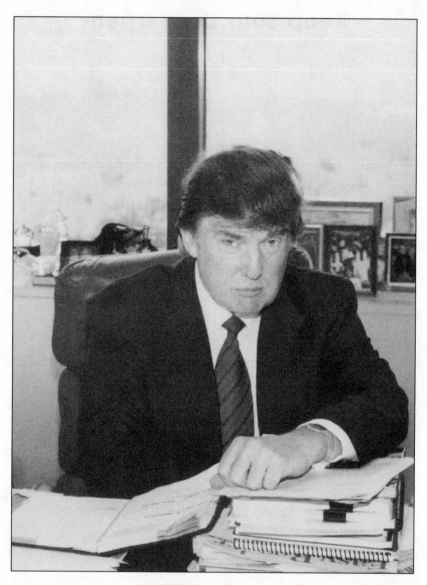

Looking for a raise? Come on in.

challenge. People ask me what keeps me going, and this is probably the closest answer to the truth. If I end the day without knowing more than I did when I woke up, it makes me wonder: What did I miss out on today? Am I getting lazy? I am a disciplined person, and this thought alone can get me going.

We've all heard the phrase *creature of habit.* That can be good or bad, depending on your habits. I've cultivated the learning habit over the years, and it's one of the most pleasurable aspects of my life. Everyone in my family knows I'm big on education—not just Ivy League education, but all education, and for people of all ages. That also applies to me, and while I got very good grades at school, I do not have time to be a scholar. Still, it's something I aspire to in my quiet time. Possibilities unfold. The world opens up.

My sister Maryanne introduced me to the writings of Aldous Huxley. He was such a learner that when he was faced with near-total blindness as a young man, he learned braille and continued his studies anyway. His description of this predicament had not a trace of self-pity. In fact, he mentioned that it had offered some benefits: He could now read in bed at night and his hands would never get cold because he could read with his hands under the covers.

Learning begets learning. I'd rather be stimulated than passive.

You can't wear a blindfold in business. A regular part of your day should be devoted to expanding your horizons.

We live in a big world, and it is important for us to be aware of cultures other than our own. I have always lived in the United States, but I make an effort to be informed about other cultures. That's easy to do in New York City, the most diverse and exciting place on earth.

Someone who had been living abroad for a few years told me, upon returning home, that a frequent comment about Americans is that you always know exactly where we're coming from. The flip side of this is that we rarely know where *anyone else* is coming from. We're very much up to snuff about our own national events, but we are less aware of what's happening in other countries. All of us need to pay more attention to events outside our own realm. We are connected to each other in so many ways—politically, commercially, socially. Perhaps one of the reasons I've been able to sell and rent apartments to people of so many foreign nationalities is that I've made an effort to understand where they're coming from.

Learn something new, whether you think you're interested in it or not. That's the opposite of having a closed mind—or a closed door. I can thank my father for the example he set. It was the key to his remaining young and dynamic into his nineties. It can do the same for you, if you make the effort.

Think Big and
Live Large

This is the final rule of the Donald J. Trump School of Business and Management. Once you have mastered it, you are ready to graduate.

It's a big world. There's a lot we don't know, which means there's still a lot to be discovered and a lot to be accomplished.

The possibilities are always there. If you're thinking too small, you might miss them.

In some ways, it's easier to buy a skyscraper than a small house in a bad section of Brooklyn. Either way, you'll probably need financing, and most people would rather invest in a great building than a dilapidated duplex on a dangerous street. With the skyscraper, if you hit, at least you hit big. And if you don't hit, what's the difference between losing $100,000 or hundreds of millions of dollars? Either way, you've lost, so you might as well have really gone for it.

I've read stories in which I'm described as a cartoon, a comic book version of the big-city business mogul with the gorgeous girlfriend and the private plane and the personal golf course and the penthouse apartment with marble floors and gold bathroom fixtures. But my cartoon is real. I am the creator of my own comic book, and I love living in it. If you're going to think, think big. If you're going to live, live large.

PART II

Your Personal Apprenticeship (Career Advice from The Donald)

Take Control of the Job Interview

I've had some interesting experiences with job interviews over the years. Norma Foerderer is a good example. I wasn't too sure about her after her first interview. It had nothing to do with her skills. But she seemed a little too prim, like she belonged on some family sitcom as the ever-so-proper type. I didn't think she could handle it here, or that she would fit with my style.

Norma persisted, seeming to recognize a good match better than I did. Little did I know how deceptive first impressions could be. Norma was actually as far from fluff as you could get. So, I thought, *Okay, maybe*. Her abilities were superior to those of anyone else I had seen. As it turned out, I called her back on the same day her mother died, but Norma gave me an offer I couldn't refuse: She'd work for me for one month at a low salary just to see whether we clicked. No strings attached.

I thought, *Aha!* She'll never last anyway, and I can decide on someone else in the meantime. After one month with me, she'd be outta here for sure. The hoity-toity type just won't fly, except out the front door.

Needless to say, I underestimated Norma completely. I was duly humbled and, I must add, grateful for being so. She was persistent and committed to getting the job, and she did it with elegance.

Ask for Your Raise
at the Right Time

When it comes to your career, certain moves should not be made without careful consideration of the old and very apt saying "Timing is everything."

For example, if you've decided to ask for a raise, look around first. So many times, employees who I like very much do the dumbest things when it comes to conversations about their salaries.

Jason Greenblatt, a young and brilliant lawyer who works for me, is terrific at everything he does, but one day, I swear, he must have been wearing blindfolds—and earplugs.

I was having an especially tough, vicious, terrible, miserable day that seemed never-ending to me and to everyone else. It was a grand-slam rotten day. No one could possibly have mistaken it for anything else.

Late in the afternoon, by which time I had had enough, I heard a polite knock on my door. I yelled out "WHAT?" in my most exasperated tone. Jason nonchalantly entered my office, completely ignoring my angry welcome, and proceeded to ask me for a raise.

I could not believe a lawyer as smart as Jason could make such a dumb move. I use his real name only because Jason knows how much

I like and respect him, despite his incredible faux pas. But I have to tell you that I was ready to kill him. Was he *joking*? It's amazing, but he wasn't. He was dead serious. I couldn't believe it.

Did he get a raise? Not that day. He almost got fired for stupidity, except that I told him to get out before I really lost my temper. I also told him that although he might be brilliant, his timing for certain things needed work—and that maybe he ought to start paying attention to what was going on around him. I remember thinking to myself, *Did I really hire such a person?* But as I said, it had been a rough day.

Jason is still with me, and he gets lots of raises because he's great at what he does. But now he always waits for sunny days, blue skies, and puffy white clouds on the horizon before approaching me. I told you he was smart.

The best way to ask for a raise is to wait for the right time. It also indicates to your boss that you have a certain amount of discernment and appreciation for what he might be going through himself. I need my people to be plugged in to what's going on with me.

What impresses me most about people is their work ethic. A certain amount of swagger is okay—it's just another form of enthusiasm—but, bottom line, I look for results. When I mentioned to a salesperson that I had to cut her salary because she'd made no sales in nine months, she just about went nuts. But some things are common sense. What would she do if she had a nonproductive salesperson on her own roster?

If you knew your company was scheduled to give a major client presentation at 3 P.M., would you approach your boss at 2:45 to ask for a raise?

Money, like comedy, is all about timing.

Be Tenacious

The Art of the Deal contained a chapter called "West Side Story," about my acquisition of the West Side yards, a hundred-acre property fronting the Hudson River from Fifty-ninth Street to Seventy-second Street. The chapter title was a deliberate double entrendre, as I knew that the popular musical *West Side Story* had taken ten years to put together. Its creative team had included no less than Leonard Bernstein, Jerome Robbins, Stephen Sondheim, and Arthur Laurents, so whenever I experienced setbacks or delays on my West Side project, I would remind myself that I had some very illustrious company.

It's now seventeen years later and it's still a work in progress, but the example set by the architects of *West Side Story* has served me well. You don't create a classic overnight.

I'm calling it Trump Place. It's a $5-billion project, the biggest development ever approved by the New York City Planning Commission. When it's done, Trump Place will have 5,700 residential units and more than five million square feet of commercial space. So far, four towers have been completed and are occupied, and two additional buildings are under construction. When we're done, there will be a total of sixteen buildings on the site.

Trump Place is a good example of why tenacity is crucial in business. I bought the property in 1974. We've hit snags along the way and made many changes over time, but for more than thirty years, we've persisted. At times, just about every executive will appear impatient, but to build something that endures, you have to take the long view.

Recently, an employee told me that the pastor of her church had used Trump Place as an example of what a firm foundation should be, whether it be in faith, family, or, as in my case, buildings. The pastor, whose church was near the construction site, would watch each building go up and marvel at the immensity of the work. Each building could be a hundred stories high, he said, considering the meticulous foundation work.

My publisher sent me an inspiring book by Bill Shore called *The Cathedral Within*, which celebrates the commitment and hope necessary to build something that endures. It might be a cathedral like the one in Milan, which took five hundred years to build, or it might be a community organization or a business.

Paul Davis, the man developing Trump Place for me and my partners, is a true cathedral builder. I have rarely seen anyone work so hard or so diligently—Saturdays, Sundays—he's there at all hours, paying close attention to every impeccable detail of the layouts, room sizes, and the quality of the fixtures. He's one of the big reasons for our success.

Some things are worth waiting for. For me, Trump Place is one of those things: Sixteen beautifully designed buildings on the Hudson River. A twenty-five-acre park. The Upper West Side as a backyard. This could prove to be my finest contribution to the city of New York. Time will tell, but I'm in no rush, and I won't stop until I'm done.

Golf is a brain game, and practice makes perfect.

Play Golf

I made a lot of money on the golf course before I ever went into golf as a business. I found solutions to problems, new ideas for ventures, and even a new career. Golf has a way of giving you an equilibrium that you can't always find in the office.

Doing what you love will always make you a winner, and after spending many happy hours on golf courses, I decided to build some of my own. I am now one of the busiest golf course developers in the United States, with two award-winning, internationally acclaimed courses fully operational and two more in the works.

My first course, the Trump International Golf Club in Palm Beach, Florida, has been home to the ADP LPGA championships for three years. When I first decided to develop the most beautiful golf courses possible, I did some research and got in touch with the most respected designers in the business—the Fazio family. Just as Michelangelo had an affinity for sculpting marble, some people have an affinity for sculpting land. In this case, Jim and Tommy Fazio designed a dream come true for any golfer, not only visually, but in terms of playability.

The course opened in 1999. With its waterfalls and landscapes unique to Florida, Trump International Golf Club is already a landmark course in the state—and the best course in Florida.

My second course was Trump National at Briarcliff Manor in New York. We moved three million yards of earth, the largest land excavation ever in Westchester County, and it was worth it. We were also dealing with stone, which was used for walls and a spectacular waterfall on the thirteenth hole—a 101-foot cliff of black granite quarried from the property—which pumps five thousand gallons a minute. The walls were built by my very talented stone mason, Frank Sanzo. Membership costs $300,000. I think it's a bargain.

My third golf course is Trump National Golf Club, in a sumptuous area of New Jersey known as Bedminster. It is being designed by the master golf course architect himself, Tom Fazio. Three times, *Golf Digest* has named Fazio the Best Modern Day Golf Course Architect, and when you see this course, you'll know why. It will be long, big, and beautiful, and I am involved daily in the design and construction. Additional plans for this property, formerly owned by automaker John DeLorean and located in the heart of New Jersey's horse country, will include a second course and a world-class clubhouse designed in the colonial mansion style.

I don't want to limit my golfing to the East Coast, so in 2002 I bought a course along two miles of the Pacific Ocean. What was formerly known as Ocean Trails in Palos Verdes will now be known as Trump National Golf Club, Los Angeles. The course had fallen into disrepair under its previous owners—the eighteenth hole fell into the ocean—so I'm rebuilding it with legendary golf course architect Pete Dye. We're also planning to build luxury estate homes on the property. When completed, this course will be the best in California.

When we announced the deal, the *Los Angeles Times* reported, "As he has so many times before, Trump has spotted a trend to tap." True, but mostly I was following my instincts and my interests.

Building golf courses is not a big business for me and it's unlikely that I will ever do another one. I want only the best.

Sometimes I will sell memberships while I am hitting balls on the

Dave Anderson, Joe Kernen, me, and Ron Howard at the opening of
Trump National Golf Club in Briarcliff Manor, New York.

practice range. People approach me and hand me checks. One recent day at my Florida course, a group of four wealthy friends came to me with checks of $300,000 each. I said to myself: *Not bad; I'm playing a game I love and going home with $1,200,000 in my pocket.*

I realize that some of you don't care much about golf. Golf is one of those things that has aficionados, just as opera has diehard fans who will fly around the world to catch a certain performance. To people who don't know or like opera, that seems absurd.

I can't make you love golf, but, believe me, once you've had the opportunity to play on a beautiful course, it could turn you into an enormous fan, or even a passionate player, no matter how poorly you hit the ball.

If anyone had told me twenty years ago that I'd become a dedicated golf course developer, I would have sent them out of the room for being ridiculous. But golf has a transforming power. It's a brain game. Yes, there is skill and technique involved, but, just as important, it requires concentration and assessment.

It's a great way to improve your business skills, to learn how to maneuver. It can even be equated with learning how to negotiate, which is an art in itself.

Golf is also, in essence, a solitary game. Being an entrepreneur, even within a large company, is a solitary game.

Ultimately, the rule here is not just to visit one of my golf courses (though you would be wise to do so) but to turn your passion into profit. The results of that passion will reward you in more ways than you ever could have expected.

Passion is enthusiasm on a big scale. It is all-encompassing and consuming. People with passion never give up because they'll never have a reason to give up, no matter what their circumstances may be. It's an intangible momentum that can make you indomitable.

Take out the passion and you will have a fizzle or, perhaps, an okay product at best. Add the passion and you will be in a rarefied realm that every other "passionista" will recognize—and one that every person would like to enter.

A friend of mine is a member of what I call "the lucky sperm club"—born into a wealthy family. He followed his father to Wall Street, but he was a total failure. He didn't like it, and he couldn't do it. Meanwhile, he became increasingly involved in his Connecticut country club. He was named the head of the greens committee and took on the lead role in rebuilding the golf course. He loved it and was great at it. The club held a dinner for him out of gratitude for his volunteer work. I asked him, "Why don't you do this for a living? You're not for Wall Street. You're getting eaten alive there." He told me his family wouldn't understand if he quit a serious job to work on golf courses.

Well, two years later he took my advice, quit the Wall Street job, and is now working full-time at renovating golf courses. He says he loves getting up in the morning, and he is doing better than ever.

Of course, you don't have to learn how to play golf to have a satisfying career. But no matter what you do, you must be passionate about it.

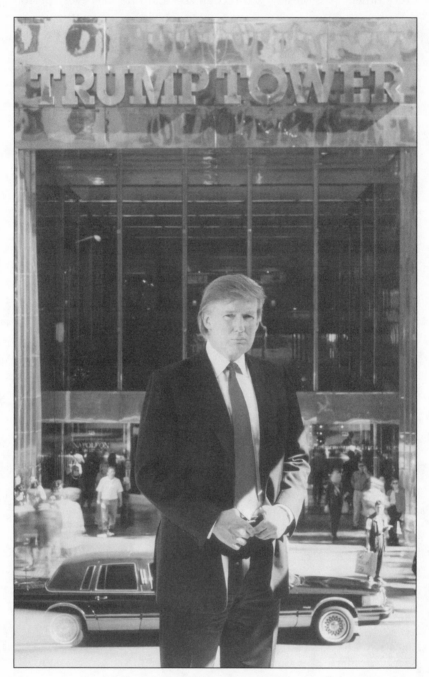

There's no place like home.

Brand Yourself and Toot Your Horn

I was originally going to call Trump Tower by another name—Tiffany Tower, for the famous jewelry store next door. I asked a friend, "Do you think it should be Trump Tower or Tiffany Tower?" He said, "When you change your name to Tiffany, call it Tiffany Tower."

We've all seen the power of a brand name, especially quality brand names. Coco Chanel became world-famous eighty years ago by naming her first perfume Chanel No. 5, and it's still going strong in a fiercely competitive market. Her fragrance, as well as her name, has become timeless. She proved that the right ingredients can create a legend.

Trump has become a great brand name, due to my rigorous standards of design and quality. We all admire Rolls-Royce cars, and I see every one of my ventures as being just that elite. Being a stickler has paid off, because my buildings are considered to be the finest in the world. That may sound like bragging, but it's also a fact. I've never been one to confuse facts with fiction. In 2003, *Chicago Tribune* real estate columnist Mary Umberger attributed the sales for Trump International Hotel and Tower in Chicago to "The Trump Factor." Umberger reported: "The sales velocity surprises even experienced real-estate players, who told me at the sales inaugural that they doubted Trump would gain enough momentum because Chicago's luxury market was—and is—in a lull."

Some people have written that I'm boastful, but they're missing the point. I believe in what I say, and I deliver the goods. If you're devoting your life to creating a body of work, and you believe in what you do, and what you do is excellent, you'd better damn well tell people you think so. Subtlety and modesty are appropriate for nuns and therapists, but if you're in business, you'd better learn to speak up and announce your significant accomplishments to the world—nobody else will.

When I'm setting the price for a luxury apartment, I consider a lot of factors—the market, the location, and the competition. Then I set my own standards. Once, when some top-of-the-line apartments weren't selling, I upped the prices, way over the competition. They started selling immediately.

I view my work as an art form and approach it with the same intensity and ego as any ambitious artist would. I never planned on becoming a brand name, but the fit of my aesthetic nature with each product I became involved with has resulted in an expanding network of interests. The success of the Trump name worldwide has been a surprise.

It's been a good surprise. For example, using my name on a building carries with it a promise of the highest quality available and at least a $5-million price tag. That's just for the name, because it will be worth it to the developers, and they know it. That building will be up to my standards. When I remember the line from Shakespeare's *Romeo and Juliet*—"What's in a name?"—I have to laugh. What's in a name can be far more than either the Bard or I ever could have imagined.

We've all noticed the ascendancy of brand names and the power they have, from Levi's to Louis Vuitton. Some people are against this widespread branding, seeing it as another form of labeling. I see it as a viable outlet for creativity.

If you're on the brink of success in your career, some snob might ask you dismissively, "You don't want to become a brand name, do you?" Anyone who asks you that does not have the big picture in focus—and they are usually just envious.

I can get a project off the ground in no time now, whereas an unknown developer would require many months, if not years, to get something going. The number of people I employ to get a project finished reaches into the thousands, and those people would not have a building to work on without a developer to give them a job. Commerce and art cannot function independently—they must work together. That is the beauty of a successful brand name.

If there is a downside to being a well-known name, it is that you become an easy target. The media needs to tear down what it builds up; that's just part of journalism—stories are about heroes and villains, or success and failure. If you're a brand name, they're going to take a shot at you. It comes with the territory, and I've learned to live with it. As we say on *The Apprentice:* It's not personal. It's business.

Fortunately, if you have the critics who matter on your side, reading the newspaper can be a lot of fun. Herbert Muschamp, the architecture critic for *The New York Times,* is a scholar and an authority when it comes to buildings. To receive a compliment from him has an intrinsic value that will never diminish. When he wrote an article on Trump World Tower and described it as "a handsome hunk of a glass tower," I was very honored. Here's more of what he wrote:

> Although Donald Trump prefers to publicize the aggressive side of his nature—it's the manly thing to do—he is also the only beauty freak at large in New York City real estate development. . . . It's not surprising that unofficial approval of Trump's building should come by way of the Museum of Modern Art. The tower embodies the Miesian aesthetic through which the Modern's design department's taste was initially formulated—I

hope Trump sticks with this material. Trump does better when he ignores his critics than when he pays attention to them.

So don't be afraid to toot your own horn when you've done something worth tooting about.

And don't believe the critics unless they love your work.

Go with Your Gut

Being an entrepreneur is not a group effort. You have to trust yourself. You may have superb academic credentials, but without instincts you'll have a hard time getting to—and staying at—the top.

This is one of those gray areas that remain an enigma even to those who have finely honed business instincts. There are inexplicable signs that can guide you to or away from certain deals and certain people.

For example, within a few seconds of meeting Mark Burnett, the creator of *The Apprentice*, I knew he was one hundred percent solid, both as a person and as a professional, which is a remarkable accomplishment in the entertainment industry.

On the other hand, I've met people that I have an aversion to for no particular reason, and while I try not to be judgmental, I have reason by now to trust my gut. Carl Jung said our conscious minds use only five percent of our brain power for daily functioning. If we can learn to tap into that unconscious, subconscious, and dormant ninety-five percent, the results can be amazing.

Be Optimistic,
but Always Be Prepared
for the Worst

There are a lot of ups and downs, but you can ride them out if you're prepared for them.

Learning to expect problems saved me from a lot of wasted energy, and it will save you from unexpected surprises. It's like Wall Street; it's like life. The ups and downs are inevitable, so simply try to be prepared for them.

Sometimes I'll ask myself why I want to take on some new, big challenge. A substantial loss is always a possibility. Can I handle it if it doesn't go well? Will I be asking myself later, *Why did I ever do that? What was I thinking?* I'm actually a very cautious person, which is different from being a pessimistic person. Call it positive thinking with a lot of reality checks.

Look Closely
Before Changing Careers

In 2000, I thought about running for president of the United States as a third-party candidate. I proposed some sensible ideas: tax cuts for the middle class, tougher trade deals, a ban on unregulated soft money in campaigns, comprehensive health care reform. I formed an exploratory committee and met with Reform Party leaders, but in the end I realized I was enjoying my business too much to run for office.

Remember the rule I mentioned earlier about how you shouldn't equivocate? That may work for business, but in politics, you usually have to watch your words. I'm too blunt to be a politician. Then, there's my long-held aversion to shaking hands. (More on this in a moment.) Had I entered the race, I wouldn't have been very popular. Even during the few months I was considering candidacy, I noticed that people began to treat me differently—in a more reserved, less friendly way. Before, I had been The Donald, someone they would wave and smile at. Suddenly, it was a different ball game, and it didn't seem like much fun to me. One guy I had been friendly with for years saw me at Le Cirque and for the first time in my life called me "Mr. Trump." He had always called me "Donald." That was a real heads-up.

A lot of successful businesspeople think they can apply their management skills to politics, but I've noticed that only a select few, like Michael Bloomberg and Jon Corzine, succeed. Most others lack the temperament for it.

There's a larger point here, beyond the obvious ones about not confusing your talent for office politics with a gift for electoral politics. Anyone with more than a little curiosity and ambition will at some point be tempted to try a different challenge on new terrain. Take the risk, but before you do, do everything you can to learn what you're getting yourself into, and be as sure as you can that you've got the right mind-set for the job.

Avoid the Handshake Whenever Possible

Some business executives believe in a firm handshake. I believe in *no* handshake. It is a terrible practice. So often, I see someone who is obviously sick, with a bad cold or the flu, who approaches me and says, "Mr. Trump, I would like to shake your hand." It's a medical fact that this is how germs are spread. I wish we could follow the Japanese custom of bowing instead.

The worst is having to shake hands during a meal. On one occasion, a man walked out of the restaurant's bathroom, jiggling his hands as though they were still wet and he hadn't used a towel. He spotted me, walked over to my table, and said, "Mr. Trump, you're the greatest. Would you please shake my hand?"

I knew that if I didn't shake his hand, he'd be saying terrible things about me for thirty years. I also knew that if I agreed, my own hands would be loaded with germs or whatever the hell he'd carried out of the bathroom. I had a choice.

In this case, I decided to shake hands, because I was a little overweight at the time and knew that if I shook his hand I wouldn't eat my meal—and that would be a good thing.

Pay Attention
to the Details

If you don't know every aspect of what you're doing, down to the paper clips, you're setting yourself up for some unwelcome surprises.

I once read about an esteemed brain surgeon in San Francisco who was known for being fanatical about detail and organization. He would go over the components of an upcoming surgery in his head as he jogged every morning. He'd visualize every detail, as if to remind himself of everything he'd learned, every difficulty and complication he might encounter.

He wasn't known for his bedside manner, but he was the best. If I had to have brain surgery, he's the kind of surgeon I'd choose. But you don't have to be a brain surgeon to pay attention to the details.

Connect with Your Audience
(The Art of
Public Speaking, Part I)

One of the problems with my schedule lately is that I am unable to accommodate most of the requests I receive for public speaking. I happen to enjoy giving speeches. I know some people dread the thought of having to give a presentation in a boardroom, let alone appearing before thousands of people. Not me. I get so much energy from my audiences that it is always fun.

I'll bet a lot of you are wondering whether I'm making that up to sound like I'm not afraid of anything. It's possible I'm forgetting a few stressful moments. Years ago I was probably nervous about facing an audience, but I got over it. Being afraid of speaking in public is something you can conquer. The following pointers can be applied by people who find presentations, whatever the size of the audience, to be a roadblock on their highway to success.

It helps if you are a naturally gregarious person. My driver, Tony, recalls a time when I was going to deliver a speech. When we were about five minutes away, I asked Tony what I was supposed to be talking about that night. Tony couldn't hide his shock. He said, "Boss, don't you *know*? There are twenty thousand people waiting for you."

Telling it like it is.

I said, "Yeah, but I've been busy. I'm sure it will be okay." I was trying to reassure him.

No go. He said, "Where are your notes? Didn't you make any notes?"

I said, "I'm making some now."

Tony was looking at me through the rearview mirror with an expression of astonishment. I think he was checking to see whether I was kidding. I wasn't.

I'd been asked to give the speech by Anthony Robbins, the best-selling author and self-help guru. I had been paid a great deal of money for the speech, but I'd never asked how many people I would be speaking in front of. As I was leaving the office to go to Philadelphia, my secretary told me I would be speaking at a basketball arena, the Wachovia Center, and that there would be approximately twenty thousand people there. I said, "You've got to be kidding. I've never spoken before twenty thousand people before!"

That situation could cause panic in some people. Instead, I thought about my audience not as a massive group of people just waiting to judge me, but as individuals who might be there because they're interested in something. Then I started thinking about what people are interested in and the kinds of questions people like to ask me.

I was ready. I suddenly had a gut feeling that we were all in for a great time.

Leaving an ashen-faced Tony in the car, I hopped out, ready to embrace the experience. Somehow the audience picked up on my energy and got much more than a speech. They got give-and-take that no one who was there will soon forget. We had a hilarious time, and we walked away having learned a few things as well.

Tony Robbins turned out to be a terrific guy. Until I met him, I didn't believe in him or trust him, but that was only because I was getting my information secondhand. Having gotten to know him and his wife, I now wholeheartedly endorse him—he is out to do good and help people. His seminars are absolutely a happening, and after our successful experience in Philadelphia, I agreed to make ten more appearances.

All in all, it was a valuable lesson in public speaking: Think about your audience first. The rest will fall into place.

Granted, having useful information to convey will help, too. But tuning in to *people* is the first step. I'm good at that, and I don't have to try too hard. Even in my office, with a few people around, the conversation will never be one-sided. I like to involve everyone and hear what they have to say.

So: Involve your audience. They will appreciate being included.

Cover These Eleven Bases
(The Art of
Public Speaking, Part II)

When you're speaking, it helps to be prepared. That may sound funny after what I've just told you, but if you read every day, you will already be prepared—maybe not for the fine points you are specifically speaking about, but usually we are asked to speak about something we are experts at or at least familiar with. Cover your bases mentally. Imagine yourself being in the audience. What are you looking for? Being able to trade places with the audience can open you up to a lot of ideas. Have examples and references in mind to back up your statements, and make them as vivid as possible for your listeners.

Notes can sometimes function as a useful reference point, especially if you're speaking to a large audience. If you're prepared, no one can tell that you're using them. Ideally, you don't want to read a speech. For some reason, no matter how good your delivery is when you read a speech, it's usually boring. Everyone sees that you're reading it and it's never quite the same as delivering it off the cuff. Notes offer the best of both worlds: They keep you focused and moving in the right direction without turning you into a stiff.

Be a good storyteller. People like stories, and they'll remember them. A speech shouldn't become a lecture. Humor goes a long way, and it will remind you and everyone else that we've all got a lot of things in common. Storytelling is a skill, so work on it. It's helpful to listen to comedians. The good ones can teach you the art of great timing.

Think about the common denominator.   How can all of us relate to one another? How can you enable your audience to relate to you and to what you're saying? People see me as a rich and powerful person, but like most people, I also have a daily routine and a family. I get stuck in traffic jams, too. I've known some real gems and some real wackos. I have cranky moments and bad days like everyone else. A lot of your experiences can be understood and appreciated by your audience because they've had them, too. Look for what you have in common and lead with it. You will create an immediate bond, because they will realize they can relate to you.

When you are on the podium, you are the entertainer.   People are there to learn something, but also to be entertained. One reason Elvis Presley was such a great entertainer is that he made every effort to tune in to his audience—it was give-and-take all the way. Wayne Newton does that, too. Even people who thought they wouldn't like Liberace became big fans after experiencing his live shows. And nobody did it better than Sinatra.

Some people call it charisma. I call it tuning in and delivering.

Study Regis Philbin.   He is relaxed and funny, and he always relates to his audiences. They love him. He's a perfect example of the give-and-take that's necessary for successful public speaking. Regis doesn't just speak—he shares. He's as magnanimous a performer as he is a person. Watch him, pay attention, and you'll learn a lot.

Be able to poke fun at yourself.   This will make you accessible to people even if you are up on the stage and in the spotlight. We've all had disasters in our lives, major and minor. To be able to laugh at them in retrospect is healthy and helpful. Use the blips that we all encounter in our lives to your advantage. I remember a particular question-and-answer period that followed one of my speeches, during the time when Ivana and I were going through our divorce and the tabloids were having a field day. The first question was from a guy who asked, "You don't mind if I call you *The Donald,* do you?"

So I responded, "Not if you don't mind if I call you Ivana."

We all had a good laugh and then proceeded to his real question.

Learn to think on your feet. Memorable public speaking involves a good deal of spontaneity. It's a lot like negotiating—you have to focus on your goals but remain flexible. A lot of people are terrific writers but not so great at getting their ideas across orally. Writing is a form of thinking, and so is speaking. The difference is that you don't have time to go back and correct yourself when you're on stage. It's not a first draft and it's not a rehearsal. Be prepared for the performance, because that's what's expected of you.

Listen in your daily life. Every day can be a preparation for a speech or a presentation. Have you ever said to yourself, "I'll have to remember that one" after hearing someone say something particularly clever or unusual? Even offhand comments that you overhear can be useful. Remember them. Make notes if you must. Everything and everyone can become material. I was in the back of an elevator once, behind a group of guys. Their conversation was so vivid, so real, that I tuned in and tried to figure out why they'd captured my attention. Aside from the fact that they had a captive audience for a short amount of time, I realized that their speaking rhythm was syncopated, quick, and to the point. What they were saying wasn't all that fascinating, but their delivery was. They made a normally mundane subject—what they were getting for lunch and how they were getting it—seem interesting.

Have a good time. It's contagious. If your audience believes you are enjoying what you are doing, they'll enjoy being in your company. If it's an obvious chore to you, forget it and find someone else to speak for you. If you're a busy executive, there's probably someone within your organization who can speak effectively in your place. Sometimes when I'm asked to speak and my schedule won't allow it, I will ask someone who works for me if they'd be interested in filling in. Charlie Reiss, executive VP of development in my organization, was a professor at Columbia University before he came to work for me. He's a dynamic speaker, but I wouldn't have known this if I hadn't asked him to help out when I was in a bind. He has a gift for public speaking because he enjoys teaching and is enthusiastic about what he does. At first I worried he might turn out to be a bit pedantic, considering his background, but he wasn't. Everyone had a good time.

Another important aspect of having a good time: Before you speak, remind yourself that it doesn't matter all that much. Don't feel that the weight of the world is on you. Most of the people in the room don't care how well or poorly you do. It's just not that important. It's merely a speech—not an earthquake or a war. You'll have a better time and be a better speaker if you keep it all in perspective.

That said, public speaking and presentations may be a necessary step on your ladder to success. For quick reference, here's my procedure for discovering a talent you thought you didn't have:

1. Think about your audience first.
2. Get your audience involved.
3. Be prepared.
4. Be a good storyteller.
5. Be aware of the common denominator.
6. Be an entertainer.
7. Be able to laugh at yourself.

8. Think on your feet.

9. Listen.

10. Have a good time.

And, of course . . .

11. Study Regis Philbin.

Change Your Altitude

When I say *altitude,* I'm not referring to my jet. It's my own interpretation of the word *attitude.* I like flying because it gets me where I'm going, fast. Likewise, if you have the right attitude, you can get where you're going, fast.

What's the altitude of your attitude? Is it high frequency or low frequency? Having a high frequency will attune you to a wavelength that exudes confidence and clear-sighted enthusiasm. I'm a firm believer that this is half the battle of any enterprise.

I'm a tough-minded optimist. I learned a long time ago that my productivity was increased by a large percentage simply by learning to let go of negativity in all forms as quickly as I could. My commitment to excellence is thorough—so thorough that it negates the wavelength of negativity immediately. I used to have to zap negativity mentally. By now, it just bounces off me within a moment of getting near me. As you may have heard, I don't like germs. I'm still waging a personal crusade to replace the mandatory and unsanitary handshake with the Japanese custom of bowing. To me, germs are just another kind of negativity.

Negativity is also a form of fear, and fear can be paralyzing. On the golf course, I've heard great athletes tell me that they can't putt. They can hit a ball three hundred yards right down the middle of the fairway, but they can't finish the hole by putting the ball three feet into the cup.

Recently, I played with a man who is terrified of putting. He hit a magnificent 235-yard shot and was seven feet from the cup. Then he looked over at me and said, "Now the hard part begins."

Another friend, also a great golfer, is paralyzed by his fear of losing his ball. Each time we played a hole near a lake, he would look down and say to his ball, "I have a feeling I'll never see you again."

I have told these two guys that they must start thinking positively or they will sabotage themselves.

Very often, negative thinking stems from low self-esteem. You have to work on this yourself. Maybe you've received a lot of hard knocks. I've learned to deal with them because I get knocked a lot. Quickly see them for what they are—knocks. But you don't have to open the door unless you choose to. I've gotten to the point where I see knocks as opportunities and as an insight into whoever is doing the knocking.

One way to chase low altitude away is to think about how fortunate you already are and how much you still have to look forward to. You can better your best day at any time. Very surprising things can happen, but you must—and I repeat *must*—be open to them. How can you fly if you've already clipped your own wings?

I don't have time to encourage as many people as I would like to, but whenever it seems appropriate, I recommend *The Power of Positive Thinking* by Norman Vincent Peale, one of my father's favorite books, and mine, too. Some people may think it's old-fashioned, but what Peale has written will always be true. He advocates faith over fear. Faith can overcome the paralysis that fear brings with it.

I can remember a time when I had a choice to make, when I was billions of dollars in debt. I had to take one of two courses of action: a fearful, defensive one or a faithful, riskier one. I carefully analyzed the situation, realized what was causing the uneasy feeling of fear, and immediately replaced it with blind faith, simply because I had nothing else to go on at the time. Then I resolved that as long as I remained positive and disciplined, things would work out.

There was not much more I could do. I didn't know how it was going to go, but I was determined to move forward, even though it wasn't easy. Within a relatively short amount of time, the situation was settled positively. I learned a lot from that and have since had a better understanding of what courage really is. Without facing my own fear, I would not have known.

When I think of someone who is tough, I also think of someone who has courage. People who persist have courage, because often it's a lot easier to give up. Some of the bravest people I've met are children with handicaps. I'm active with United Cerebral Palsy. What those kids deal with is humbling, but they are enthusiastic and thrilled with every day they've been given.

You've been given a day, too. When you're down, look at it that way. Another day can equal another chance. Sometimes, as obvious as it sounds, we really do have to take things one day at a time. Immediately after the events of September 11, we didn't know what was going to happen, but we all kept going, one day at a time, and we're still moving forward.

Maybe you've gotten to the point where you think you can't get through another day. That's shortsighted of you. You're missing the big picture. You're on the runway, but your fuel supply is the problem. You won't get off the ground without it. Feed yourself some positive thoughts and you can take off at any time.

Ever wonder what makes certain people keep going? I do. Abraham Lincoln encountered a steady procession of setbacks, but he just kept at it. Nothing deterred him. He must have had a lot of faith, because he didn't receive much encouragement along the way. He's an excellent example of someone who never gave up.

The other extreme is the person who seems to run into obstacles with the unerring aim of a marksman. I knew a guy who was remarkably accident-prone. If there was something to run into, he'd find it. If there was a hole in the ground, he'd break his foot by stumbling into it.

Once, he was in such a slam-bang accident that he was hospitalized for six months before being completely patched up. Finally, the day of his release from the hospital arrived and it was decided that he should get an ambulance ride home, just to be on the safe side. As the ambulance was taking him home, it crashed into a car—another spectacular slam-bang accident. My friend was immediately brought back to the hospital, in a new ambulance dispatched to the scene of the disaster. What can I say? Maybe he's just a really unlucky guy. Or maybe he's a loser. I know that sounds harsh, but let's face it—some people *are* losers.

The altitude level of losers is so low that they should walk around in scuba gear all day. They are below sea level on the altitude map. We all know people like that, and they might make great comedians because they have so much material—but first they'd have to learn to be funny. Honestly, I've known people who are such accomplished losers that I think that's what they devote their time to:

How can I be the biggest screwup possible?

How can I prove the born loser *theory to be correct?*

How can I defy the law of probability to make it an absolute *disaster every time?*

How can I achieve a perfect record of total wipeouts?

How far can I get at zero miles per hour?

How can I reach the lowest frequency possible?

How can I operate so that radar could never possibly find me even if I get lost, which I probably will?

These people need a new speedometer.

Get going. Move forward. Aim high. Plan for a takeoff. Don't just sit on the runway and hope someone will come along and push the airplane. It simply won't happen.

Change your attitude and gain some altitude. Believe me, you'll love it up here.

Start Visualizing Positively

Positive thoughts will create positive visuals. Have you ever heard someone say "I can just *see* it!" when they are enthusiastic about something? I know from experience that if I can see something as a possibility, it has a much better chance of happening than if I can't see it happening.

Give your higher self a chance once in a while by giving your possibility quota a boost.

Keep a book of inspiring quotes nearby, so you can change a negative wavelength the moment it descends on you. Here are some of my personal favorites:

> Know everything you can about what you're doing.
> —My father, Fred Trump

> I know the price of success: dedication, hard work, and an unremitting devotion to the things you want to see happen.
> —Frank Lloyd Wright

> A leader has the right to be beaten, but never the right to be surprised.
> —Napoleon

"I remember when *I* was the Donald!"

Cartoon *in* The New Yorker

*(© The New Yorker Collection 1993, Lee Lorenz from
cartoonbank.com. All Rights Reserved.)*

Let's avoid subtlety on this one.
—CHARLIE REISS, *Executive Vice President of Development,*
The Trump Organization

He who looks outside his own heart dreams, he who looks inside his
own heart awakens.
—CARL JUNG

Exciting is a dull word for the business we're in.
—FRED TRUMP

You're the only guy who can wear a cashmere overcoat to a baseball
game and get away with it.
—REGIS PHILBIN

Imagination is more important than knowledge.
—ALBERT EINSTEIN

Continuous effort—not strength or intelligence—is the key to
unlocking our potential.
—WINSTON CHURCHILL

I remember when *I* was the Donald.
—DONALD DUCK

Read Carl Jung

I find reading psychology and self-help books useful. Carl Jung's theories fascinate me and keep my mind open to my own—and the collective—unconscious.

Reading his books can also be a good form of self-defense.

There's a lot we don't know about ourselves. Likewise, there's a lot we may not know about everyone else. Jung used the word *psyche* to refer to both the conscious and the unconscious processes. (That's where the word *psycho* comes from, by the way.) I first became aware of Jung through an acquaintance who had endured some extreme ordeals, yet he remained calm. I couldn't fathom where he got this sort of "grace under fire" demeanor, so I asked him, and he told me that Jung's ideas kept him centered.

My friend put it like this: "Donald, I've learned from my experiences. As a safety factor, I very often see other people as a revolver that could be pointed at me. They are the gun. I, however, am the trigger. So I speak and tread carefully. It's an effective visual aid to avoid conflicts, as I was unwittingly among people who were actually psychos underneath their dignified personas. We never know what will trigger another person's killer instinct. It can be something that happened when they were five years old. So avoid being the trigger, and the revolver will not be a threat."

This synopsis of his philosophy made such an impact on me that I immediately started reading about Carl Jung. I'm glad I did, because it helped me in my business as well as in my personal life. We are all evolving human beings, and being aware of this gave me a big boost toward maturity. It also made me less inclined to be surprised by so-called aberrant behavior. I have to stress that I am not cynical, but I am aware. I hate being in situations where I'm asking myself, *How could this have happened?* This reminds me of my favorite quote from Napoleon about being surprised: A good leader shouldn't be.

You have to know yourself as well as know other people to be an effective leader. For me, reading the work of Carl Jung was a step in the right direction. If someone had told me in business school that studying psychology would be important for financial success, I would not have believed it. My friend's story changed that, and I am grateful to him for such cogent advice. The relatively small number of hours I've spent reading Jung have been more than worth it. Start with his autobiography, *Memories, Dreams, Reflections,* and you will be in for a fascinating time while simultaneously fine-tuning your intuition and instincts. You will also gain a technique for seeing into—versus reading into—the people around you. Believe me, this will serve you well on many levels.

The word *persona* has an interesting root. It comes from the Latin word meaning "mask." This, however, is not derogatory. It's necessary. Each of us has a persona. We need it for survival. It's the face we put on for public use, and it can be intentional or unconscious. For example, a salesman who has lost his entire family in an accident is, naturally, devastated. But to work effectively with his customers, he must appear cheerful and confident. That's part of his persona. It's a survival device.

The only danger is when people become their personae. That means something has been shut off somewhere along the line, and these people will end up hiding behind the false personality that works professionally. As I am very much in the public eye, this hit home and I gave it considerable thought. Fortunately, I am aware of my public side as well as my private side, and, while I'm not one for hiding much, I know there are several dimensions in which I operate. That's one reason I feel at home at The Trump Organization. The people I work with day in and day out know I'm not entirely a glam guy. They see how hard I work. One person said I am very much like a Mormon, which I took as high praise.

Anyway, reading Jung will give you insights into yourself and the ways in which you and other people operate.

Have an Ego

As you know, this rule has been easy for me to follow. But hear me out—I've got a good reason for it.

Having a well-developed ego, contrary to popular opinion, is a positive attribute. It is the center of our consciousness and serves to give us a sense of purpose. I remember saying to someone, "Show me someone with no ego and I'll show you a big loser." I was trying to stir things up and provoke a reaction, but I later realized the basic idea is on target.

The ego works to keep our conscious and unconscious aspects in balance. Too much either way can be detrimental. No ego means very little life force, and too much means a dictatorial personality. Keep your ego in a healthy balance, for your own well-being as well as for those around you. Strive for wholeness. It's an intelligent approach to life and business.

Understanding how egos work can be a great tool. Did you ever notice how you can deflate an opponent by simply saying, "Yeah, whatever you say . . ."? By doing this, you are gently assuming a no-ego position, which disarms the other person while at the same time taking the wind out of their sails. It gives you the peace of mind necessary to allow you to concentrate on something more important than dealing with someone who is playing God.

Sometimes, rather than confronting a tyrant or a psycho directly, it's more effective to keep the knowledge to yourself and proceed accordingly, behind the scenes.

We've all heard the saying that knowledge is power. The intelligent use of that power is crucial in the business world, and it's just as important in your personal life. Your mind can build castles—just make sure the foundations are in place first. You, and the people around you, will be grateful for that.

Keep Critics in Perspective

In any job, you will be criticized at some point. Let's face it: Nobody but a total masochist wants to be criticized.

There is constructive criticism, and then there is destructive criticism. Here's how to assess both types:

1. First of all, consider the source. Should this person's opinion even matter to you?
2. If it does matter to you, take a few minutes to consider whether anything helpful can result from the criticism. Others can often see things that we have overlooked. Use their keen eyes to your advantage.
3. Critics serve their purpose. Sometimes they serve a larger purpose, and sometimes they serve their own purpose. *American Idol* judge Simon Cowell can be critical of the performers on the program, but he's fair and he's honest, and I don't think *American Idol* would work without him. Simon was nice enough to compliment *The Apprentice* in an interview. "I think it's absolutely fantastic," he told the *Daily News*. "I think [Trump] is superb on the show. He's not hamming it up. He's just playing himself and that's very hard to do on television." As I said, Simon is a fair and honest critic, and I am a fan of his.

4. Everyone has an opinion. In most cases, it's not worth the paper it's written on.

5. If the opinion is worth the paper it's written on, and it's written in a paper people are buying and reading, then realize that if people didn't find you interesting enough for public consumption, they wouldn't be taking the time to criticize you. Think of their criticism as a compliment, proof of your significance.

Homework Is Required and There **Will** Be a Test

People who think achieving success is a linear A-to-Z process, a straight shot to the top, simply aren't in touch with reality. There are very few bona fide overnight success stories. It just doesn't work that way.

Success appears to happen overnight because we all see stories in newspapers and on TV about previously unknown people who suddenly become famous. But consider a sequoia tree that has been growing for several hundred years. Just because a television crew one day decides to do a story about that tree doesn't mean it didn't exist before.

In 1955, Glenn Gould, the classical pianist from Toronto, rocketed to international fame by recording Bach's Goldberg Variations. He was young and unusual, but he had already been practicing the piano for close to twenty years. He may have seemed like an overnight sensation to the general public, but anyone who's been working at something for twenty years isn't likely to agree with that assessment.

I have to admit that my knowledge of classical music is limited, but from what little I've read on the subject, I know that the process of becoming a classical musician is a long and demanding one. The amount of practice hours required to master an instrument is astounding, and also never ending. How do they do it? I'm not sure, but I would guess that passion plays a large part.

Every industry and profession has its bottom line for what is required to succeed. If you can't stand to practice every day, being a musician is out of the question. If you hate to exercise, being an athlete is not for you.

In business—every business—the bottom line is understanding the process. If you don't understand the process, you'll never reap the rewards of the process. You'll never last long enough to achieve your "overnight" success.

Part of the process is doing your homework. You have to know what you're getting into first. That was one of my father's strongest beliefs. We've all heard the phrase "You're barking up the wrong tree." It brings to mind a funny image, but in reality it can be embarrassing. Not doing your homework can result in something analogous, so do a few things first to avoid this.

We can learn from our mistakes, but it's better to learn from our successes. When I hear people say, "Well, it was an *interesting* experience," I can usually safely assume they are referring to something that didn't work out the way they'd planned. I don't find my goof-ups to be amusing or interesting.

Can you imagine hearing a surgeon say, "Well, it didn't go quite right, but I sure learned a lot"? I wouldn't want that guy operating on me. The same applies to anyone in business, because if you're in business, it's not just *your* money involved, but very often the money and well-being of others as well. In my business, I can't take chances. If something is not quite right with the design or construction of a superstructure, a lot of people could be injured or killed. I've *got* to know what's going on. Bottom line, it will be my responsibility.

People see the finished product. Wow, a skyscraper! What goes into it is another story. Construction isn't glamorous. It's a serious and often dangerous endeavor. Fortunately, I understood this from my earliest days in the business, so there's a certain gravity in my approach to the construction of any building.

That's where having learned to do my homework comes in handy. It's a necessary requirement, not an extracurricular course to enhance my productivity. Not only do I have to know exactly what I'm doing, but I've also got to make sure I find contractors who know exactly what they're doing as well. That's why I'm tough on them, and that's why I'm equally tough on myself. A lot of lives are at stake in our work. We don't want any "interesting" experiences!

We all know what it's like to pretend to study. There are some courses in school that just don't hold your attention. If you are choosing a career, keep that in mind. What most holds your attention?

Consider a pyramid. Did you ever notice how large and solid the foundation is? Did you notice the carefully graduated levels that eventually lead to the pinnacle? Now turn the pyramid upside down. That's a representation of topsy-turvy thinking. You don't start at the top. You start with the foundation—the stronger, the better.

The world moves along at such a fast clip that we have little patience when things are slow, whether it's the line at a supermarket or Internet access. We've become intolerant of those things that cannot be accelerated or skipped entirely. I can't speed up the foundation work for a building, nor can I expect to play piano like Glenn Gould just because I want to.

Know the limitations as well as the possibilities of everything you do. Find out as much as you can *yourself* about what you plan to do, and don't expect anyone to act as your favorite grandmother in wanting what's best for you. Most people want what's best for *themselves,* not for you. If those people have already spent a great deal of effort on their homework, why should they share it with you?

Listen to a
Ping-Pong Game

I learned a long time ago to listen, but to listen judiciously. You can learn a lot from the people around you—you just have to be discerning about the information that comes your way. A lot of the so-called information I receive turns out to be someone's personal opinion. We're all entitled to our two cents' worth, but sometimes that's all it amounts to.

Be aware of the marketplace. Know what's going on now. That's one reason I devote several hours a day to reading. That's how long it takes to both keep up with current events and learn from the greats in history. How can you expect to be successful if your idea of what's happening in the world is vague or nonexistent? That's like saying, "I know that September 11 happened, but I choose not to acknowledge it. It gets in the way of my positive outlook on things." That approach is fine if you're a professional fairy-tale writer.

There's another side to everything, so develop your ability to see it—or even hear it. I once met a young woman from Hong Kong who worked on Wall Street in emerging markets. She had an uncanny ability to predict certain events in the marketplace—it seemed almost like a psychic gift to me.

One day, I asked her how she could be so on target in her work and she likened knowing and predicting the global markets to *listening* to a Ping-Pong game.

At first, I thought she was joking, or perhaps just being evasive, but she went on to explain her theory.

"I'm not kidding you, Donald. When I was growing up, we had a Ping-Pong table in the den, and I could hear the games my brothers would play, sometimes for hours, when I was studying in my room. I discovered that I could discern the tilt of the paddle, and the outcome of the volley, just by the sound of the Ping-Pong ball being hit, and the sound of it landing on the other side of the net. I knew the results, the repercussions, and the recovery that would be required to successfully handle what had been dealt.

"Later, I applied this to my work in emerging markets and found I could often predict what would be happening just by concentrating on world events and thinking of the sound of Ping-Pong balls being hit around the globe. Ping-Pong is really the reason behind my success."

I was astounded. *That's* my idea of tuning in.

I must add that this young woman had all the education in finance that her position required. She was a bright student. What set her apart from everyone else was the way she applied her knowledge and her keen analysis of the game of Ping-Pong to her work. She may even have done this on an unconscious level initially, but tapping into this resource gave her an uncanny edge. The lesson I learned from her story is never to underestimate the power of awareness.

Find out what other people have done to succeed, and then be prepared to do ten times more. There are no guarantees.

Comparing ourselves to others is a waste of time. I've heard people say, "Well, Mr. Lucky had a million dollars before he was thirty and I've worked just as hard as he has." Well, Mr. Lucky has nothing to do with you, your possibilities, your success, or your failure. Don't let anyone else be your yardstick. That's taking power away from yourself in a big way.

You've got your own personal blueprint to attend to. We can't all be Tiger Woods, J. Lo, Bill Gates, or whoever it is you would like to be, and sometimes that's a hard fact to face. You may have already experienced defeat. That happens. It happens a lot! But the fact that you have aspirations to begin with is putting you on the road to success right now. No matter how defeated you may feel, you've still got a chance. But it won't happen by itself. Get to work!

I'll sum up with two of my favorite quotes:

There are no short cuts to anywhere worth going.
—BEVERLY SILLS

The harder I work, the luckier I get.
—GARY PLAYER

Reflect for
Three Hours a Day

I read an article recently in which European exchange students living in the United States all agreed on one aspect of American life: The noise level here is very high. We seem to avoid quiet moments. Even lapses in conversation are quickly filled with banter or some kind of interference.

It made me realize how much I need a certain amount of quiet time—usually about three hours a day—in order to stay balanced. It's time I use to read and reflect, and I always feel renewed and refreshed by this. It also gives me material to feed my extroverted nature.

For me, the early morning hours are best for this kind of reflection. I'm an early riser, usually up by 5 A.M., which gives me a few hours to read newspapers and magazines of all sorts—local, national, and international.

In the evening, after a black-tie dinner, I'll unwind by stopping at my local Korean grocery for snacks—potato chips and pretzels. That will be my dinner. I rarely get to eat at those black-tie events, and I'd rather have the junk food, anyway.

Once I'm home, I read books—usually biographies. Now and then I like to read about philosophers—particularly Socrates, who emphasizes that you should follow the convictions of your conscience, which basically means thinking for yourself, a philosophy I tend to agree with. It may not make you too popular, but it's essential for lucid thought, and it's a good way to avoid being part of a herd mentality of any sort.

I read as much as I can, but not as much as I'd like, because there are so many constraints on my time. I am grateful for the contribution Oprah Winfrey has made to our country in regard to reading. In my book *The America We Deserve,* I wrote about the deplorable state of reading in this country. Since Oprah decided to do something about it, there has been a noticeable upswing in book sales, and writers are once again considered to be cool people rather than dinosaurs. I cannot thank Oprah enough for what she has done, and I hope every person in this country realizes the positive influence she has had. We all owe Oprah a big thank-you, and I'd like to lead the crowd in saying so.

I like movies and television as much as anyone else, but reading is a form of replenishment for me. The potato chips and pretzels help, too.

Dress for Your Culture

I used to pride myself on buying very inexpensive suits and other clothing. It just didn't make sense to pay thousands of dollars for great clothes when you could buy something for a hundred dollars. Who would know the difference?

Over the years, I've learned that this is wrongheaded. I now buy very high-quality shoes, and they seem to last forever, whereas the cheapos used to wear out quickly and always looked as cheap as the price I'd paid for them. The same is true for suits. These days, I go for Brioni, whose service and attention to detail is second to none. They supplied most of the clothing for *The Apprentice,* so I have tremendous loyalty to them (and I got a good deal). They also make great overcoats.

The way we dress says a lot about us before we ever say a word. To me, dressing successfully means understanding your environment: knowing the culture and making an effort to reflect—and respect—it.

The "look" in Beverly Hills may be attractive, but that same look may be met with scorn on Wall Street. Success is hard enough to achieve without showing up on casual Friday in a three-piece suit. Don't put up unnecessary hurdles for yourself.

Make it easy for people to take you seriously. I would wonder about someone who arrived for a meeting or an interview and was dressed inappropriately for the culture of that particular workplace— for example, a guy showing up at Trump Tower in a cowboy hat, boots, and a fringed cowhide jacket. It's more about culture than style. Be aware of your surroundings and dress accordingly.

Some people can get away with anything. Most people can't. Micha Koeppel, who works at The Trump Organization, usually looks like a Canadian Mountie in full regalia. To look at him, you'd think he was about to lead an expedition through the Rockies. Then again, my buildings are tall, and he scouts the right locations for them, so maybe there's a reason for his getups. It works for him, and he does a good job, so I don't mind.

It's certainly not groundbreaking news that the early victories by the women on *The Apprentice* were, to a very large extent, dependent on their sex appeal. The fact that sex sells is nothing new. However, women are judged harshly when they go too far, so be careful in how you present yourself. If you want to be acknowledged for your intelligence as well as your beauty, don't stand in your own way. Not everyone can tune out a knock-em-dead appearance. Think of how you would like to be perceived, and proceed from there.

I tend to notice what people are wearing only if they look exceptionally well put together—or exceptionally badly put together. It has more to do with style than which designer they may or may not be wearing. As I said, expensive clothing usually looks like it was worth the price.

Have you ever noticed how we tend to pigeonhole people in certain professions by their appearance? It's a form of shorthand to just be able to say "your basic accountant type" or "a typical advertising type" when describing someone. Every profession has a certain look or standard. Just say "banker" and you've saved yourself a hundred words. It's not always fair, but that's how it works.

However, you don't have to be a typical anything.

For example, Frank McKinney looks like a cross between a rock star and a surfer dude. You would never guess by looking at him that he's a real estate entrepreneur who sells ultra-high-end residential real estate in Florida. When he speeds by you on his motorcycle in his Versace vest with his two feet of blond hair blowing in the wind, you can bet he's on his way to a business meeting. But that's Frank's style, and he's very successful.

I'm a conservative dresser due to business considerations and to save time. I enjoy flamboyance in other people—I'm more interested in what a beautiful woman might wear than in anything I might ever put on.

Be aware that your attire can literally become a costume. I've known a lot of terrific-looking scoundrels and a lot of well-dressed bums.

Being tasteful is being tasteful, no matter what line of work you're in. Sure, it helps to have the money to buy great clothes, but a little style can go a long way.

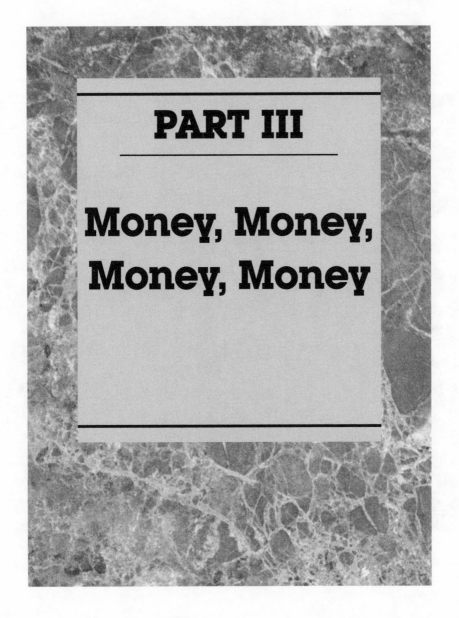

PART III

Money, Money, Money, Money

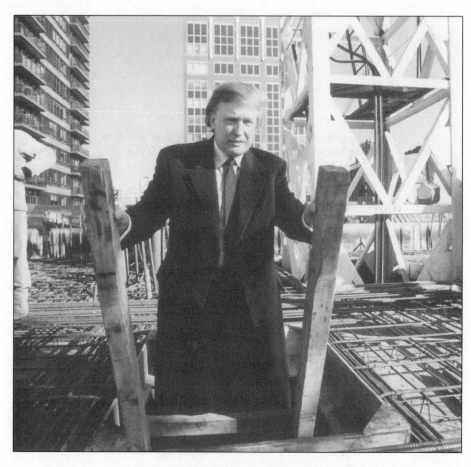

Here I am on top of Trump World Tower at the United Nations Plaza. I like to check up on things, even without my helicopter.

Be Your Own
Best Financial Adviser

Many people go out and hire financial advisers, but I have also seen a lot of those advisers destroy people.

Athletes, in particular, make a great deal of money at a very young age. Too often, some manager squanders the athlete's fortune and they wind up in their thirties with nothing left but their past glory—and are forced to get jobs just to survive.

A good friend of mine and truly one of the greatest basketball players who has ever lived, Kareem Abdul-Jabbar, was in the NBA for over twenty years, only to find that some bad advice had destroyed much of his wealth. I don't know whether it was theft or stupidity, but it was a shame.

Herschel Walker is an athlete who signed big contracts, with both the USFL and NFL. One day, he came to me and told me he was going to invest in a fast-food franchise. I told him, "Herschel, you are a friend of mine, but if you do that, I will not speak to you again." Because of the relationship we had (and continue to have), he decided not to make the investment. The company went bankrupt two years later. Herschel is now a wealthy man, and he thanks me every time I see him.

When it comes to picking a financial adviser, rely on your own judgment based on what you read in reliable publications like *The Wall Street Journal, Forbes, BusinessWeek,* and *Fortune.* They are usually terrific, even though, on occasion, they say some negative things about me. I'm angry at *Fortune* at the moment—and for good reason—but even *Fortune* sometimes manages to awake from its stupor to report something worthwhile. I'm particularly impressed with an editor there named Geoffrey Colvin, who is also the host of *Wall Street Week* on PBS and has written perceptively about corporate restructuring.

The *New York Post* has developed a truly great business section—and one that is fun to read. Lately, *The New York Times's* coverage of business has gone right to the top!

If you read these financial publications for a while, you will start to pick up on the cadence and get a feel for what's happening in the market, which funds are the best, and who the best advisers are.

Stay with the winners. Often, you will read about somebody who has made money quickly and then relies on one of his friends to invest his fortune. That friend has no track record, and if it weren't for his connection to a rich investor, he wouldn't have any money. Beware of instant stars in the world of finance. Trust the people who do it again and again, and who are consistently ranked high by the four best institutional business media outlets. But trust your own common sense first.

Invest Simply

There are numerous firms that provide comprehensive charts and other information on the best returns from certain financial advisers and funds. Study those charts, not over the short term (maybe they just got lucky) but over a fifteen- or twenty-year period.

Invest with the help of a major firm like Goldman Sachs, Morgan Stanley, Bear Stearns, or Merrill Lynch. These are your hard-earned savings at stake. Don't take unnecessary risks.

Generally there is a reason for success. When you look at legends like Alan "Ace" Greenberg and Warren Buffett and marvel at how good they are, you will likely see that what makes them so successful is the same quality you should apply to every one of your own investments—common sense.

I've read many of Warren Buffett's annual reports. In every case, what fascinates me is that he is able to reduce things to the simplest of terms.

Many accomplished Wall Street gurus can make you dizzy with talk of intricate financial maneuverings. They might impress you with their sophisticated computerized trading results, their fifty percent returns from options on products that may not even exist yet. Fortunes are won and lost every day in these markets, but as far as I'm concerned, those folks would be just as successful if they ditched their hedge funds and put all their money on their favorite roulette number at the Trump Taj Mahal Casino in Atlantic City.

You paid good money for this book, and I know you're expecting sophisticated investment advice. The wisest thing I can tell you is to invest only in products you understand, with people you know you can trust. Sometimes the best investments are the ones you don't make.

Get a Prenuptial Agreement

I've said it before—I even wrote a chapter on the art of the prenup in one of my other books—but I'll say it again for anyone about to propose: A prenuptial agreement doesn't mean that you won't always love your spouse. It doesn't mean that you have doubts about the person's integrity or questions about the relationship. All it means is that you recognize that life, especially the parts involving love and business, can be complicated. People have a right to protect their assets. If you own your own business and you're facing a difficult divorce without having secured a prenuptial agreement, your negligence could jeopardize the livelihoods of your employees. I know plenty of women who are supporting their husbands, and this advice applies equally to both sexes.

If I hadn't signed a prenup, I would be writing this book from the perspective of somebody who lost big. We needed a bus to get Ivana's lawyers to court. It was a disaster, but I had a solid prenup, and it held up.

A friend of mine is married to a woman who stands only five-foot-two, but he's petrified of what she will do to him in court, all because he didn't get a prenup. Before he met this woman, he'd had four unsuccessful marriages, yet he told me, "Donald, I'm so in love with this woman that I don't need a prenuptial agreement." I didn't have the courage to tell him what I was thinking to myself: Loser!

A year later, the marriage was over and he was going through hell. When I saw him, he looked like a frightened puppy.

There's nothing wrong with common sense. Be like Thoreau and simplify.

Cut Out
the Middleman

Wayne Newton is a great friend of mine, and he made a lot of money over the years. Unfortunately, given terrible advice, he lost his money and was forced to declare bankruptcy. Meanwhile, his lawyers were eating him alive.

He called me and said, "Donald, I heard you owed $9.2 billion to a hundred banks in the early nineties and you never went bankrupt. How did you do it? Because I just can't seem to get out of this mess. My lawyers are making a fortune and the banks are impossible."

I asked Wayne how many banks were involved. He told me it was three. "You're lucky," I said. "I had ninety-nine banks and I made a point of becoming best friends with everybody at every bank. You have to do the same."

I gave him some more advice, which he has generously acknowledged in many interviews. I told him, "Wayne, you are a major celebrity. Have your secretary call the three banks and get the person who is really in charge, not the figurehead, and personally talk to all three people. Arrange a meeting with them, ideally a dinner with them and their families. Get to know them. At the end of this period of time, they'll like you. They'll be impressed by you because you are a celebrity. They may control a lot of money, but they don't control fame, and people are impressed by fame. Forget your lawyers. They are never going to want to settle the case, because then their legal fees stop. You must do it yourself. Call the bankers. Become friendly with the bankers. And make a deal."

Wayne called me three weeks later. He'd had dinner with all three bankers and said they were among the nicest people he'd ever met. They brought their wives and children. Later, he cut deals with every one of them. The banks were taken care of over a period of time, the lawyers didn't get any richer, and today Wayne is doing fantastically well.

You're probably wondering how this rule applies to your life if you are not headlining a major Las Vegas show. Here's how: Wayne took control of the situation. He appealed to the people in charge. Most of us need lawyers at some point in our lives, and we all have to deal with large bureaucracies. But sometimes you need to go right to the top, and you need to do it yourself. You don't have to sing "Danke Schoen" to make a sincere personal approach.

Of course, there will be times when lawyers are essential. Some people are scoundrels.* In those instances, sue the bastards. But whenever possible, settle. It saves a lot of time for everyone involved.

---

*I have come to hate doctors. I think that, generally, they are a bunch of money-grubbing dogs. I can tell you about countless instances when doctors have ruined people's lives. As an example, a person I am very fond of had a foot injury that I believe should have healed naturally, but instead, the doctor operated on it, fitting pins and plates into the foot. Now, after over a year of convalescence, this person is having a hard time walking. I think that suing a doctor like this would qualify as a worthwhile legal expense. (Recently, the patient saw this doctor walking on the very expensive and chic Worth Avenue in Palm Beach and spending lots of money.) This is one of many bad doctors I know of—there are too many others to name. I just can't stand the bastards.

Teach Your Children the Value of a Dollar

My kids know the value of money from example. They see how hard I work. I don't talk about it with them because I don't have to—they have eyes.

They see the way I live. I turn off the lights whenever I leave the office. I'm always happy to get a good deal, whether I'm buying a building or buying supplies at Duane Reade. (Trust me: You can get a good deal on shaving cream there.)

I always remember the example my parents set for me. I could *see* their determination and discipline. They didn't have to harp on it. I try to be the way they were.

My parents were frugal in the sense that they knew it wasn't easy to make money, and that it should be treated with respect. They lived well but simply, and were not flamboyant in their spending. We rarely went out to eat. We took relatively few elaborate vacations.

They emphasized schooling and education. We had a solid family life, and I remember feeling very fortunate. Each of us was expected to contribute something not only to the family as a whole, but to society. That is a Trump family value that is ingrained in me, and one I've tried to live up to.

With my mother at
New York Military Academy.

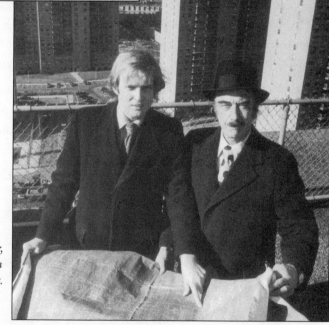

With my father,
Fred Trump, in
the early days.

My children have benefited from affluence, as I did, but it's surprising how unspoiled they are in many ways. They have budgets and live within them. They have limits on their credit cards, and they have them more for protection in an emergency than for anything else. When they were growing up, both of my sons earned extra money during their summer vacations by mowing lawns, cutting trees, moving stones, and doing landscaping work at the Seven Springs estate in Westchester. Ivanka attended the School of American Ballet, which requires an enormous amount of discipline and training.

College kids today are more money savvy, perhaps, than kids from earlier generations. They seem serious about their money. This is a good sign, because the sooner you understand the value of money, the more likely you are to possess large amounts of it.

If your children see you being careless with money, they will assume it's okay for them to be careless. Children watch. That's how they learn. Your priorities will often become their priorities. Any family can have a wild card or two, but on the whole, it's been proven that children will learn from what they see.

If you obviously enjoy going to Las Vegas to gamble, it's likely they'll think this is a good thing and will follow suit. If you like going to Carnegie Hall and bring the kids along, they'll think this is an exciting event because you do. Children inherently like to please, so think about the values you exhibit. Sooner or later, kids will form their own tastes, but the initial exposure is important.

I spent a good deal of time with my children—Don Jr., Ivanka, and Eric—when they were growing up, because we all lived together. We remain very close. I spend less time with Tiffany, as she lives in California with her mother. I do try to include them in my travels and activities as much as possible.

They know they are always welcome to join the family business. Don Jr. began working full-time at The Trump Organization in September 2001. "Trumps are builders," he told Barbara Walters in a

With my three eldest children—Don Jr., Ivanka, and Eric—and Barbara Walters for an appearance on 20/20.
(© 2004 Virginia Sherwood/ABC Photo Archives)

With my youngest daughter, Tiffany.

recent interview. I hope Ivanka, Eric, and Tiffany might also consider a career with us, but it's their decision entirely.

I have very high standards, but so do my kids. They're all high achievers who enjoy working and are not goof-offs in any sense of the word. I wonder why I'm so lucky.

Not teaching your kids about money is like not caring whether they eat. If they enter the world without financial knowledge, they will have a much harder go of it. Make sure you let them in on your way of thinking about money—how you manage expenses, how you save, where you invest.

Let them know that having money isn't necessarily a sign of greed. It's an important element for survival. Just getting a first apartment can be a lesson for your kids: They suddenly learn about security deposits! Equip them for life as best you can. Buy them a subscription to *Money* or some other personal-finance magazine. Give them incentives for saving their allowance.

If they don't learn about money from you, who's going to teach them?

PART IV

The Secrets of Negotiation

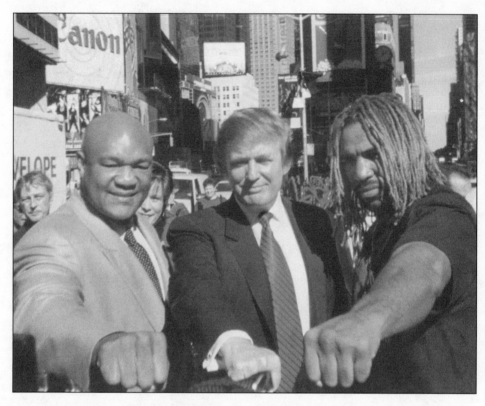

Negotiations, anyone? Here I am with George Foreman and Shannon Briggs.

If You Have Them
by the Balls,
Their Hearts and Minds
Will Follow

In this part of the book, I want to tell you about some of my favorite deals and the essential rules of negotiation they exemplify.

First, though, here's my basic philosophy of how deals are done: It's all about persuasion, not power.

Power is merely the ability to convince people to accept your ideas.

Just because I am a successful businessman doesn't mean I always get my way. It's true that I don't have to be as vociferous about things as before. I don't have to act like a bulldozer to get attention. But I have to coax and make my case just like any other negotiator.

An interviewer from Brazil recently asked me what the best parts and the worst parts of having so much money and success were. I had the same answer to both questions: the effect it has on people. Anyone in a position of power will probably agree with me. There are pluses and minuses.

The plus side is that people will listen to you more readily than if you aren't on the map financially. The minus side is that they will reduce you to one dimension and keep you there.

Power is not just about calling all the shots. It's about ability. You can call all the shots, but if they're bad ones, no one will take much notice after a while. *Know what you're doing.* That's where the real power comes from.

Convincing others has a lot to do with understanding negotiation. Study the art of persuasion. Practice it. Develop an understanding of its profound value across all aspects of life.

Don't expect people to believe your blarney simply because you're good at delivering it. The boardroom is not the pub down on the corner.

Make it easy on the people you are trying to convince. Give them readily accessible metaphors and analogies. If you are too far over their heads, they'll feel frustrated or, worse, inferior. Let them know you're all on the same level in some way. Use humor. It's a great icebreaker. I sometimes tell people that I wish our meeting had been yesterday, because I was having a great hair day and they missed it!

Convincing other people of how wonderful you are and how lofty your ideas are is a good way to convince them to tune out or, better yet, to escape from you as soon as possible. We all need to have a healthy dose of confidence to be convincing, but don't bulldoze. If you do, you may see a lot of people in front of you at first, but the room will soon be empty.

As the adage goes, "There's a fine line between acceptance and resignation." You want people to *accept* your ideas, not merely be *resigned* to them because they think they can't fight back or are just plain exhausted by you. Don't browbeat them into believing you. Let them think the decision is theirs. It will give them a feeling of control.

Here is the golden rule of negotiating:

He who has the gold makes the rules.

If you walk into a negotiation and know nothing about the other party, let *them* talk, listen to their tone, observe their body language, and determine whether they really want to make a deal or just show you how smart they are.

Most negotiations should proceed calmly, rather than in a hostile manner. However, sometimes a negotiation works best after a few screams and some table pounding.

The best negotiators are chameleons. Their attitude, demeanor, approach, and posture in a negotiation will depend on the person on the other side of the table.

If the other party to the transaction wants to acquire something you own, let them convince you that you really don't want it or need it. In doing so, they'll convince you of just how badly they want it.

Money is not always the only consideration for exchange in the sale of an asset. Think beyond the traditional boundaries.

Learn the value of saying no. View any conflict as an opportunity.

Most important, know the party on the other side of the table before sitting down with them. Research who you're dealing with, how they negotiate, and what they want from you.

Now you're ready to deal. The following stories illustrate these basic rules.

The Trump Building at 40 Wall Street.

Consider What
the Other Side Wants

One of the best deals I ever made was the acquisition of the tallest building in lower Manhattan, a 1.3-million-square-foot landmark known as 40 Wall Street.

I got it for $1 million, and the negotiation was all about timing and intuition.

In the 1960s and 1970s, 40 Wall Street was truly a hot property—a fully occupied building. Then in the 1980s, it was bought by Ferdinand Marcos, who was busy dealing with a revolution in the Philippines. The skyscraper at 40 Wall Street fell into decline, proving once again that a business should never be run by a dictator, especially a real one about to be booted from power.

Then the Resnicks, a prominent real estate family, descended on 40 Wall Street, but after a long period of negotiation, it became clear that the Resnicks and Citibank weren't going to make a deal and that 40 Wall Street would be back on the block. I wanted very much at this time to make my move, but this was in the early 1990s and I was in no position to do so. The real estate market was terrible, and my own financial straits were woeful.

The next buyer was the Kinson Company, a group from Hong

Kong. They made a great deal, and after the purchase was complete, I requested a meeting with them to discuss a possible partnership. They weren't interested in a partnership, but they did want to make 40 Wall Street the downtown equivalent of Trump Tower, including a public atrium. It sounded like a beautiful idea. However, what they would do with the steel columns that supported a seventy-two-story building never seemed to enter their minds. I was dumbfounded.

As you can probably guess, the Kinson group proved to be relatively clueless about renovating, running, and leasing out a New York City skyscraper. They weren't in the real estate business to begin with—they were mostly in apparel—and they were in way over their heads. They poured tens of millions of dollars into the building but were getting nowhere. They had problems with tenants, contractors, suppliers, architects, even the owners of the land, a prominent family from Germany, the Hinnebergs. Eventually, Kinson wanted out, and they called me.

It was now 1995 and the market still wasn't so good. Kinson had every reason to want to get out, and they wanted to do it quickly and quietly. So the negotiations began, with me offering them $1 million in addition to assuming and negotiating their liens. I also made the deal subject to a restructured ground lease with the Hinneberg family.

They accepted my terms without question.

Why? Because they wanted out—and fast. They knew it and I knew it, and because I knew it, the negotiation was easy.

There was another crucial aspect to this deal, which proves the importance of knowing what the other side wants: All of the prior leaseholders had dealt with the agent of the Hinneberg family. The agent insisted on increasing the rent and raised other financial obstacles that he said the owner insisted upon. I had to see for myself what the Hinnebergs wanted—was it money, or something else? If you want the truth, go to the source and skip the translation by the intermediary.

I flew to Germany with Bernie Diamond, my general counsel, for a face-to-face meeting with the owner, who seemed impressed by the fact that I would travel across the Atlantic to see him. I learned that what he really wanted was peace of mind in connection with his ownership of the land, but all he was getting was aggravation and litigation. I told him I would agree to turn the present disaster into a first-class office building if he would forgo all rent during the renovation period and revise the lease to permit rental to quality subtenants and bank financing for part of the building improvements. He agreed—and it was the first of many instances that confirmed my belief that Walter, Christian, and Walter Hinneberg Jr. are among the finest people with whom I've ever done business.

Very soon after acquiring 40 Wall Street, the markets turned for the better, and the downtown area experienced a renaissance in terms of both commercial and residential properties and developments.

I make a great deal of money from 40 Wall Street. Aside from owning the most beautiful building in lower Manhattan, I have the added attraction of owning a particularly lucrative one, all because I watched the property carefully for decades, waiting for my moment, and knew what the other side was thinking.

Be Reasonable and Flexible

A good negotiator must be flexible to be successful.

When I bought 40 Wall Street, it was virtually vacant. I told the existing leasing broker, a friend of mine, that I was going to renovate the building and get tenants. I offered him the chance to be my exclusive rental agent. The broker had been the agent for the previous owners of the building, who had been having big problems getting tenants. He was so sure I would fail that he said he would take the job only if I would pay him a retainer of $60,000 per month, starting immediately. He said he would deduct his future commission from that guaranteed fee.

His offer was impossible for me to accept. I owned a vacant building with existing losses, and the broker, who had been unable to produce in the past, was asking me to pay cash up front. I told the broker that his offer showed a total lack of faith in my ability to be successful—a broker getting paid without producing a tenant was unheard of.

The broker remained inflexible in his position. We parted company.

I hired another high-quality broker, who willingly accepted the opportunity on the usual terms—no lease, no commission. I renovated the building. The broker made millions in commissions in the next two years. The original broker's inflexibility cost him a small fortune, plus he lost any future business from me.

Trust Your Instincts

When I took over 40 Wall Street, my associate Abe Wallach, who orchestrated the purchase, was certain that the only viable solution was to convert the building to a residential cooperative apartment house. His reasoning made sense, given the depressed market for office tenants and the incentives the city was giving for residential development downtown. All of the real estate brokers shared his view that leasing to office tenants wasn't feasible. They said the floor sizes were either too small or too large for renting. They complained that the lobby, elevators, and building systems required extensive renovations with questionable results.

I was leery of their recommendation because the cost of residential conversion was high, plus the five floors occupied by a law firm would have to be bought out for megabucks and that would screw up any construction timetable. My instincts told me the building could become the prime office location it once had been, and that there had to be a way to make it work.

I asked George Ross to see whether he could devise a workable scenario, and he came up with an interesting new approach. He suggested we envision the 1.3-million-square-foot building as three separate structures on top of each other:

- The top 400,000-square-foot tower had small floors with spectacular views, and he was convinced it would quickly be rented to boutique tenants who would pay higher rent for the prestige of being a full-floor user on a high floor.
- The middle 300,000 square feet could be rented for less per square foot, but those rents would still more than cover the purchase price and the cost of renovation.
- The bottom 400,000 square feet might be tougher to rent, but even if those floors were completely empty, the building would still be profitable, assuming our projections about renting the top 700,000 square feet were correct.

Emboldened by George's plan, I discarded the idea of residential conversion and relied on our construction expertise to turn 40 Wall Street into a successful office building. We redesigned and modernized the lobby and building systems, and when the rental market improved, we were ready. Now, the building is worth hundreds of times what I paid for it.

I guess my instincts were right.

Know Exactly
What You Want
and Keep It to Yourself

If you're careful about what you reveal, you'll have more flexibility as you gather more information about the contours of the deal.

In order to complete Trump Tower as I envisioned it, it was necessary for me to control an adjoining site on Fifty-seventh Street owned by Leonard Kandell and leased to Bonwit Teller, a dying department store chain. Len Kandell was a shrewd real estate developer whose ultimate desire was to own land in strategic locations forever. I tried to gain a long-term lease, but Kandell was asking for too much in rent, and we were stalled.

Meanwhile, during negotiations to buy air rights from the adjoining Tiffany store, which would allow me to build a larger Trump Tower, I learned that Tiffany also had an option to buy the Kandell property at a fair market price. This was news to me, and a crucial piece of information, but I didn't let anyone know how important that news was to me.

I led Tiffany to believe I was interested only in air rights, without calling any special attention to their option to buy the Kandell property. They sold me their air rights and basically threw in the option as part of the deal.

Then I told Len Kandell that I was no longer interested in a lease on the land. I was going to buy it, using the Tiffany option.

Kandell didn't want to sell, and I really didn't want to buy. With my new leverage, I suggested reconsideration of a long-term lease. This time, Kandell agreed, and we quickly closed on a mutually acceptable lease, beginning a friendship that continues to flourish with his heirs.

Don't be confined by your expectations. Sometimes, what we think we want and what we actually want are two different things.

On more than several occasions, I have discovered in the middle of negotiations that what I had wanted was the wrong thing. Sometimes, my negotiating partners have given me ideas I hadn't thought of. Even adversaries have given me new ideas. Sometimes, a big question suddenly comes into my mind and I begin to think in a new direction.

Cut yourself some slack. It's okay to change your mind and suggest a different approach—as long as you haven't made any commitments to the other side.

Some people, while admitting I'm a good negotiator, have said I'm devious. I'm too busy to be devious. I just assimilate new information quickly and move forward in unexpected ways—unexpected to the other party as well as to myself. That's one reason I find negotiating exciting.

Perhaps because I'm a Gemini, I believe there is a duality to negotiating. You have to balance reason with passion. Reason keeps you open. Passion keeps your adrenaline going.

Before you begin any negotiation, write down your objectives. Then try to anticipate what the other side might want. Find a way of talking about the deal and setting up parameters that will keep either of you from getting locked into an impossible position.

Know what you want, bottom line, but keep it to yourself until a strategically necessary moment. Once all of the issues are on the table, you'll have a better approach to navigating your way to your desired solution.

Make Sure Both Sides Come Out Winning

In *The Art of the Deal*, I described how I acquired the Hilton property in Atlantic City, now known as Trump Marina, for $320 million. It was the biggest gamble of my career at the time, and it became front page news because the property was also sought by Steve Wynn, the largest casino owner in Las Vegas, who launched a hostile takeover bid before Hilton chose me as its white knight.

I like all of my Atlantic City hotels, but Trump Marina is where I prefer to stay when I'm in town, because acquiring this property was a victory to savor. It reminds me of an essential negotiating skill: Let everyone come out a winner. There was no rancor in this triumph.

There was drama, however—especially when Steve Wynn got involved. It became a competition of heavy hitters, and I loved every minute of it. I'll bet Steve did, too. To this day, we are good friends.

Interestingly enough, we are now both fodder for an HBO movie in development about Atlantic City. I got a copy of the script and it takes plenty of shots at me and Steve. It is highly inaccurate.

Steve, in essence, provided a catalyst for both the Hiltons and myself to get what we wanted. Was Steve the loser? No. I got the property I wanted, but Steve is thriving. The battle for the property enlarged his reputation and probably helped him move on to even bigger deals.

If the HBO movie ever makes it to the small screen, don't believe what you see. You'll get a better view of reality from other TV shows on the air. In a good negotiation, all sides win.

Let Your Guard Down, but Only on Purpose

Offer a calculated nugget of information, or a provocative opinion, to see what the reaction is.

If you say something seemingly off the cuff, you may get a revealing response. I might make an outrageous comment in a meeting just to see whether the other people play along or take a stand and disagree. It's a good way of assessing the mettle of the folks across the table. Do they want to be liked? Are they comfortable with unpredictability? Are they capable of candor?

Know that your negotiating partner might bluff, too. But when it comes to serious endeavors, you don't want bluffers of any sort. Study the person's history.

I'm always surprised when newcomers to the real estate industry think that talking big and fast will get them somewhere with me. Construction of a big building is painstaking work and that's the kind of person I want doing it—someone who will take the time to do it right. I don't want people who think they can get it done in record time. That can spell disaster.

I remember one contractor who tried every angle to convince me how fast he was. His time estimates were so far off that I couldn't take him seriously, but I let him keep trying to pitch me just to find out how full of it he really was. He must have thought he caught me on a bad day or with my guard down, but my guard wasn't down—I was just incredulous. Finally, I told the guy that what he was saying was exactly what I never wanted to hear. He was the first person whose bid was ruled out.

Being Stubborn
Is Often an Asset

My first big deal, in 1974, involved the old Commodore Hotel site near Grand Central Station on Forty-second Street in New York City. The hotel was vacant, except for a sleazy club called Plato's Retreat and some rundown street-level stores.

The land was owned by the Penn Central Railroad, which was bankrupt and owed New York City $15 million in back taxes that the city desperately needed. The city was about to default on its bonds, and banks would not consider real estate loans in Manhattan.

My idea was to transform the Commodore into a state-of-the-art hotel. I had a six-point plan:

1. Buy the land from the railroad.
2. Induce the railroad to use the purchase price to pay the City of New York the back taxes it owed.
3. Convince a New York State agency with the power of eminent domain to accept a deed to the land to condemn all existing leases.
4. Persuade the city to accept a fixed rental and a share of the profits in lieu of taxes.
5. Find a big hotel operator to join me in the project, since I had no hotel experience.
6. Convince a bank to loan me $80 million to build the hotel.

When I first told my lawyer, George Ross, of my plans, he told me I was crazy to attempt something so bold in such a bad economic environment. I told him I was determined to get it done. He agreed to help.

For two years, I stuck to my guns. Eventually, it paid off.

The railroad sold me the land for $12 million and used the money to pay the city its back taxes.

The Urban Development Corporation accepted the deed to the land and agreed to condemn all existing leases, provided I would pay all damages to the displaced tenants.

The city agreed to the lease from UDC with a fixed rent and a share of the profits.

Hyatt became my partner in the deal and funded half of it.

I got a loan from the Bowery Savings Bank to cover the cost of acquisition and construction.

The hotel became the Grand Hyatt.

The fact that I was stubborn and had achieved a result others deemed impossible jump-started my career as a developer.

Be Patient

I like to move quickly, but if a situation requires patience, I will be patient. The speed depends on the circumstances, and I keep my objective in mind at all times. This alone can be a patience pill. I've spent from five minutes to fifteen years waiting for a deal.

One good tactic for speeding up a deal is to show a lack of interest in it. This will often make the other side rekindle their efforts to get something going. I was very interested in a deal once, but I had a hunch that it wasn't a good idea to look too eager to these people. I would put off their calls and do my best to appear aloof. Then I said I'd be traveling for a couple of weeks and would get back to them after that. While I was "traveling," they used the time to modify their position and present to me almost precisely what I'd been hoping to get. It saved us all a lot of negotiating time.

A good tactic for slowing down a deal is to distract the other side. One way is to drop hints about whether a certain aspect of the deal should be looked into further, or to mention other deals and properties as examples. That will set them off in a direction that consumes their time and focus. While they're off on a tangent, you'll still be on target.

One time, I was in the middle of a negotiation that seemed to be speeding out of my control. I suddenly asked the other side if they knew the history of a particular development, implying that their understanding of it might be crucial. They figured the development must have had some bearing on what we were trying to accomplish together, so they backed up a bit, took some time to investigate it, and gave me control of the negotiations with enough time to assess everything at my leisure. I got the upper hand.

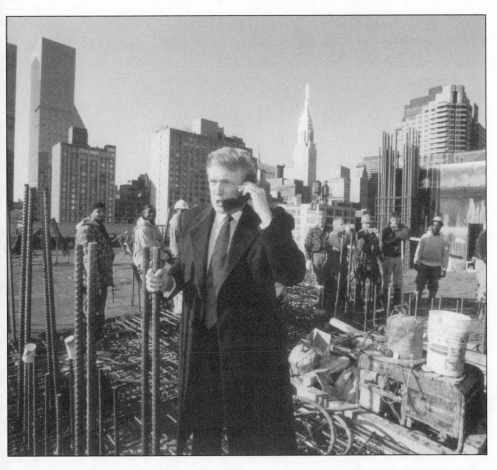

Life at the top means the phone calls never stop.

Be Strategically Dramatic

In 1999, I began construction on the tallest residential tower in the world, Trump World Tower at the United Nations Plaza.

The location was terrific—the East Side of Manhattan, close to the United Nations, with both river views and city views. It was hot stuff, but not everyone was happy about it, especially some diplomats at the United Nations, who didn't want their thirty-eight-story building to be outclassed by our ninety-story tower. According to CNN, UN secretary general Kofi Annan acknowledged talking with New York City mayor Rudolph Giuliani about the project and how to stop it.

"It will not fit here," the Ukrainian ambassador, Volodymyr Yel'chenko, told CNN, "because it overshadows the United Nations complex."

When the protests became vocal, I used my own brand of diplomacy and refused to say anything critical of the United Nations. I predicted that many ambassadors and UN officials would end up buying apartments in the building. Sure enough, they have.

But as soon as we were in business, the city hit us with an enormous tax assessment, costing us over $100 million more than we thought we should pay. We decided to take the only action possible.

We sued the city for $500 million.

For four years, we fought this case. The city lawyers held their ground, and we held ours. We could have given up. It's not easy to take on the government and win, especially when the issue is taxes, but I knew we had a case.

Finally, after many conversations, we reached a settlement. The city agreed to cut our taxes seventeen percent and give us the ten-year tax abatement that we sought if we would agree to withdraw our lawsuit and subsidize two hundred units of affordable housing in the Bronx.

The lawsuit saved us approximately $97 million. We never would have gotten any of it if we hadn't taken dramatic action.

Sometimes
You Still
Have to Screw Them

For many years I've said that if someone screws you, screw them back. I once made the mistake of saying that in front of a group of twenty priests who were in a larger audience of two thousand people. I took some heat for that. One of them said, "My son, we thought you were a much nicer person."

I responded, "Father, I have great respect for you. You'll get to heaven. I probably won't, but to be honest, as long as we're on the earth, I really have to live by my principles."

When somebody hurts you, just go after them as viciously and as violently as you can. Like it says in the Bible, an eye for an eye.

Be paranoid. I know this observation doesn't make any of us sound very good, but let's face the fact that it's possible that even your best friend wants to steal your spouse and your money. As I say every week in *The Apprentice*, it's a jungle out there. We're worse than lions—at least they do it for food. We do it for the thrill of the hunt.

Recently, I've become a bit more mellow about retribution and paranoia. Although I still believe both are necessary, I now realize that vengeance can waste a lot of time better spent on new developments and deals, and even on building a better personal life. If you can easily dismiss a negative from your life, it's better to do so. Seeing creeps as a form of corruption that you're better off without is a great time-saving device.

Still, sometimes you've just got to screw them back.

For example, a while ago I agreed to invest a small amount in a new restaurant venture. I did this with the full expectation that I was throwing this money down the drain, because most of these clubs are not successful. I liked the two young guys who approached me to invest and figured I'd give them a break—plus a good friend of mine had asked me to help them.

When the restaurant opened, it was a smash hit. Crowds of people lined up to get in. Money was pouring in. It was incredible.

About a year later, I realized that I hadn't received a single dollar from the owners—no repayment of my initial investment and certainly no profit. I called two of the guys who got me into the deal and said, "Fellas, come on, I know success when I see it. You ought to pay back your investors."

One of them said, "Oh, we're working so hard, and the money just isn't coming in fast enough."

My response: "Bullshit! I don't believe it." From my perspective, they seemed to be living like kings.

Eventually, I received my first "equity distribution" from them, for a fraction of my investment. I was furious and sent an angry letter to the managing partner, in which I asked for a public investigation of their records.

I'm an instinctive businessman and I hate being screwed. I can't prove they did anything wrong without spending more money to investigate them than my investment is worth, but my hunch is that investors like me should have been repaid six times their initial investment by now.

Now whenever I see the guys I tried to help, they wave to me and I just turn my back. The sad thing for them is that had I felt that they treated me (and their other investors) fairly, I probably would have backed them for millions on their next deal.

Maybe I'll sue them anyway, just to prove my point. Business can be tough, but you've got to stay true to your principles.

Sometimes
You Have to
Hold a Grudge

For years, I supported the governor of New York Mario Cuomo. I was one of his largest campaign contributors. I never asked for a thing while he was in office. For my generous support, he regularly thanked me and other major contributors with a tax on real estate so onerous that it drove many investors away from the city. It became known as the Cuomo Tax.

After he was defeated for reelection by a better man (and governor), George Pataki, I called Mario to ask for a perfectly legal and appropriate favor involving attention to a detail at the Department of Housing and Urban Development, which at the time was being run by his son Andrew.

Mario told me that this would be hard for him to do, because he rarely calls the "Secretary" on business matters.

I said to him, "Mario, he is not the Secretary. He's your son."

Mario said, "Well, I think of him as the Secretary, and I refer to him as that—he's got a very serious job to do."

I understood Mario's concern about impropriety, but I wasn't asking him to do anything even slightly questionable—this was a simple, aboveboard request, the kind of favor that takes place between friends in the private and public sectors all the time. Finally, I asked Mario point-blank, "Well, are you going to help me?"

In a very nice way, he essentially told me no.

I did the only thing that felt right to me. I began screaming. "You son of a bitch! For years I've helped you and never asked for a thing, and when I finally need something, and a totally proper thing at that, you aren't there for me. You're no good. You're one of the most disloyal people I've known and as far as I'm concerned, you can go to hell."

My screaming was so loud that two or three people came in from adjoining offices and asked who I was screaming at. I told them it was Mario Cuomo, a total stiff, a lousy governor, and a disloyal former friend. Now whenever I see Mario at a dinner, I refuse to acknowledge him, talk to him, or even look at him.

I will say this, however. Mario's wife, Matilda, is a fine woman and was a terrific friend to my mother. It's not her fault that her husband is a loser.

Another failed politician who disappointed me is a man named Pete Dawkins, sometimes referred to as General Pete Dawkins. He led a charmed life—West Point cadet, Heisman trophy winner, Rhodes scholar, but as I found out, Pete was also a stiff. When he was running for the U.S. Senate in New Jersey against Frank Lautenberg, a magazine called *Manhattan, Inc.* published a damning profile of him, and Dawkins folded up like a broken umbrella.

One day, Dawkins came to my office and asked me to help him build the Vietnam Veterans Memorial in lower Manhattan. He asked for a million dollars (or more) because he said he was having bad luck raising money.

I decided to help because no soldiers have ever been treated worse than the courageous people who came back from Vietnam, wounded and maimed, attacked physically abroad and psychologically at home.

I provided over a million dollars in matching grants, and, almost as important, I helped get it built by using the best contractors in the city, along with unions who made sure it was constructed swiftly, properly, and cost-effectively. At the opening, Pete Dawkins took the credit.

Many years later, he was working as a high-ranking executive at Citibank and I phoned him to ask a small favor, to find something out for me. He didn't respond for a while, so I called him two more times. Finally, he said, "I really can't do it for you, Donald, and I really don't want to get involved." I told Dawkins that the *Manhattan, Inc.* article about him had been true. I consider him to be one of the most over-rated people I have ever dealt with.

Sometimes you have to hold a grudge.

The hugely successful Miss Universe Pageant. From left to right: Charles Gargano, Stephanie Seymour, Evander Holyfield, Miss Universe Wendy Fitzwilliams, me, and NFL great Bruce Smith. Also pictured: Kylie Bax (third from right) and Sirio Maccioni (far right).

Learn the Value
of Saying No

I purchased the Miss Universe Organization in 1996 and immediately sold half of the company to CBS; so not only were they our broadcaster, they were a co-owner as well. This kind of arrangement, where the network actually owns the end product, was a fairly new concept and should have been a win-win situation, since CBS would actually be able to eliminate the middleman and pay a lower license fee while, in theory, the network, as an owner, would look to maximize all promotional opportunities.

The partnership was a great concept, but after five years, it had not gone as planned. CBS was not willing to promote the shows to my satisfaction. As more and more cable competition ate into the network's market share, on-air promotion became all the more important to sustain viewership, but it just wasn't happening. To make matters worse, CBS tried to change the shows drastically by making them MTV-style music specials and dramatically cutting the time allotted to show the women competing. I am not a network programmer, but it seemed to me that people might be tuning in to a beauty competition to see beautiful women.

I am not saying a television musical performance is a bad thing;

there have been some great ones over the years. A perfect example was the 1999 Miss Teen USA pageant: A year earlier, the teen show had introduced a little-known boy band called 'NSync. By 1999 they were the biggest band around. As a sign of appreciation, they agreed to appear on the Miss Teen USA pageant again. In the middle of their summer tour, 'NSync rented a jet and flew in for eight hours the day of the show, performing two songs. They were terrific. Unfortunately, no one knew about it because CBS had chosen not to run a single promotion for the show.

So in February 2002 we were all reevaluating how we wanted to approach the network license renewal. Citing the current ratings, which were caused by the lack of promotion and the fact that CBS would always air the pageant against the toughest competition, Les Moonves, the head of the network, said he was not willing to begin negotiations until the end of the season. Obviously, with the season ending in August, the network schedules would be set and there would be absolutely no room for negotiation with any other network.

I sent a letter to Les telling him I wanted an option to buy CBS out of the partnership, exercisable up until a week after the broadcast of the Miss Universe pageant in May. I feigned disinterest in continuing with the pageants and told him if I did not exercise the option, we would commence with selling or dismantling the company. A few days later, I believed we had a deal.

I immediately signed with Jim Griffin of the William Morris Agency to begin shopping the pageants to other broadcasters. I also called my good friend Bob Wright, chairman and CEO of NBC, to tell him the pageants might become available. I knew that NBC had recently acquired Telemundo, and the pageants are huge in Latin markets. It looked like a great opportunity for cross-promotion.

In the meantime, CBS had given up and allowed us free rein to get back to the basics on the production and put more emphasis on what had worked in the past: beautiful women. We also convinced them to schedule the pageant for a night outside of the all-important ratings sweeps, which would ensure more on-air promotions.

As a result, our 2002 Miss Universe pageant hit ratings gold. Overall, it was number seven for the week and number one in demographics. The pageant even trounced the NBA playoffs on NBC. The Miss Universe pageant quickly became a very hot property.

I immediately sent a letter to Les Moonves telling him I was exercising my option to buy out CBS. To my shock, Les took the position that we had never agreed on an option. NBC was waiting in the wings, and after a weeklong bidding war I bought out CBS and created a new partnership with NBC.

At the first meeting of the new board, I asked the Miss Universe staff to dust off some of the cross-promotional ideas they had pitched to CBS over the years. Within minutes, Jeff Gaspin of NBC approved the production of a Miss USA *Fear Factor* to lead into the Miss USA telecast. In addition, the *Today* show agreed to do five-minute live shots from each pageant location. The results were amazing. For years the pageants had tried to get a plug on the third-rated *CBS Morning Show* and couldn't get as much as a returned phone call. Now they were getting major promotion on the nation's number one morning program and an Internet tie-in through NBC.com.

The Miss USA *Fear Factor* was the highest rated in the series and the 2003 Miss USA and Miss Universe pageants received the highest ratings since I had bought the company. Additionally, the Telemundo simulcast of the pageant was one of the highest-rated programs in the network's history.

The cross-promotional concept I visualized in 1996 was finally realized in 2003, and it never would have happened if I hadn't been willing to walk away from CBS, say no, and pursue a better opportunity elsewhere.

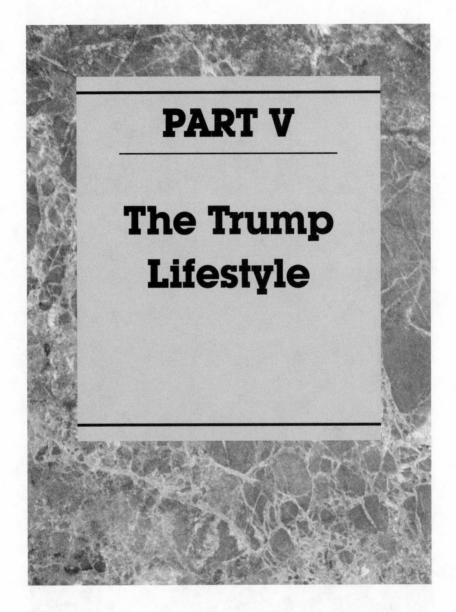

PART V

The Trump Lifestyle

The art of the hair.

The Art of the Hair

Over the years, I have been criticized for the way I comb my hair, but never so much as since the opening show of *The Apprentice*. *New York* magazine wrote that I'd "perfected the pompad-over." *The New York Times* called it "an elaborate structure best left to an architecture critic."

David Letterman and Jay Leno regularly do quips about it. Matt Lauer, who with Katie Couric has taken the *Today* show to new heights, told me I should just give up the ghost and shave it off or give myself some kind of buzz cut like the one he has. Likewise, Pat O'Brien, the star of *Access Hollywood*, told me he had heard about Matt Lauer's comment and totally agrees with him.

Personally, I think it looks good, but I've never said my hair was my strongest point. I told Pat and Matt that I'm just not ready to change my style. I've been combing it this way for a long time and I might as well keep doing it. The ratings of *The Apprentice* are sky-high, and maybe they would drop if I changed the look at this point.

I'm amazed by how often people ask me whether or not I wear a hairpiece, a wig, or a rug, as it is affectionately known.

The answer, for the record, is emphatically and categorically no: I do not wear a rug. My hair is one hundred percent mine. No animals have been harmed in the creation of my hairstyle.

However, I must admit that the day may come when I will wear a hairpiece, wig, or rug—but only if I go bald, which I hope never happens. The reason for this is because I, like most men, am very vain. Many times over the years, I've heard people say that men are vainer than women, and I believe it. Guys don't like to talk about it, but Random House is paying me a fortune for this book and specifically requested a chapter on "the art of the hair," so I will admit to my vanity.

I will also reveal some of my hair-related secrets.

The reason my hair looks so neat all the time is because I don't have to deal with the elements very often. I live in the building where I work. I take an elevator from my bedroom to my office. The rest of the time, I'm either in my stretch limousine, my private jet, my helicopter, or my private club in Palm Beach, Florida. If Matt Lauer had my lifestyle, he might not have changed his hairstyle—although his hair looks great now.

If I happen to be outside, I'm probably on one of my golf courses, where I protect my hair from overexposure by wearing a golf hat. It's also a way to avoid the paparazzi. Plus the hat always has a big TRUMP logo on it—it's an automatic promotion.

I will also admit that I color my hair. Somehow, the color never looks great, but what the hell, I just don't like gray hair.

I wonder how much longer my hair will be a national topic of conversation. Letterman and Leno have been funny, but one person I don't like is Joy Behar, a woman who works for Barbara Walters on *The View*. For weeks, she was attacking me, insisting that I wear a wig, so Barbara and her staff called me and asked if I would surprise them and appear on the show. I did, and when I ran my hand through my hair and proved that it was real, everybody laughed and that was the end of that.

After *The Apprentice* premiered, Joy Behar was on *The Tonight Show* along with the rest of the cast of *The View*. Out of the blue, Jay Leno started talking about the great success of *The Apprentice*. Star

Jones raved about it, as did the others—except for Joy Behar, a woman with no talent and a terrible accent, who again attacked my hair. I've always said that show would do better without her. I did her a favor by going on the show, and it was not appreciated. Being nice to some people never pays off.

I suppose it's possible that I could rethink my look for the second season of *The Apprentice*. But probably not—it seems to be working!

Gossip

Whether you're building a luxury apartment or producing a beauty pageant, you've got to give the people what they want.

In a book like this one, that means some good advice, some wisdom, a little bit of gossip, and a glimmer of fame.

I've done my best to give you some wisdom and advice. Now, here's a Palm Beach morality tale about gossip and fame:

I had a friend who was rich and successful and very married. For months, I kept hearing a rumor that he was having an affair with an equally successful businesswoman who was also very married. It was hard to believe. She was drop-dead gorgeous and could probably have had any guy she wanted. My friend was not a likely choice.

The rumors persisted, and then one day my friend invited me out to dinner with the gorgeous woman and her husband. I told him the invitation seemed strange to me. "For a long time, I've been hearing you're having an affair with her. Wouldn't you find it a little uncomfortable having dinner with her in front of her husband?"

Surprisingly, my friend confirmed that he was having the affair, that the woman's husband didn't know, and that he (my friend) was totally in love, something which he felt his wife, who was as tough as nails, would not exactly appreciate or understand.

Without revealing any of my friend's secrets, I told my girlfriend, Melania, to prepare for a wild evening.

We had dinner at a restaurant. Normally, I would have been watching the scene with great amusement, but the businesswoman's husband was also a friend of mine, and so I was in a precarious position. There we all sat, as though nothing was happening, but we could all feel tension in the air. As we left, I watched my friend grab the businesswoman around the waist in a more than familiar fashion. Her husband was out of sight when this happened, but it was clear to me that, despite my disbelief and amazement, there was something going on between the two.

Over the next few weeks, my friend called me incessantly, proclaiming his love for the woman. He said he would do anything to be with her, and that she was also in love with him. His calls became so frequent that Melania asked, "Why does he keep calling you? What's going on?" When I told Melania about the affair, she also found it hard to believe. As I said, this businesswoman is an amazing beauty and my friend is not exactly Brad Pitt—although he is very rich and some women find him handsome.

Finally, after a number of phone calls, I said, "Look, are you bullshitting me or is this for real?"

He said, "It is! It is! I want to come over and see you and I'll prove it." He didn't have to prove anything to me. What difference did it make? But I invited him over anyway.

When he arrived, he told me how they'd met, how the relationship was going, all the sordid details. I still wasn't sure I believed him, but then he played an answering machine tape of a call she had made to him. She said the kind of intimate things only a lover would say. It was truly down and dirty, and I definitely recognized her voice. There was no longer any doubt in my mind about what was taking place.

For a while, my friend continued to call me to say how much he loved this woman. If I was in Palm Beach when he called me, I would just watch the television and politely listen to what he was saying. I felt more like his psychiatrist than anything else.

Then the shit hit the fan! The woman's husband had found out, phoned my friend, and threatened to kill him. But what really bothered my friend was the next call he received—from the woman, saying she would never see him or talk to him again, and that if she did, her husband would tell my friend's wife everything about the affair. My friend was devastated. Afterward, he repeatedly tried to reach his ex-lover, but she refused to respond.

As usually happens, my friend's wife found out. Probably, the businesswoman's husband had called her, but who knows?

About six months later, I saw the businesswoman at a gallery and she confronted me. "Donald," she said, "I hear you've been spreading rumors all over town about me. It's terrible what you've done, and the rumors about me and [X] aren't true. Can you imagine me going out with him?" After listening to her accusations and denials for fifteen minutes, I realized she is one of the greatest salespeople I have ever known, because if I had not heard her voice on that answering machine tape, I would have completely believed her. She told me she couldn't believe people would even think she would go out with my friend. "Why would I want to? What did he have? Give me a break!"

I figured that was the end of it, but then I realized that my friend had not called me in some time. I was wondering how he was doing, so I phoned him to say hello. He wasn't in and didn't return my call. I phoned again, and again he didn't call back. I was worried, so I called a third time and a fourth time. No response.

Later, I found out that his wife had blamed me for the entire affair. She thought I had introduced him to this woman. Apparently, she told him that if he ever spoke to me again, she would divorce him.

It turns out he had used me as a scapegoat. The funny thing is, I wouldn't have minded and would have helped him out and played along if he'd had the decency, as a good friend, to call me and say,

"Look, I have a problem. Can I blame it on you?" Even if it meant he wouldn't have been able to see me or speak to me again, I would have accepted it and been glad to have helped keep his marriage together. But he never made that call to me. He did everything without an explanation.

Now when I see him at a restaurant or an event, nothing is said. But he knows, and I know.

I heard he was still suffering through his marriage. As a means of reconciliation, he bought his wife some tremendous jewelry. Apparently, she made him return it because it wasn't big enough or expensive enough. He had to go back and buy her something even bigger and better.

Page Six, My Way

The *New York Post* is a popular daily newspaper in this city. I read it every day, as do lots of other people. It contains a two-page spread called Page Six, which is not located on page six but is a must-read. Over the years it's been edited by a highly talented guy named Richard Johnson. He's got insight into everything, and he knows more about what's going on in New York than anyone I know. For better or for worse, I make Page Six a lot. I hope the day never comes when they don't find me interesting enough to mention. Meanwhile, here's my version of Page Six for my readers, so you'll be up on the latest.

I'm sure a lot of you have heard of **Ivana,** my first wife, who christened me "The Donald" and launched a thousand missiles—I mean smiles—in my direction. Well, I'm happy to report that she's doing well and at this moment is in the south of France, having, I hope, a great time. We are on good terms and speak often. We are still neighbors in New York City, and with three incredible children to share, we consider ourselves to be very fortunate people and good friends.

Marla, my second wife, is living in Los Angeles and is as beautiful as ever. Our daughter, Tiffany, is now ten years old, and continues to charm everything and everyone in sight. I don't see her as much as I'd like, but every minute is worth a bundle when I do.

With Richard Johnson of Page Six fame.

With the exquisite Melania Knauss.

I've spent the last five years with the exquisite **Melania Knauss,** a model from Slovenia. Anyone who has ever met her will never forget it. She's just as beautiful on the inside as she is on the outside. Despite her great beauty, she is a very calm and soothing person who has brought a sense of stability to my very turbulent life. I am lucky to be with her!

My eldest son, **Don Jr.,** joined The Trump Organization in September 2001 and has already proven himself to be a valuable member of our team. He, like me, graduated from the Wharton School at the University of Pennsylvania, and has since decided to join the family business and see what he can learn from his father. He's a good guy and will be a successful one, too.

Ivanka, my eldest daughter, is currently attending the Wharton School. She has already had a successful modeling career and is a heartbreaker in every way. She will do well no matter what she does.

Eric, my youngest son, is at Georgetown University and doing well. We have great expectations for him, and since he's already six feet six inches tall, that shouldn't prove to be a problem. He, like Don Jr., is an avid outdoorsman.

I remain very close to my brother **Robert** and to my sisters, **Maryanne** and **Elizabeth.** All are thriving, successful, and productive.

My parents, **Fred** and **Mary,** passed away in 1999 and 2000, respectively. The void they left will never be filled. But what each gave to me, by way of example, will remain with me every day of my life.

I love my family. They are very much my motivation. They always have been, and they always will be. Am I a rich man? Yes, very rich.

I also feel blessed to have some terrific friends and business associates.

Barbara Corcoran is a wonderful woman who did a tremendous job in creating the Corcoran Group. She then sold it for a substantial profit and has done well ever since. I will never be surprised by how well she does. A friend of mine recently sent me an article about Bar-

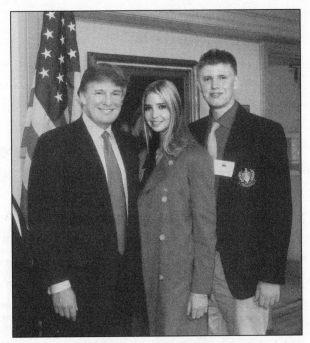

*With my daughter Ivanka and my son Eric
at Georgetown University.*

With Don Jr. and Eric at the Mar-a-Lago Club in Palm Beach, Florida.

bara in which she was asked about my influence on the residential market. She said, "Donald Trump has had singularly the greatest possible influence on Manhattan luxury real estate, simply because it was his marketing chutzpah that changed the perception of living in Manhattan." It's always nice to be complimented by pros, and Barbara is a total pro.

Another good friend is **Mohamed Al Fayed,** chairman of Harrods in Knightsbridge, London. Mohamed has gone through quite a rough time over the last several years—it was his son Dodie who was dating Princess Diana. To many of us, it looked like they would be getting married at some point in the not-too-distant future, until their lives ended in that tragic car crash in Paris. Mohamed is an extremely loyal father who has fought so hard for his son and the memory of him. I wish people understood him better. He is a truly good man.

Jack Welch is a particular favorite of mine. Now he's writing a book, and I'm going to be the first on line to buy it. Few people, if any, have ever done a better job of running a corporation.

I always enjoy being with **George Steinbrenner.** Quite honestly, there's no one like him, and he hasn't been appreciated to the extent he should be. I remember the Yankees when they couldn't win a game, when nobody went to Yankee Stadium, and the team was a total disaster. George puts a championship team on the field every year and does what it takes to win, whether people like him for it or not.

When we were taping *The Apprentice,* I told NBC that I would love to get George to give the candidates a lecture on winning. They looked at me and thought I was crazy, because the scene had to be shot that day and the World Series was beginning the following day. Knowing what a good friend George was, I was sure he would do it, and when I called him at Yankee Stadium he immediately picked up the phone and agreed. We were at Yankee Stadium thirty minutes later, and even the top people at NBC were impressed. The kids walked into this legendary office with its pictures of Babe Ruth, Joe DiMaggio, Mickey Mantle, and many other Yankee greats on the walls, and their eyes were wide open, as though they'd never seen anything like it before. George was incredibly nice. He sat with the kids for a long time, until I finally had to be the one to say, "George, you're busy as hell—let me get them out of here." He's really a great guy. People will appreciate George Steinbrenner only when they no longer have him, and when the Yankees are wallowing in last place.

Another sports owner who is one of the great winners is **Bob Kraft,** who helped lead the New England Patriots to a second Super Bowl victory. I've gotten to know Bob over the last two years, and there is no finer gentleman. He and his wife, Myra, are totally unassuming. With his sons, Bob has methodically and brilliantly built a strong franchise in New England that was a total disaster before Kraft's ascent. **Tom Brady** is the best quarterback in football. There are other quarterbacks with impressive stats, but when you need someone to throw four or five completions in the final minutes of a game, there is nobody better than Tom. With all of their upcoming draft choices and the great players they already have, this team is only going to get better over the next few years.

Two other terrific team owners are **Jerry Jones,** owner of the Dallas Cowboys, and **Bob Tisch,** owner of the New York Giants. Tisch has done so well in every capacity, whether it's business or sports. He's in his seventies, but he's got the attitude of someone in his twenties, thirties, or forties.

Larry Silverstein, the developer of the new World Trade Center complex, is a good friend of mine, but I really hate what's being designed for the site. It resembles a skeleton, and I can't believe Larry really wanted to evoke that image. In actuality, Larry is being forced to do certain things that he would not do under normal circumstances, but he has to go with the flow. Nevertheless, I'm sure he'll do a terrific job.

Finally, since Page Six often takes a few digs at people, here are mine:

Dan Rather is not one of my favorite people. A few years ago, he wanted to profile me for *60 Minutes.* As we toured Mar-a-Lago and Trump International Golf Club in Florida, he couldn't have been nicer or more respectful. I was sure the interview would be a total home run.

When the interview aired, it couldn't have been nastier. He showed me giving a speech to an empty room at a poorly planned event, when the day before I'd given the same speech to a standing-room-only crowd. But *60 Minutes* didn't air that speech. They just wanted me to look as bad as possible.

Dan Rather is an enigma to me. He's got absolutely no talent or charisma or personality, yet year after year, CBS apologizes for his terrible ratings. I could take the average guy on the street and have him read the news on CBS and that guy would draw bigger ratings than Dan Rather does. When I see Rather at Yankee games, I stay away from him. However, I will say one nice thing about him: Recently, he was the emcee at a Police Athletic League dinner for District Attorney Robert Morgenthau, one of the great men in the history of New York City. Dan called me and told me he felt very uncomfortable being the emcee of a dinner for which I was the chairman. I told him I appreciated the call and that it would be fine with me if he was the emcee. He did a nice job, but I'll never forget what he did to me on *60 Minutes.* People don't change their stripes.

I'll conclude this with a story about **Howard Cosell,** a spectacular sportscaster who I got to know during the last ten years of his life. People either loved Howard or hated him—there was no in between—but he was really the best at what he did. As Howard grew older, though, he became nastier, even toward the people who loved him and had helped make him a success. He always felt that being a sportscaster was beneath him. He longed to run for the U.S. Senate.

Howard could sit on a dais with sports figures he hadn't seen for thirty years and quote their exact statistics. His memory was amazing.

Then he wrote his final book and knocked almost everyone he knew, from Roone Arledge to Frank Gifford, one of the finest people around. It did a lot of damage to him, because all of his friends turned against him. I remember saying to him, "Howard, you can knock twenty percent of the people, maybe twenty-five percent or thirty percent of the people, but you can't knock everybody. You didn't say anything nice about anybody in the book. It was the wrong thing to do. I believe in knocking people, but you can't knock everybody."

That's a rule I try to follow, in this book and in my life.

A Week in the Life

In *The Art of the Deal* and in my other two memoirs, I included a chapter about a typical week in my life. When I met Mark Burnett, the creator of *The Apprentice,* he told me it was his favorite chapter in the book, and a lot of other readers have told me the same thing. So, back by popular demand, here's an example of what an average eventful week was like in the fall of 2003.

This chapter doesn't have any specific advice on how to get rich, but it will show you how I have fun, and I doubt I'd be as successful as I am if I weren't having such a good time.

MONDAY

9:00 A.M.   I have a meeting with architect Costas Kondylis, an elegant way to start the week. Costas and I have worked on several very successful projects together, including the Trump World Tower at the United Nations Plaza, Trump Park Avenue (at Fifty-ninth Street and Park Avenue, just completed), and, together with Philip Johnson and Skidmore Owings and Merrill, Trump Place, my sixteen-building development along the Hudson River. Some of you might remember that site as the West Side yards, which I have been involved with since

1974, when I first secured the option to purchase them from the Penn Central Railroad. That was my first major deal in Manhattan. Close to thirty years later, here we are discussing the fifth and sixth buildings under construction. (Never give up.)

My eldest son, Don Jr., is also at the meeting. We are on schedule with construction, and the first three condominium buildings have proven to be very successful. However, neither Costas nor myself is likely to ever rest on his laurels, and we are troubleshooting, going over every detail. If Costas hadn't been an architect, he'd have made a very good surgeon—he's just that meticulous. We get along famously, and I'd put him up there with Philip Johnson as one of our most outstanding architects.

We are also discussing the reaction to the city park I developed and donated to the city, which is on the West Side yards property. I hate to disappoint people, but my detractors were not pleased about this twenty-five-acre gift. What can I say? Except that you can't be all things to all people, no matter how hard you try.

I look over some kitchen and bathroom fixtures, and we decide to go with the top of the line. My name and work have become synonymous with quality, and there's a reason for it. We don't skimp on anything, ever or anywhere. Don Jr. mentions looking forward to the topping-out party for Building #4. That's a big day for builders, and it's a celebration when the frame of the building, the superstructure, is completed, and everyone involved meets at the top for a party.

9:30 A.M. Norma comes in to tell me that Oscar de la Renta is on the line, and Costas and I decide to meet again in a couple of weeks. Our new Miss Universe, Amelia Vega, is from Santo Domingo, which is also the birthplace of Oscar de la Renta. He wants to meet her, and I don't blame him. She's a beauty, all six feet of her. We're proud not only of her, but of the Miss Universe contest, which has become extremely successful since I bought it seven years ago. We beat out the competition in television ratings and we are highly regarded internationally as well. Ecuador has paid millions of dollars to host the 2004 contest, and we're looking forward to a great time there.

Back to Oscar—he's a class act all the way. His impeccable work speaks for itself.

9:45 A.M. I make a call to some wiseguy contractors who've been trying to cheat me. This can be a crummy business because of the scum of the earth it attracts, but you have to do what you have to do. Screaming at them is what I have to do.

10:00 A.M. I have three calls waiting: Mark Brown, the CEO and president of my three casinos in Atlantic City; Woody Allen's office; and Mayor Bloomberg. I take the mayor's call first, much as I respect Woody Allen and Mark. I think the mayor is doing a great job, considering he's got one of the toughest jobs on the planet. Running a corporation is one thing; running a city is another, especially this one.

Woody Allen may go down to Florida and stay at the Mar-a-Lago, my club in Palm Beach. I've been in one Woody Allen film, and I never miss any of his movies.

10:30 A.M. I have my first Diet Coke of the day. I know I should drink mineral water, and I do sometimes, but I really like Diet Coke. Irina Dvorovenko calls in; she's a ballerina at the American Ballet Theatre. She's not only a sensational dancer, but also an incredibly beautiful woman. I'm not exactly a ballet fan, but because of Irina, that might be a possibility.

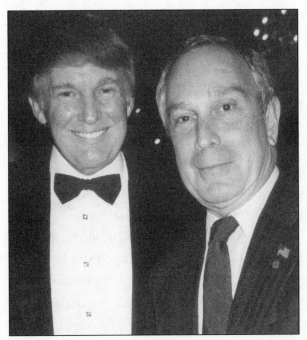

Our wonderful mayor, Mike Bloomberg.

With another great mayor of New York City, Rudy Giuliani, in 2000.

The television crew from Neal Cavuto's team is ready for an interview. I ask what it's about, and then we're ready to go. After decades of interviews, they are easy for me to do, especially with someone like Neal, who is not only personable but also very knowledgeable. He and his team are pros all the way. And he gets the best business ratings on cable TV.

11:00 A.M. I received seventeen calls during the interview, and I begin to return them, in between the incoming calls. After so many years in business, knowing how to prioritize is second nature. It's also a key factor in keeping up your momentum, even during a typical workday, which is crucial if you intend to become or remain successful. Everyone's heard of the New York minute, but by now that's outdated—it's become the New York second. That's no exaggeration. Seconds count when you have hundreds of phone calls a day to handle. One bogged-down conversation, and your momentum could be interrupted for an hour. So when I say momentum is crucial, I mean it. You'll know when you've got it, and you'll know when it's being disrupted.

I return Joe Cinque's call; he's an executive with the American Academy of Hospitality Sciences, which presents the coveted Five Star Diamond award. My properties have received several of them. Joe is a high-spirited and generous man, but he's difficult to please and discerning when it comes to giving out awards. He's just returned from Sardinia and mentions that he still thinks the Mar-a-Lago Club in Palm Beach is the most beautiful resort he's ever seen, worldwide. Coming from him, that's saying something. I always liked Joe, and now I like him even more.

I return Regis Philbin's call. He and his wife, Joy, are among my closest friends, and he's even more fun off-screen than on-screen, if you can imagine that. I always look forward to spending time with them—they are both solid-gold people. We're on for dinner at Jean-Georges Restaurant, which is in the Trump International Hotel & Tower and is considered to be one of the finest restaurants in the world. With Jean-Georges Vongerichten in charge, how could it not be?

I take a call from Mark Burnett, the brilliant creator and producer of the reality show called *Survivor*. It was his idea to do *The Apprentice,* and we are busy working on the details.

11:30 A.M. I take a call from Sony; they'd asked me to be a sponsor for the 150th celebration of Central Park in July, featuring rising opera stars Salvatore Licitra and Marcello Alvarez. The event was a huge success, with many thousands of New Yorkers turning out to hear some magnificent singing on a perfect night under the stars in the park. On nights like that, you have to thank your own lucky stars just to be alive. We were all proud of how successful the evening was, and I was equally proud to be a sponsor.

Mike Donovan, my trusted pilot, calls in to update me on the checkup of my 727 jet. I have both a helicopter and a jet, and they get a workout throughout the year. With my schedule, they aren't luxury items, but necessities. Turns out the jet will be ready in two weeks.

Norma comes in to go over the media requests of the morning thus far, which include two from Holland, three from Germany, two from Canada, one from France, one from England, and seven from the United States. Handling media requests alone can require negotiation skills, and we do our best to accommodate them.

11:45 A.M. I have a meeting with Charlie Reiss, Jill Cremer, Russell Flicker, and Don Jr.—my development team. We are busy with a building in Chicago, and Don Jr. has been working very effectively and in many capacities on Trump Park Avenue. We have a lot on our plates already at The Trump Organization, but, not being a complacent type, I know there are many opportunities out there and this team tends to that. They do a great job and have some interesting projects to brief me about.

12:30 P.M. I order lunch from our terrific new restaurant at the Trump Tower atrium, which is doing great business. Some of you may have seen the commercial I did for McDonald's. I didn't have to act— I like McDonald's and am a loyal customer. Some days I have pizza, sometimes a ham and cheese, some days nothing, but I rarely go out for lunch. I still consider it an interruption in my workday. I review news clippings and articles during my lunch minute.

12:35 P.M. I speak to Bernd Lembcke, the director of the Mar-a-Lago Club. As you might remember, Mar-a-Lago was once my private home, and I restored it and turned it into a breathtaking private club. Anything that beautiful should be shared, and it has been an immense success. Bernd has tended to it, and I've been named to the Benefactors Board of Directors by the Historical Society of Palm Beach County. It's nice to see painstaking work being noticed and rewarded. We discuss the upcoming season and the latest improvements to the grounds.

12:45 P.M. I walk down the hall to visit George Ross. George will always tell you the way it is, which I appreciate. His thoughts are sharp and insightful, and we have a longish conversation of, perhaps, three minutes. I am thinking about putting him on *The Apprentice*.

12:50 P.M. Back in my office, I take a call from Hugh Grant. I had a brief role, as myself, in his movie with Sandra Bullock, *Two Weeks Notice*. Hugh's an avid golfer, and my course in Westchester is at his disposal whenever he's in New York. He's a nice guy on top of being a

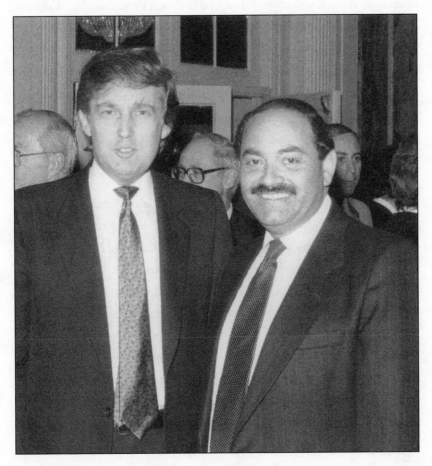

With Allen Weisselberg, my CFO.

gifted actor. In fact, I'm glad he lives in another country—he's got too much on the ball to have around all the time.

1:00 P.M. Norma comes in to go over the invitations to parties and openings, and for speeches. I don't have much time available. I decide on a party at Le Cirque.

1:30 P.M. I put in a call to Trump National Golf Club in Los Angeles. This course is on the Pacific Ocean and has the potential to be better than Pebble Beach. "Spectacular" will be an understatement. It's a gem, and we're working hard on it. All is going well, but every detail is important and there are a lot of them to take care of.

2:30 P.M. I make a call to an expert on trees. I saw some beautiful ones and would like to have them on my golf course in Bedminster, New Jersey. I ask a few questions and find out a lot. When I want to know something, I go for it, and only on rare occasions will I take a second-hand opinion. This tactic has served me well over the years—there's nothing wrong with knowledge, whether it's about trees or sinks.

3:00 P.M. Allen Weisselberg, my CFO, comes in for a meeting. He's been with me for thirty years and keeps a handle on everything, which is not an easy job. He runs things beautifully. His team is tight and fast, and so are our meetings.

3:30 P.M. I return the fourteen calls that came in during the meeting, which include those from lawyers, publishers, reporters, and friends. The only thing worse than having so many calls is not having any calls, so I'm not complaining.

I take a call from the concrete contractors, who have completely screwed up and are trying to tell me they haven't screwed up. Everything they've done is a mess. So instead of having the nice conversation they expected, I tell it to them the way it is—that they've made a mess of everything and they'd better get it right. The amazing thing is that they act like they know what they're doing. When people hear me yelling, believe me, there's a reason why.

4:30 P.M.   I go to the conference room for a photo session with Platon, a young and very accomplished photographer. The photos are for *Forbes* magazine. He is fast and efficient, very much like Richard Avedon was when I did a shoot with him last year. I look forward to seeing the prints.

5:00 P.M.   I return the seven calls received during the shoot, including one to my sister, Maryanne. She's still a judge and as wise as ever, and she has just returned from a trip to Rome.

5:30 P.M.   Norma comes in to go over more invitations and media requests, and I read a few letters. There's one from a nine-year-old boy in Minnesota who has a business proposal for me. After describing his business idea, he makes me a very tempting offer: "And what's in it for you, Mr. Trump? A chance for you to make millions, just by becoming my partner!" He also adds that I can call him anytime, as long as it's before 9:00 P.M. I'll keep that in mind.

6:00 P.M.   I decide to return to my apartment upstairs, where I make more calls, until 7:30 or so. At 8:00 P.M., Melania and I meet Joy and Regis at Jean-Georges Restaurant for a perfect meal.

TUESDAY

8:30 A.M.   I arrive at the office. I read between five and seven newspapers every morning before I get into the office. One thing I enjoy

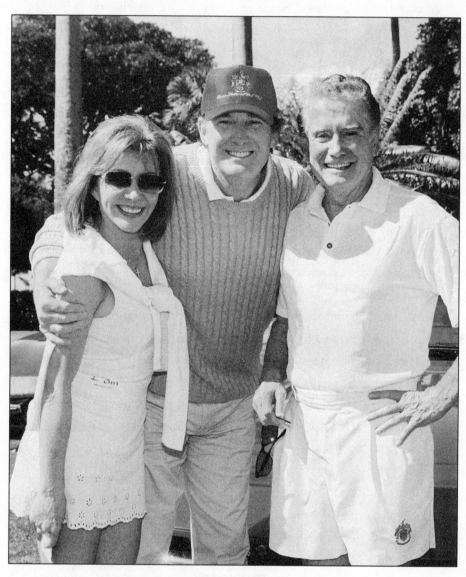

At the Mar-a-Lago Club with Joy and Regis Philbin.

doing is clipping articles of interest, whether they're about me or not; then I either save or distribute them. I also receive between ten and twelve magazines a day, which I review in my apartment at the end of the day. Keeping up on things worldwide is of great importance if one is to keep the big picture in mind. Yes, I'm a New Yorker, but there's a big world out there and I try to stay informed about it. If you see the entire planet as an emerging market—which it is— you'll discover that you've got a lot of homework to do every day. It's not an indulgence, but an absolute necessity. So I spend the next fifteen minutes of relative quiet assessing world developments. Call it multitasking, call it whatever you will, it works and it focuses me for the day ahead.

8:45 A.M. I take a call from the guy trying to jack up the prices on the fixtures for a new building. Doesn't he know I *know* the market prices for everything I'm doing? These jerks think I don't do my homework—that's what it boils down to. Which means they're all in for a big surprise, and if I have to yell to get my point across, that's what I do.

9:00 A.M. I ask Rhona to call Bob Wright, the chairman and CEO of NBC. In addition to being a great admirer of his business acumen, I am friends with Bob and his wonderful wife, Suzanne. We've done some deals together, and in the seventeen years since he went from General Electric to NBC, the network has seen enormous improvements in quality control as well as growth in the right directions. Bob takes my call and we chat about a lot of things. Have you ever noticed that some people have a knack for enlightened conversation? Bob is one of those people. He's never been boring for one second of his life. I'm glad he takes the time to talk to me, and, considering his schedule, it's a good sign that maybe I don't bore him either.

Norma comes in to remind me that I have a Police Athletic League Board of Directors meeting next week. I am active with the Police Athletic League and have been for many years. They do a great job in New York and benefit many people and neighborhoods.

9:15 A.M. I take a call from Alfons Schmidt, who is someone I hold in very high esteem, not just because he's a great golfer and businessman, but because he's a remarkable person. Those who know him will agree with me. We'll meet on Friday for a round of golf at Trump National Golf Club in Briarcliff Manor. It's a high for me to play on the course with someone like Alfons. We'll be joined by former president Bill Clinton as well, who is a member. He lives nearby and likes the course, and we welcome him at any time. He's managed to become a good golfer, and, considering the schedule he had for so many years, that's saying something. If he keeps up this rate of improvement, he'll get really good very fast. Joining us will also be David Granger, the editor in chief of *Esquire,* a dapper guy on and off the golf course. It's a rare occasion that I take an afternoon off, but considering the company I'll be in, it will be worth it.

9:45 A.M. Ivanka, my beautiful daughter, calls to tell me about her most recent trip. She's on holiday and is taking off for somewhere else tomorrow. Keeping track of her isn't easy, but she's good about keeping me informed, and I'm happy she's enjoying herself. I'm a lucky guy with a daughter like this.

10:00 A.M. I have a board meeting in the conference room with Mark Brown and Bob Pickus from my Atlantic City team. John Burke and Scott Butera join us. We have these meetings every three months, to iron out any problems, to go over numbers, and to keep an eye on the future. Considering how large our operations are in Atlantic City— I have three casino hotels—our meetings are relatively brief; they rarely

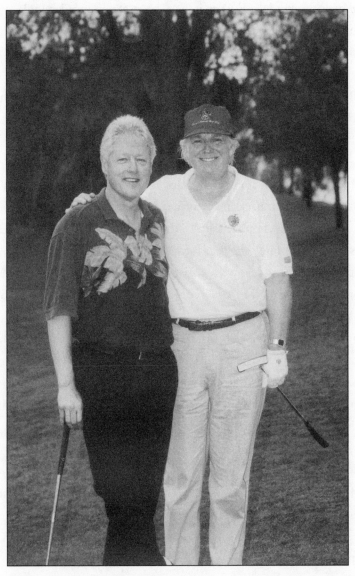

*With Bill Clinton at Trump National Golf Club
in Briarcliff Manor, New York.*

last more than two hours. My team knows the value of time and exactly how not to waste it. People often comment on the brevity of my meetings, but if everyone knows what they're doing, they don't need to be long or long-winded. Fortunately, I have experienced people on my teams, and they know how I operate, so they get to the point, and quickly.

12:00 P.M. We have sandwiches from the Carnegie Deli in the boardroom. Ever had one of their ham-and-cheese or corned beef sandwiches? They're great. When you visit New York, try one.

12:15 P.M. I'm not antisocial, but to me, fifteen minutes is a very long lunch. So I'm back in my office, getting back to business, perusing the thirty-seven phone calls that came in during the meeting. These are the phone calls that have already been screened, first by the receptionist, and then by my assistants. I get hundreds of calls a day from around the world from people who just want to say hi or to tell me something. My security team takes some of the calls as well, because the number of calls can be overwhelming. But these are thirty-seven legitimate calls that must be dealt with, and I begin returning them. First I return Bob Kraft's call. He'd invited me to a private Elton John concert, which was terrific. Elton John just gets better and better; he's amazing. Bob Kraft is a first-class act all the way and always a delight to talk to. It's a good way to start the afternoon.

12:30 P.M. Joe Torre stops by for a surprise visit. He's the manager of the New York Yankees and always a welcome guest. He takes the time to sign autographs on his way in and on his way out. A real champ.

12:45 P.M. I return Rudy Giuliani's call. He was a great mayor, and he saw New York City through some difficult times. In addition to my respect for him professionally, we are also friends and we keep in touch. I will always wish him the best—and his wife, Judy, is tops!

1:00 P.M. The TV team from the National Geographic Channel are here for an interview. They've done great work, and I decide we should go up to my apartment for the interview. I don't often do that, but they are pros, and it goes very well. For the most part, I get along very well with media people. I respect them and the jobs they do, and they usually respect me and my time limits. It works both ways, and it's a rare occasion when we clash.

1:45 P.M. I take a call from Mohamed Al Fayed, the owner of Harrods in Knightsbridge, London, and the Ritz in Paris. He's one of a kind, a gentleman all the way, and I always make a point of visiting him when I'm in London. He's remained a kind and loyal person despite the tragedies in his life, and I am honored when he calls.

2:00 P.M. I call my brother, Robert. He's a great guy, and a good brother to have. We keep in close contact, and I consider myself lucky to have the brother and sisters that I've got.

Melania calls to remind me that we are going to see *Chicago* on Broadway tonight. I've seen it before, but Melanie Griffith is currently starring in it, and we want to see her. I already know she'll be terrific—she's a natural.

I return twelve calls in rapid succession, most of them concerning my different properties in New York and Florida. Each time, I ask what the problem is, and we get to it immediately. I like to keep a handle on all my properties, and the problems are to be expected. The time I worry the most is when there aren't any problems. That's usually the result of misinformation or wishful thinking on someone's part.

Here's one of my greatest wishes: I would like a computer chip that I could attach to the brains of all my contractors so they'd know exactly what I wanted, when I wanted it, and at what price. This would save me a lot of time, a lot of phoning, and a lot of yelling.

3:00 P.M. I take a walk over to Trump Park Avenue, my new super-luxury building on Park Avenue and Fifty-ninth Street. This was the former Delmonico Hotel, which has historical merit, and the location is about as prime as you can get in New York. It's a prize building, and I make almost daily visits to see how it's progressing. I visit Laura Cordovano in the sales office, then check out the construction. They are taking too long, and the lobby doesn't look up to my standards yet. They get an earful, and they deserve it. When my name is on something, it'd better be great. Could it be any simpler?

It's funny, the reaction I get from people when I walk down the street and get recognized. Sometimes it's a double take, sometimes there's no acknowledgment, but often it's a wave and a familiar and friendly "Hi, Donald!" from total strangers. It still takes me by surprise. Once I was stuck in a horrible traffic jam in my limousine, and I had a few members of Mark Burnett's team with me, so I decided to try an experiment. It was one of those traffic jams where we hadn't moved an inch in ten minutes, and tempers were red-hot, with taxi drivers yelling and everyone else as well, and every car seemed to have its horn on permanent full blast. I decided to step out of my limousine and just stand there in the middle of this chaos. The reaction? At first, dead silence. Then the fuming drivers and passengers started waving and shouting "Donald! It's The Donald! Hi, Donald!" I had to laugh. At least we had some relief from the honking horns for a few minutes.

4:00 P.M. Back in my office. I make a call downstairs, as I'd noticed some of the lobby door handles weren't as polished as I'd like them to be. I want my buildings to be impeccable, and the people who inhabit them appreciate that, even if I might seem a bit extreme at times.

I receive a letter from a U.S. serviceman overseas, Terry Simmons. His morale-building idea for his unit is to receive an autographed photograph from me. I am very touched by this request, and we send it off right away. These men and women are putting their lives on the line to protect something I cherish, which is this country. One of the great moments of my life was being honored, along with General John M. Keane, by the USO in 2002. In my speech I mentioned that accepting this honor put me in the finest company imaginable, because every member of the United States armed forces was being honored alongside me. I meant it then, and I still mean it today. We send our best to Terry Simmons.

4:30 P.M.   Giuseppe Cipriani, who has one of the best restaurants in New York, calls. As someone who goes out to dinner a lot, I have very particular tastes, and Giuseppe is someone who will never let you down. I am trying to get him into my Park Avenue building.

The mysterious Jeffrey calls in. As mysterious as Jeffrey is, he's one of the few people I know who can get by on just a first name. My staff never asks for a last name in his case, which in a way puts him up there with Elvis. Not that Elvis calls in much these days, but you never know. That's why I have a floor for security. Sometimes we need it. We've had some calls you wouldn't believe.

Norma comes in to tell me she's had it with *The Apprentice* TV crew looking like "ragamuffins" and that if they show up tomorrow in their usual gear she's going to send them back to their hotel "to dress properly for a change." She means business and I know it, so I try to explain that they're from California and working on a TV-show set, not in our corporate office, but she'll have none of it. I think they're in for it, and I don't envy them.

I call Vinnie Stellio, a longtime employee whose wife has just had a baby boy. Vinnie could've been a movie star with his looks and swagger, but, fortunately, he works for us. He also could've written his own scripts, but he's busy enough as it is.

5:00 P.M. I call Arnold Schwarzenegger to congratulate him on his recent decision to run for governor of California. I've also received several media calls asking me for my opinion on his decision. I've always liked Arnold, and I think he'll make a great governor, not just because I like him but because he's got the smarts and energy to run a state like California.

I read an article by a journalist who spent a day with me a few months ago. I remember him saying that he felt one day wouldn't be sufficient, and I remember telling him that most people felt that one day with me was enough. At the end of the article, he admits I was right—that one day with me was enough—he was completely exhausted. It's funny, because to me it seemed like a more relaxing and low-key day than I usually have, and I was certainly on my best behavior. Anyway, it's nice to be right.

5:30 P.M. Norma comes in to review media requests, charity requests, and invitations. Since September 11, requests for charity have increased sharply, and we do what we can. We comment on how we receive a consistently high number of letters from Canada. One letter is from two ladies in Saskatchewan who have invited me to have a cup of coffee with them at their local coffeehouse, which has two tables. If I decide to accept, they will do their best to reserve a table for me. Due to my schedule, I have to decline, but their offer is genuine and kind, and if I had the time, I'd go.

Sometimes I answer media requests myself, when I have time. Once I called a guy named Phil Grande in Florida. He has a small radio program, *Stock Trading & Money Talk,* and he had faxed me an interview request. I picked up the phone and called him myself. When he asked who was calling, I said, "Donald Trump," and he said, "Yeah, and I'm J. P. Morgan." It took some convincing on my part, but he finally believed me, and we chatted for some time. Afterward, he called my assistants to verify that I had indeed called him, and to this day he sends them flowers every Christmas. People like Phil can make our jobs a lot of fun.

6:00 P.M. Asprey, the jewelers who occupy the corner of Trump Tower on Fifth Avenue, are expanding, and they've invited me down to see the renovations. They will have three floors, and it will be stunning—much like their jewelry. They are the jewelers to the royal family in England, and their new space will reflect that status when it's done. I also decide to check on my new tenants, Mark Burnett Productions, on the way down to the lobby, to see that everything is up to par. I have a great management team, but I like to check things out for myself as much as possible. I make a quick call to Melania to check on dinner plans before the theater, and I leave the office.

WEDNESDAY

9:00 A.M. Melanie Griffith was terrific in *Chicago* last night, and we visited her afterward to tell her so.

I take a call regarding placing antennas on The Trump Building at 40 Wall Street. Since the World Trade Towers are gone, 40 Wall Street is once again the tallest building in lower Manhattan. It's not a fact that particularly appeals to me, but it is a fact. Whatever will best serve the Financial District is fine with me.

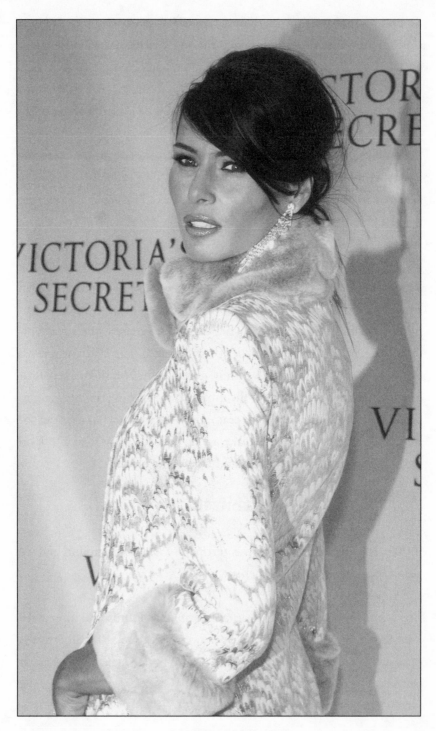

Melania Knauss

I have to say one thing about New Yorkers, and that is that after September 11, they just continued to move forward and do their best. That took courage, and I think it shows what makes New York City such a great place.

I place a call to Governor Pataki, and take a call from John Myers, president of GE Asset Management. We've done some deals together and he's a great guy—and a very smart one.

9:30 A.M. Kevin Harris, a supervising producer for Mark Burnett, is ready to take me on a tour of the sets built in Trump Tower for *The Apprentice*. He has on some sort of a new vintage bowling shirt, deconstructed jeans with more holes than fabric, and some very original footwear that I can't begin to describe. This guy could make Helmut Lang look old hat, but we make a quick getaway before Norma can see him.

The construction site also includes living quarters for the sixteen contestants, which is an incredibly stylish ten-thousand-square-foot loft, probably the only such living space in midtown. I am pleasantly surprised at the quality of the work, and my trust in Mark Burnett is again confirmed.

10:00 A.M. Back in my office, I begin returning calls. People are surprised at how many hours I put in at my office each week, since I seem to have a busy social life as well. I also like to plan my business trips for the weekends whenever possible, to avoid missing office time. I love what I do, so it doesn't seem like I'm missing out on any fun. Last year I took a transatlantic weekend business trip that included breakfast in London with Mohamed Al Fayed and dinner in Slovenia with Melania's parents before flying back to New York. We were back in time for me to be in the office by 9:00 A.M. Monday.

I talk to Jay Goldberg, a brilliant lawyer and an old friend. He and his wife, Rema, will join me in my box at the U.S. Open.

This is a good one: The pushiest broker in New York calls in for a chat about the availability of some of my prime apartments, as if I couldn't guess why she was calling me in the first place. She tries to tell me what my apartments are worth, and I try to control my temper, but she's full of bullshit. Finally, I ask her if she realizes who she's talking to and, surprisingly, she immediately becomes reasonable. Almost every day, I have to remind someone that maybe I know what I'm doing, and while that may sound like I'm tooting my own horn, believe me, it saves a lot of yelling time.

10:30 A.M. The German TV team is ready for an interview in the conference room. They'd done a wonderful job in covering Mar-a-Lago a few months ago, which I appreciate, and so we're doing a New York interview. They are professional and enthusiastic, and all goes well. You see, I've done so many interviews that at times they can be boring for me, so if the people are interesting, it helps a lot. Just this year, both of my sons did their first TV interviews, and that was exciting. The *Today* show did a Father's Day program, and Matt Lauer interviewed Don Jr. and myself, which was great fun. Both Matt Lauer and Katie Couric have a knack for making anything entertaining, and I enjoy them tremendously. *48 Hours* interviewed my younger son, Eric, and myself, and aside from some slumping on his part, Eric did a great job. The media really isn't anything new to my kids, although they've been protected from it to a certain extent.

11:00 A.M. I receive an invitation to attend the show of Oscar de la Renta's new collection, and I call Melania. We decide to attend. I've never gotten tired of fashion or fashion shows. To me, it's an unbeatable combination—beautiful women and beautiful clothes, especially Oscar's.

My agency, Trump Model Management, has managed to put itself on the fashion map in a relatively short time. I started it about five years ago. We've got some top models, and I enjoy watching this business become more and more successful. I call John Tutolo for an update, and we discuss a few things that we think could be improved.

I call Paula Shugart, president of the Miss Universe Organization, to go over a few things with her. An interviewer recently asked me what motivated me to buy the rights to the Miss Universe pageant. My answer was that I love beautiful women and I'm also a businessman, so it seemed like a good idea, which it has turned out to be. Sometimes things are that simple. I realized early on that I was an aesthete by nature, being attracted to beauty in both people and buildings. My work has shown that some early self-knowledge was right on target.

I take a call from Ricardo Bellino, a businessman in Brazil. We are working on the Villa Trump together in Brazil, and he's also asking me some questions for his upcoming book on the power of ideas. I mention that ideas are door openers, the first step. Without a first step, there won't be any other steps to take you where you want to go. It's a visual process. Perhaps that's why I'm a visionary, but a well-grounded one. When it comes to great ideas, the first questions I ask myself are: *Yeah, but is it possible? Will this be feasible?* If I can see something being accomplished, I know it is a possibility. I guess that's why I'm a builder. I start from the ground and go up from there.

I write a congratulatory note to Kitty Carlisle Hart for her ninety-third birthday. In addition to being multitalented, she's been a true philanthropist, and New York is lucky to have her. I always liked to watch her on television. Those of you who remember the television show *To Tell the Truth* will know what I'm talking about.

I write another note to a high school that has asked me for advice, and also asked who my favorite U.S. president might be. I decide to start with a quote by Abraham Lincoln, who would have to be my first choice: "I will study and prepare, and perhaps my chance will come." Always humble, always hardworking, always studying, Lincoln is a great example for high school kids.

11:30 A.M. The Entertainment Channel is ready for an interview regarding *The Apprentice*. It goes quickly and well, and we're done in five minutes.

12:00 P.M. I call an employee at a large property who has not been as attentive as his position demands. I tell him that his bad performance is not his fault, but mine: I simply hired the wrong person by overestimating his capabilities. I add that if he'd like to change my mind about my initial mistake, it's up to him. He promises to take care of things right away, and I think he means it.

I ask Andy Weiss to come in. His office is about 110 feet down the hall, but he can hear me. The reason we don't have an intercom system is because we don't need one. This often startles visitors, but, as I see it, why have more gadgets than necessary? Andy's been with me a long time, and we get right to the point. The meeting's over in less than five minutes.

I call Beverly Sills, one of the most wonderful opera singers of all time, and an equally wonderful person. I may not enjoy sitting through an opera, but I have always respected opera singers and enjoy the highlights of opera. Beverly is remarkable in every way, and I always enjoy talking to her.

12:30 P.M. I decide to have a slice of pizza for lunch, and I read a few of the letters that have come in. Here's one from a young man in the

Bay Area of San Francisco who writes, "This letter is in appreciation for inspiring us in hard times. Please continue writing your books and influencing people to live their dreams." He'll be happy to know that's exactly what I'm doing, even as I eat my pizza and read his letter. Here's another one from a family in Germany, who thinks I should run for president and invites me to stay at their home. A business proposal comes from a group in Wales who would like me to work on a housing development with them.

12:45 P.M. I call Brian Baudreau, my executive of security, and tell him I want to go over to Trump Place, my development along the Hudson River. We go over to the West Side and check out what's going on with construction. We meet with Paul Davis, the CEO of the Hudson Waterfront Associates, and take a walk around. I get daily reports, but there's nothing like seeing things for yourself. Paul has a big project on his hands, and he's doing a terrific job.

I've encountered a lot of opposition from staunch West Siders about this development, but gradually they are beginning to see that these buildings will be an enhancement to their neighborhood. The West Side is thriving like never before, and even as an East Sider, I've got to admit that the West Side is a great place to be.

2:00 P.M. Back in the office, I start returning the twenty-two calls that came in. That's another reason I don't like to be out of the office too much—the backlog of calls can get out of hand. The first call I return is to United Cerebral Palsy, as I'm on the advisory board. One of the biggest perks of being financially successful is being able to be generous. I like giving money to good causes like United Way and the Police Athletic League. It really is a great feeling every time I can be of help, and, for the most part, that's a private part of my life. Some of my charities are public knowledge, and some of them aren't.

2:30 P.M.   Robin Leach and his team are here for an interview. Robin is well known for a reason. We have a great time, and it's a job well and quickly done.

3:15 P.M.   I have a meeting with Carolyn Kepcher, executive vice president and director of Trump National Golf Club in Briarcliff. We are building some magnificent villas on the grounds, and there are a lot of details to attend to. Fortunately, both of us are perfectionists, and our meetings never have to be long.

3:30 P.M.   I take a call from David Schner, president of *Leaders* magazine. I'd been interviewed a few months back and we still keep in touch.

Craig Semandl, the director of Trump National Golf Club, Los Angeles, calls in. He gives me an update on what's happening, and we go over some details. I will visit California later this month to see the progress for myself. It helps to have people you can trust when you're three thousand miles away.

This is something that still amazes me: Here's another person requesting my autograph on the March 1990 issue of *Playboy* magazine, which featured an interview and a cover photo of me. To this day, thirteen years later, I receive several requests a month for my autograph on this issue, and, granted, the girl I'm photographed with is a beauty, but I never thought this interview would remain so popular with people who follow my career. I'll have to reread it one of these days. Meanwhile, I sign the cover and it's sent back to the owner, and I sign a few books that have been sent in as well.

I make a call to Tiffany, my youngest daughter, who is giving me an update on her latest activities. She has enough going on for five people. She must take after me. She is excited about her upcoming birthday and her plans to have a party aboard the *Queen Mary* in Long Beach, California.

I write a note to the Veterans of Vietnam of Ward 4CD of Valley Forge General Hospital. I am cochairman and builder of the New York Vietnam Veterans Memorial Fund, and still continue to do what I can for these brave people.

4:00 P.M.   I take a call from Susan James, director of sales for Trump International Hotel and Tower on Central Park West. She has a great job—this is one of the most successful condominium towers ever built and the top-rated luxury hotel in New York City, all in one building. This is also where Jean-Georges Restaurant is located. All in all, it's a gem, and I'm proud of it. It's near Lincoln Center on Columbus Circle, and those of you who know architecture will find it interesting that Philip Johnson designed both this building and the State Theatre at Lincoln Center, home of the New York City Ballet. I'm sort of young to be considered historical, but some things point in that direction, and this building is one of those things.

I go over the invitations and requests of the day with Norma. I decide on an event given by Anna Wintour of *Vogue* magazine and leave the other decisions until later, when I can give them more time and consideration.

Charlie Reiss comes in and we go over current project developments in Chicago, Toronto, and London. Bernie Diamond and Jason Greenblatt, my terrific in-house attorneys, are in on the meeting as well. Contrary to what people may think, I listen to and take advice from a lot of people before I make a final decision on anything. I like to be as well informed as possible. However, when it comes to making a decision, I am aware that the full responsibility for that decision is, and will always remain, mine. That is why I proceed with caution, even if my image may be more flamboyant.

4:30 P.M. I have a meeting with Matthew Calamari, my chief of operations. He's always a busy guy, but with *The Apprentice* starting up soon, he's busier than ever. I'm not concerned, because after knowing Matthew for more than twenty years, I am certain he can handle anything.

My son Eric stops by to say hello. He's in college now but is visiting New York City for a couple of days. He sits in on my meeting with Matthew and then we chat for a bit. He's got a great grin. I love it when my kids visit, and we decide to have dinner together tonight.

5:15 P.M. I write a welcome-back letter to the members of the Mar-a-Lago Club. We are finishing a new ballroom, and it will be magnificent. One visitor to the Mar-a-Lago Club remarked that F. Scott Fitzgerald and his friends would feel right at home there. I had to agree. I'm looking forward to the new season, and I fly down most weekends during the winter.

I return a few calls, including one to Larry King, one of the sharpest interviewers of all time; another to a reporter for the *Star-Ledger* in New Jersey; and one to a reporter doing a story on the wonderful and very smart Russell Simmons.

John Myers, the president and CEO of GE Asset Management, calls in. He's a terrific guy in every sense of the word, and we are active together with the Damon Runyon Cancer Foundation, along with Dale Frey, who preceded John at GE and likewise did an absolutely fantastic job. These are two guys worth knowing. Over the years, General Electric has been my partner in a number of my developments, including the very successful Trump International Hotel and Tower at 1 Central Park West.

6:00 P.M.   I call Melania to see where we should take Eric for dinner. We decide on the "21" Club.

Norma comes in and we review some details of my deals, invitations, letters, and media requests, including those from a surprising number of international television programs and publications. Last year I did an interview for the number one program in China, which drew a huge audience. These facts continue to surprise me, probably because I am so focused on my immediate and daily responsibilities. I never found myself to be particularly fascinating.

The phones have quieted down, so I decide to go through a box I keep beside my desk where I put articles and letters of interest to me. Sometimes I'll keep certain articles for years if I like them. I also keep letters and quotes, such as "Hope is not a strategy." I saved an invitation from a speech I gave to the Wharton Business School Club about the future of New York City. I am always honored to speak to Wharton students and alumni.

I find nice notes from Dr. Jerry Buss of the Los Angeles Lakers, one terrific guy; Ed Malloy, an old friend I call "Blue Eyes"; and Harrison Tucker LeFrak, the next generation in a remarkable real estate family. Richard LeFrak, the son of Sam LeFrak, has done an amazing job in the real estate business. Likewise, his son Harrison will be one of the really great young people to watch. I have no doubt he will go right to the top.

There's a clipping from Liza Minnelli and David Gest's wedding, which I was honored to attend, even though I didn't think the mar-

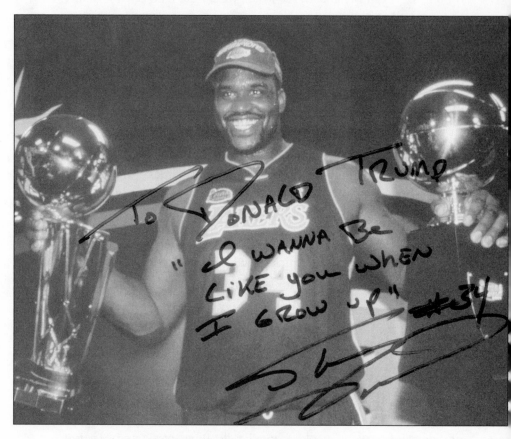

"To Donald Trump—'I wanna be like you when I grow up.' Shaq."

riage had a chance, and letters from John F. Kennedy Jr. and Howard Schultz of Starbucks, as well as one from Clint Eastwood, a great guy and golfer. He was my guest at Mar-a-Lago. He liked my course in Florida and wrote to tell me that.

I come across a fax from Roger Ailes of Fox Network News. What a job he's done, taking them to heights they'd probably never dreamed of.

During the march toward war in Iraq, someone sent me this joke: "You know the world has changed when you realize the best rapper is a white guy, the best golfer is a black guy, and Germany doesn't want to go to war."

A review to savor, from Rick Remsnyder upon the opening of Trump National Golf Course: "Trump National's par 3 thirteenth hole, which features a breathtaking 100-foot man-made waterfall behind the green, is one of the most challenging and spectacular holes in the world." Music to my ears.

I love sports. I have one of Shaquille O'Neal's oversized sneakers on display in my office and a signed baseball from my favorite team, the New York Yankees. I keep it near Tiffany's drawing of a house. She's already into real estate.

Speaking of real estate: I've saved an article about how I sold the land under the Empire State Building for $57.5 million in March 2002. New York real estate can be a wonderful business. I've also clipped a profile of another great success story, developer Steve Witkoff, who owns the Woolworth Building and the News Building, in addition to valuable property in London. In an interview with a London newspaper, Steve described me as "the only real estate person in this world who can brand his name individually. In my opinion, it's not going to happen again. Donald is a master at marketing. But you can't market and be a master at marketing unless you've got great product—it doesn't work like that. They say 'Coke are masters at marketing Coke,' or 'Nike, they're masters at marketing Nike.' You know what? They've got the best drink and the best sneakers. Well, Donald develops the best buildings. It's a fact of life. He's a great developer. No one wants to give him credit for that."

Finally, I come across a postcard from my gorgeous daughter Ivanka and an old postcard from my parents. I miss them. I still have two-thirds of the box to go through, but I'm on for dinner with Eric and Melania and I don't want to be late.

7:00 P.M. I pick up a large pile of documents to take with me, say good night to Norma, turn off the lights, leave my office, and head up to my apartment. It's been a good day. Business tip: Keep a box by your desk for mementos of the people and events that matter in your life and career. Reviewing the contents every now and then will keep you aware of your good fortune.

THURSDAY

8:30 A.M. This morning I have an interview with the legendary Barbara Walters, regarding the upcoming anniversary of September 11. All goes well; she's professional and to the point, which always helps. I am also planning a surprise visit this morning to Barbara's show, *The View*, as I have been the center of their discussions for a few days. They've been waiting for me to call them, which I haven't done, as I think a personal appearance might be more fun, although they don't know about it yet. If someone challenges you, always try to take the challenge and run with it.

9:15 A.M.   I have a meeting with Elaine Diratz, the director of sales at Trump World Tower at the United Nations Plaza. This condominium tower experienced a lot of opposition while it was being built, but it has literally been a triumph, both nationally and internationally. Even though Herbert Muschamp of *The New York Times* has lauded it and it has recently won a coveted European award for design, that doesn't mean we sit back in wonder at our good fortune. Everything requires upkeep, especially something of this caliber—plus it is in constant demand as a location site for films and television shows. Elaine and I troubleshoot the latest details.

9:45 A.M.   Don Jr. comes in to update me on his work. He's sharp and has some good insights on a few of our developments. It makes me think that maybe he's paid attention all these years after all. Norma comes in to tell me I should get going.

10:00 A.M.   Brian and I go over to the ABC studios on the West Side, to tape a special segment with Regis Philbin. It's a beautiful day and the city is sparkling—and as ever, so are Regis and Kelly.

11:00 A.M.   I am lurking in the studios of Barbara Walters's show *The View*, where I see Sharon Stone, who is a scheduled guest. At the top of the program, they are still discussing my hair and why I haven't called them back. Joy Behar mentions that here she is, still waiting for some guy to call, and Meredith Vieira mentions that expecting Donald Trump to call her back might be expecting too much. This conversation continues for a while—will he call?, won't he call?—and then I decide to just walk out onto the set. The audience shrieks when they see me, and Joy is, well, not exactly overjoyed but certainly surprised. I receive a very warm welcome from Barbara, Star, and Meredith, and I think Joy is relieved to know that I'm not at all in a huff over her remarks. I even let her touch and rearrange my hair and explain that while it may not be great hair, it's mine, and it's fine with me. We have a good time, and I think we'll all have to agree that a visit is better than a phone call.

12:00 P.M.   Steve Wynn is here to visit me. We chat for a while and then I take him on a tour of *The Apprentice* sets being built downstairs. Steve and I are close friends—again!

12:30 P.M.   This is an unusual day, even for me. Sandra Bullock is here to visit, so she comes into the conference room where I'm having a meeting, just to say hi. I think the guys in the room are very impressed, and so am I, but I try to act cool. After all, my life isn't exactly dull, but getting a visit from Sandra is a highlight for everyone—especially the contractors, who cannot believe that it is actually her.

1:00 P.M.   Robin, one of my assistants, is eating a great-looking salad, so I ask her to order one for me. Then I start returning calls that came in while I was out, including one to Bob Tisch, owner of the Giants and Loews Hotels. The Tisch family has been a tremendous force for good in New York City, and I like Bob a lot. Most of the people I know don't take lunch hours, so when I return calls at lunchtime it means I actually want to talk to them.

I talk to Ashley Cooper, director of Trump National Golf Club at Bedminster, New Jersey, for an update on progress. I'll visit next week by helicopter to check things out for myself.

I call Sirio Maccioni, the owner of Le Cirque, one of my favorite restaurants in New York. We've decided to have a business dinner there tonight; while getting a table isn't a problem, I like to talk to Sirio just to catch up on things. He has the instincts required to run a great restaurant, as well as the manners. I always look forward to seeing him.

1:30 P.M. I see Norma in the small conference room, meeting with the Bank One executives about a credit card, the Trump card, which I am starting. Everyone tells me this will be a great success, and it is going very well.

Aretha Franklin's assistant calls to see if I can attend her concert at Radio City later in the month. Aretha is one of the all-time greats, but, unfortunately, I will be out of town on business. That's one of the downsides of having a busy schedule, but it's flattering to hear from Aretha.

One of the things I think about when my schedule gets a little crazy is a labyrinth. Labyrinths date back to the ancient Greeks and usually imply something intricate or complex. Thinking about them helps me, because my schedule can make a labyrinth look like tic-tac-toe, so it becomes a soothing visual for me. That may be some convoluted psychology, but it works. Later on, I learned that there are some famous labyrinths still around today, such as the one at Chartres Cathedral, in France, and that they serve some meditative purpose, but the motive for me has always been to gain perspective on my own agenda.

As they say, whatever works.

2:00 P.M. I attend the board meeting for one of my residential properties in the small conference room. I think anyone who lives in any of my buildings is fortunate, not just to be in a great building, but because we take pride in upkeep and service. We try to cater to the people living and working in my buildings in every way possible, so these meetings are important to me, and here's the reason: Past, present, and future tenants and owners have one very important quality in common. They all want the best for their money, which allows me to give you a simple formula for success: Deliver the goods.

A lady in a building across from one of mine actually called in to complain to us. Her complaint? The constant cleaning and polishing of my building was making her crazy. Every time she looked outside and across the street, someone was cleaning something, which she thought was excessive and unnecessary, and that I must have some sort of a problem that should be taken care of. Ever hear of New York stories? The funny part is that we don't have to make them up.

2:45 P.M.   I decide to take a tour of the office. First I visit Bernie Diamond, my general counsel, who is conferring with Sonja Talesnik. Then I see Andy Weiss and Don Jr. about something they're working on. I pass Scott Etess, who is on the phone, and see Charlie, Jill, and Russell in the conference room. I stop by to visit Micha Koeppel, VP of construction, and notice that Nathan Nelson and Anna DeVincentis are both busy on their phones. I ask my accounting team, Jeff McConney and Eric Sacher, to meet with me and Allen Weisselberg at 4:30. I see Ramon dealing with an enormous pile of mail, which we get plenty of around here. Everyone looks busy to me, and there's a nice hum to all the activity. On my way back, I stop to chat with George Ross and Jason Greenblatt. I notice some doorknobs need polishing and that the copy room needs to be cleaned up a bit, but on the whole, the office is looking good. We've been in our Trump Tower offices for twenty years, and they still look brand-new.

3:00 P.M.   I agree to go to Ferragamo's new store opening and the Luca Luca fashion show at Bryant Park, and we're trying to arrange my weekend schedule, which at this point is a whirlwind, even with a helicopter. It's a good thing I'm an active type, or this might tire me out.

Reggie Jackson stops by for a quick visit. He is always welcome here, and my staff loves it when he visits. We chat for a few minutes, and I remember all the incredible moments he has given us as a Yankee. Truly a great.

I return calls to Jay Neveloff, David Scharf, and my brother Robert, and make a call to Wollman Rink to see how we did with our summer attraction, Victorian Gardens. We used the ice rink space as an upscale amusement park for children during the summer months, and since this is our first season doing so, I'm interested in a firsthand account.

3:30 P.M.   I take a walk over to Trump Park Avenue, at Park and Fifty-ninth. As I said, I like to keep my eye on things, and I never find property checks tedious. This is such a beautiful building. I remember being interviewed last year by *The New York Times* about both the building itself and the real estate market in New York. I told them "People would rather invest in real estate than in Enron and WorldCom. You can touch it, feel it, smell it. As opposed to Enron, which you can only smell." Costas Kondylis mentioned that this building also had an advantage over properties that boast of being prewar-like, in that this building is definitely not prewar-like. It *is* prewar. Anyway, the work is coming along and it's looking good.

I guess someone saw *The View* on TV this morning, because, as I'm walking back, a lady says "Hey, Donald! Your hair looks great!" Whoever you are, thanks.

4:30 P.M.   I take a call from Joe Cinque regarding Sardinia. That's pretty far away but he says that next to Mar-a-Lago, it's his favorite place, and this guy travels all over the world. I'll have to check into it a bit.

I have a short meeting with my finance group, Allen, Jeff, and Eric. I should have a picture of these guys for you—what a crew! However, they do good work. People often ask me where I find the people who work for me. I think it must be divine intervention, if there is such a thing. But somehow, it all works. Remember how I once said that you should try to get people you like to work for you? These guys are a good example of that advice.

4:50 P.M.   Rhona comes in to tell me that Jim Griffin is on the line. Ever heard of the William Morris Agency? He's the guy to know. Jim is another example of someone who will always tell it like it is, which I appreciate. He'll give you the facts, and fast.

5:00 P.M.   I get a lot of letters from students of all ages who ask me specific things—either for school projects or for their own interest— and, while I can't respond to them all, I like to review their letters. Sometimes the simplicity and directness of their questions can keep me aware of small and simple things. As Benjamin Franklin once said, "Beware of little expenses. A small leak will sink a great ship." In business, nothing is ever too small to notice.

5:30 P.M.   I review a pile of legal documents, making short notes on them for response by my assistants tomorrow morning. If we didn't keep up with our correspondence several times a day, we'd be sunk. I receive requests from people in every industry under the sun, moon, and stars combined. My daily delivery includes submissions from artists, musicians, screenwriters, architects, authors, poets, comedians, chefs, designers, actors, shoemakers, and more. That's a condensed list. I also receive bundles of cookbooks from a lady in Illinois several times a year. Why she does this is beyond me. She must know that one of the few things I don't do is cook.

6:30 P.M.   Enough ruminating. I check my faxes and go upstairs.

FRIDAY

8:30 A.M.   The electrical contractors call in with some bogus claims about why they're way off schedule. They've been slacking off on the job. I've been watching them carefully and know exactly what their problem is, and proceed to tell them so. They get the message and promise me they will get back on track. We'll see. I believe about twenty percent of what contractors say, and that's on a good day. They know what I mean.

9:00 A.M.   I take a call from Dick Levy, a real gentleman, then I ask for a Diet Coke. Another call concerns an ad I placed about slot machines at the racetracks in New York, which I'm against. Without countless layers of security, it will not be in the public's best interest, and I therefore mention that it is obvious the ground under our racetracks is most fertile for growing organized crime. The ad contains a photograph of Al Capone, with the caption "He would have loved it." The bottom of the ad says, "Paid for by a Committee of one, who may not always be right, but knows what's wrong." I think the point is made.

Rhona asks about the Giants game next week, and I decide to go. I return calls from Bo Dietl, Vinnie Stellio, and Ivana, and place a call to Jim Griffin of the William Morris Agency. David Granger calls; *Esquire* magazine is using an apartment in Trump World Tower as an example of the ultimate man's apartment, the Esquire Apartment. I have to agree with him that it's the ideal place.

I take a call from a writer doing an article on motivation and leadership. One of the questions asked is how I handle a person who consistently makes the same mistakes. I tell them the truth: I don't. They're working for someone else now.

9:30 A.M.   I take a moment to glance out the window, which I rarely do, even with the spectacular views from my office. There is something inspiring about New York City, and I feel fortunate to live here. Just as I'm thinking this, a call comes in from *Los Angeles Confidential Magazine* for a comment on their publication. I tell them that Los Angeles is as viable a cosmopolitan center as New York City, which it is, and that I think their magazine has a lot of integrity. I always enjoy my trips to California, and with my new golf course in Los Angeles, I'll be able to spend more time there in the near future. I decide to call Jason Binn, just to catch up on things with him. He's a successful magazine publisher, and I haven't spoken to him for a couple of weeks. I enjoy his take on things.

Tom Fazio calls in to go over some course plans and to give me an update on my New Jersey golf course. He loves what he does and that's made apparent by his attention to detail. John Mack of Credit Suisse calls in. Despite his great accomplishments, he remains an unassuming man—the work is what matters to him. These are two easy and informative calls. People have to understand that I've been dealing with all kinds of people and industries for a long time, so I can pretty readily discern who the goof-offs are and who the solid-gold people are. So if you hear me blow up in my office at someone or something, there's usually a reason for it. It can be as clear as day to me, and I see no reason to tolerate someone being inefficient or irresponsible. I do my best, and so should they.

I heard someone who had worked with me for a long time describing me as a generator—someone who revs up, keeps going, gathers momentum, keeps going at a higher level, and all is well—except for the boiling point. Because when something causes me to explode, believe me, there will be a lot of energy behind it. But, hey, at least I can be honest about it, and his assessment is accurate. A great Palm Beach lawyer, Paul Rampell, called me a reverse tornado—I build everything in my path, instead of destroying it.

Robin comes in to tell me the copies I want are delayed because our copy machine is on the blink again. I can't believe it. With all the amazing inventions of today, can't they design a copy machine that won't break down every three minutes? This is one thing that can make me lose my temper. I personally call Pete Strada, our director of purchasing, and ask him when the lease is up on this terrible machine. I want it out of here.

10:00 A.M. Norma comes in and we go over the event I'm hosting with Heidi Klum and Jonathan Tisch for the Elizabeth Glaser Pediatric AIDS Foundation. It will be held at Sotheby's next month. We also discuss some interview requests and invitations, seeing if and how we can fit them into my schedule. Every week we think that week can't be topped, then the next week is even more hectic, so what's happened is that our stamina has increased. I am much busier now than I have ever been. That's one reason I don't complain much. I literally don't have time to.

I take a call from Tony Senecal, the head butler and historian at Mar-a-Lago. This guy is terrific and a great asset to Mar-a-Lago. He fills me in on the latest, and I'm glad he has X-ray vision when it comes to details.

Jean-Georges Vongerichten calls in. In addition to being a genius when it comes to food, he's also a visionary. He's a celebrity in his own right, but I can tell you that what really matters to him is cooking— and when you visit any of his restaurants, you'll find out what I mean.

10:30 A.M. Tina Brown, of publishing fame, calls. We weren't always on such good terms, but we put our differences aside. I enjoy talking with her. She's quick and insightful.

I ask George Ross and Carolyn Kepcher to come in. I've decided they should play themselves in pivotal roles on *The Apprentice*. They both agree and do not seem put out at all. There won't be any acting involved, because to them it will be another day on the job. Maybe a longer day on the job, but just another day. Total pros.

I take a call from Jim Dowd, senior press manager at NBC, regarding *The Apprentice,* and one from Jay Bienstock, a producer on *The Apprentice.* Both guys know exactly what they're doing, which is a relief to me. Then I yell at some contractors for a while. It's too boring to tell you about this, but it's something that is absolutely necessary in real estate development and construction. I spend much of my days doing this.

I take a call from Eliot Spitzer, the New York State attorney general. He is one smart guy, who has an even more brilliant future ahead of him. He is just amazing!

11:00 A.M. I go down to the large conference room to see some plans for a possible new development. Charlie, Russell, Jill, and Don Jr., my development team, go over them with me. This could be a go, but I'll have to think about it a bit more. I don't have a formula for making decisions—each situation is unique, and I allow my assessment to be equally unique, with no time constraints. When it's right, it will be right. I may have the reputation of being brash, but I am very restrained in regard to making decisions. People don't see the process—they only see the results.

11:30 A.M. I return nine calls and realize I'm looking forward to having lunch at the golf club and a round of golf with Bill Clinton, David Granger, and Alfons. It's a beautiful day, and I love checking out the course. That's one reason I don't feel too guilty about taking a Friday afternoon off—I'll still be working.

Someone sends in a big box of Godiva chocolates. This will be tough, but I'll just look at them for a while and then put them outside for my staff. Who says I'm not a nice guy? Ditto for those Belgian truffles. Life can be tough.

12:00 P.M. I ask George Ross to come in, and we go over a few things. George brings the word *laconic* to life. Five minutes with him equals one hour with your average lawyer.

12:05 P.M. I decide to call Mike Donovan. I want to see how the work is going on my 727. He says it will be ready next week, which is good news, as I want to visit my golf course in California.

12:15 P.M. Mark Burnett and his two producers, Jay Bienstock and Kevin Harris, come in for a meeting, to go over the assignments to be given to the sixteen candidates on *The Apprentice*. This is an interesting process. We want to make sure that each assignment has a purpose beyond entertainment. These guys are not only nice, they're intelligent. I really feel they've got their bases covered. Any apprehensions I had about the TV show have evaporated.

12:45 P.M. I go through twenty-seven requests, including invitations from Norway, Peru, and India. Norma tells me I should view the video made for Trump Park Avenue before I leave, which has some beautiful footage. It's a great video.

1:00 P.M. I collect my papers and faxes and ask Rhona to call the elevator and to tell Eddie to have the car ready in fifteen minutes.

I make my exit. It's been a great week. I just hope the car is ready. Otherwise, Eddie's in for it—big time.

PART VI

Inside
The
Apprentice

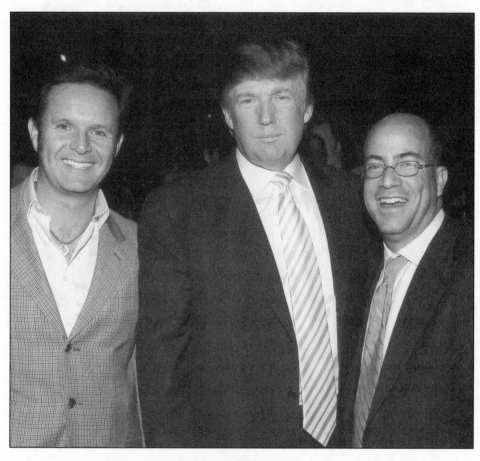

Here I am with Mark Burnett, creator of The Apprentice, *and Jeff Zucker, president of NBC Entertainment.*

Prime Time

Over the past few years, since reality shows came into vogue, television networks have been trying to get me to do one. They approached me with offers for substantial amounts of money, but the concept was always predictable. They wanted to follow me around with cameras, watching me make deals, brush my teeth, and, most certainly, comb my hair. None of this appealed to me at all.

One day, I was approached by the head of CBS Entertainment, Les Moonves, who wanted to broadcast the live finale of the hit series *Survivor* from Wollman Rink in Central Park, which I control through a long-term lease. It sounded like a great idea to me, especially when they told me they were going to build a jungle to replicate the one in which the *Survivor* contestants had been living.

When I arrived at Wollman Rink that night, I was amazed to see what they had been able to do. They had transformed a city skating rink into an exotic wildlife scene. As I was heading toward my seat, an attractive young man approached me and said, "Hi, Mr. Trump, I'm Mark Burnett and I'm the creator of *Survivor.*"

I said, "Mark, you don't have to tell me that. Everybody knows who you are, but it's really nice to meet you."

He said, "You know, Mr. Trump, I have an idea and I'd love to see you at your earliest possible convenience."

A week later, he came to my office. Before he got to his formal presentation, he did what any smart entrepreneur would do: He made sure he established a connection with me.

He did this by telling me that I'm a genius. Some people may consider such flattery excessive, but when you're on the receiving end, it's usually okay.

In the most passionate terms, he told me how, fifteen years ago, when he was selling shirts on Venice Beach and barely making a living, he had read a copy of *The Art of the Deal*. He said it had changed his life.

"If that's so," I said, "why haven't you given me twenty percent?"

He laughed heartily. I knew he was setting the table, but he was setting it brilliantly. I was impressed.

Then he told me his idea for *The Apprentice*—a series set in the jungle of New York City, the toughest jungle of them all, where people tear each other apart just to get an inch ahead of the competition.

His idea was terrific: Have sixteen people compete in a televised thirteen-week job interview, where the winner gets to become my apprentice. Whoever won would get a six-figure job at The Trump Organization for one year—maybe longer, if he or she was worth it.

What appealed to me most was that the premise of *The Apprentice* would be educational to viewers. People would be able to see how the real business world works and what it takes to survive in it—or to even have a chance to survive in it.

I asked Mark what kind of a time commitment he would need from me.

Mark's words, which I will never forget and will always remind him of, were: "Donald, believe me, the most time we would need is three hours a week."

I can affectionately say that I was a real schmuck for believing that line.

The first few episodes took about thirty hours each. But it turned out I didn't mind. As time went by, I started to realize that this show could be really big, and I wanted to devote the kind of time to it that Mark needed me to give.

When we pitched the project to the top networks for bids, everyone wanted it. They loved the concept. We chose NBC, which also broadcasts my Miss Universe, Miss USA, and Miss Teen USA pageants, so it was a quick and easy deal. Neither side had to be convinced of anything, and from the very first meeting, the relationship has been a strong one. Bob Wright, the chairman of NBC, and Jeff Zucker, president of NBC Entertainment, are the best in the business. They worked hard to promote the show and were rewarded with rave reviews and the best ratings of any new show of the season. I know this sounds like typical showbiz hype, but it's all true.

Once I got used to the time commitment, working on the show came naturally, because, in effect, what I do on *The Apprentice* is what I do in life: I hire people. I fire people. I make things work.

One of my favorite aspects of the show are the dramatic entrances and exits I get to make—from limousines and planes, or into the boardroom. It's good to be the CEO, and it's even better to be the CEO on national TV. It was also great to enlist the services of special guest stars such as George Steinbrenner and Donny Deutsch, the best advertising man in the business, as well as Regis, of course.

When we announced the show to the media in one of the most publicized job listings in recent memory, the reaction was instant and huge. In the first week, we received over 86,000 website hits. Over 70,000 applications were downloaded—the first one from Hamburg, Germany. The tally reached 215,000 before we finally stopped counting. This might have been the biggest job application in history.

Fortunately, Mark and his team knew what they were doing. After reviewing the twelve-page applications and videotapes required of

The Apprentice *auditions in August 2003. I'm greeting these brave people in front of Trump Tower.*

prospective contestants, ten casting directors and five assistant casting directors studied the materials further, narrowing the field to those deemed strong possibilities.

Their screening process was comprehensive and thorough. In the spirit of fairness, open calls were held in ten major U.S. cities. Tens of thousands of people showed up. In New York City, at Trump Tower, those thousands stood in the pouring rain for hours just to get a few moments of consideration. Obviously, most of them didn't make it, but they've got what it takes to succeed because they've got the guts to go for it.

Seeing their enthusiasm really revved me up for the show. It also bowled me over. I thought to myself, *All these people want to work for me?* It was incredibly flattering. Then again, I doubt those people knew what they might have been getting themselves into. I heard through the grapevine at my office, on one particularly rough day, that the name for *The Apprentice* competitors who didn't win spots on the show was "The Lucky Fifteen."

There were some amusing moments before we began taping. Mark Burnett brought his adoring father, Archibald, to visit one day. After meeting me, he said, "You're much more handsome in person than I would have thought. Maybe you don't photograph so well. Good luck with the show." Mark quickly interjected that his father was from Scotland and tended to be on the blunt side. I think he's terrific.

Mark is a lot of fun to be around—the British equivalent of a Green Beret. He has no fear and tremendous positive energy, which is my idea of a great leader. We're both big Neil Young fans, so one night, I took him to a concert at the Taj Majal in Atlantic City and introduced him to Neil backstage. Then we went to Naomi Campbell's party in New York City.

I always made a point of mentioning *Survivor* when I introduced Mark to people, but later I realized I was getting some confused looks when I did it, particularly from a Chinese poker winner we met at the

Taj Majal. It took me a moment to figure out that *Survivor* probably isn't on TV in China. The poker winner thought Mark was a cancer survivor and didn't know what to say.

When the crew of the show first appeared at Trump Tower, they created a bit of a buzz. Our ordinary routine was altered by just their presence. It was unusual to see all of those cameras. But within a couple of weeks, it became part of the routine. Jay Bienstock and Kevin Harris, two of Mark Burnett's producers, became fixtures of our organization. Then NBC executive Jim Dowd became a regular. If anything, it was when they weren't around that it seemed like something was amiss. They were never an imposition, and we even missed them when taping was over.

Unlike a scripted movie or TV show, *The Apprentice* that you have seen on NBC is pretty much the way it was behind the scenes. That's the idea—behind the scenes is in front of your eyes. Right away, I can hear you saying, "But we heard the boardroom was a set, and not your boardroom at all." That's true, but the only reason we built another boardroom was because my own boardroom at The Trump Organization is in constant use, and having a film crew in it every week for several months would have disrupted my business. So we built a replica on the fourth floor of Trump Tower. The reception area was also built there because the comings and goings of the sixteen apprentices and a TV production crew would have been a disturbance to our employees and our guests, some of whom may not have been expecting a close-up.

The set was built in Trump Tower so I could take an elevator and be there in fewer than two minutes. My regular business schedule is hectic, so traveling to and from an off-site location could have caused problems. Using the space we had on-site proved to be a good decision.

The living quarters for the sixteen applicants were also built on the fourth floor, and the equipment necessary for filming was installed there. It was an amazing setup, with sound rooms, tech rooms, lights, cameras, and what seemed like miles of cables. When I first saw it all, I realized the immensity of the preparations that went into this show, with designers, decorators, technicians, assistants, producers, and directors all working like mad. At any point, there could be twenty-eight cameras going at once. This was a big operation.

One day after seeing this, I paused silently for a moment. What if the show was a flop? All this work, all this energy . . . well, it just had to work. And I was determined to do my best to make it a hit.

The reassuring thing was that I didn't have to act. That gave me some comfort. Mark Burnett told me that my value to the show would be in just being myself. Is there such a thing as acting like yourself? I don't know, but I try not to think about it. I'm just myself.

I didn't have to read any scripts or learn any lines. Despite having a great memory, I don't have time for that, anyway. Mark would apprise me of the assignments for the applicants each week and we'd go from there. I enjoyed the spontaneity of the process, because we don't rehearse episodes in our daily business life. What happens, happens.

What went on in the boardroom or anywhere else was not fabricated in any way. If it seemed dramatic, that's because business *is* dramatic. There's nothing boring about it. There's nothing passive about it, either—even for viewer.

Seeing the eagerness and anticipation of the sixteen winning applicants was a rush in itself. I never used the word "contestants" in describing them, because this was not a game. People who think their jobs are a game aren't people I want to have around. A lot of these people already had lucrative positions or businesses of their own, so they weren't in it merely for some prize money. We made sure they were all serious about learning something not only after the process but during it. This also ensured that each applicant would be a winner, no matter what the outcome of their quest turned out to be. How many other reality shows have you seen that has only winners? That was another reason *The Apprentice* was so appealing to me. There would be no losers in this win-win situation. My kind of show.

I know what you're thinking. *But you fired fifteen people!* Yeah, but look what they got to do. Look what they got to see. Look what they learned.

All of the tasks required of my would-be apprentices required negotiation skills of one type or another. I was particularly interested in the way the applicants approached the task of achieving maximum savings from a list of items we told them to buy. Items ranged in value from $10 to $550. The highest-ticket item that could be discounted was a luxury golf club, a Callaway driver. The winning team homed in on this item. The losers spent their time trying to buy gold, a relatively fixed-price commodity. The winning team learned an essential lesson in negotiation and business: If you win on the big point, you don't sweat the minor ones.

The sixteen applicants quickly became people I liked and cared about—in the way a boss cares about his employees. They were all dynamic individuals with a lot on the ball. It wasn't easy to fire any of them.

Heidi Bressler, 30, an account executive from Philadelphia, Pennsylvania. Heidi is strong, and she kept her objectives in focus in her dealings. She used her account executive background to her advantage in keeping herself balanced.

Jason Curis, 24, a real estate entrepreneur from Detroit, Michigan. Jason has a lot on the ball, but he's young and a little rash. For those of you who missed the episode, Jason cut me off, in midsentence, in the boardroom. You *never* interrupt the boss in a meeting. You *never* interrupt the client in a meeting, either. But he will continue to learn and achieve.

Katrina Campins, 24, a real estate broker from Coral Gables,

Florida. Katrina is very accomplished already as a broker, which is a different scenario from that of being the president of a company. I think she will continue to prove herself in her field, possibly becoming an entrepreneur. She will be a success in life.

David Gould, 31, a health care venture capitalist from New York City. David has an exceptional educational background, with both an MBA and an MD, but business is not yet his forte. He surprised me in the first episode when he said salesmanship was not one of his skills. Why volunteer any deficiency? He was the first to be fired.

Jessie Conners, 21, owner of a chiropractic marketing and management company from New Richmond, Wisconsin. Jessie was an interesting mixture of sophistication and innocence. She competed like an experienced player, then did herself in by taking unnecessary abuse from a colleague. You've got to fight back if you want to be successful in business. But don't underestimate her.

Bowie Hogg, 25, an account executive at FedEx, from Dallas, Texas. Bowie has great determination, but when it came to selling, he fell short. He learned a lot, and I'm confident he'll be successful in his career.

Kristi Frank, 30, a real estate broker and restaurant owner from Bel Air, California. Kristi knows a lot about the real world in many ways, due to her business experience, but her failure to stand up for herself showed a lack of one hundred percent focus on her immediate goal. She will do well for herself if she focuses more.

Kwame Jackson, 29, a Harvard MBA and investment manager at Goldman Sachs, from New York City. He is smooth and collected, and will do what is necessary to succeed. Kwame raised some eyebrows when he signed basketballs at Planet Hollywood, implicitly suggesting to customers that he was famous. Was it unethical? When you're desperate, you sometimes have to push the envelope. Kwame was on a desperately failing team. His judgment wasn't admirable, but I don't think he crossed the line: He was supporting his team members.

Amy Henry, 30, a manager at a high-tech start-up in Austin, Texas, who owned millions of dollars in options and lost it all in the dot-com bust. Amy is extremely bright and has great spirit, team and otherwise. I don't think much can get her down, and she will excel.

Troy McClain, 32, a mortgage lender in the insurance business and a real estate developer, from Boise, Idaho. Troy is optimistic and realistic at the same time. It's a great combination, and I expect him to do big things. Plus it takes a brave man to have his legs waxed. That showed me how much he really wanted the job.

Tammy Lee, 36, a stockbroker at Merrill Lynch in Seattle, Washington. Tammy's experience gives her a realistic view of the world. She watches out for herself and keeps her goals clear. Her strength is one of her greatest attributes, and it will help her throughout her career.

Bill Rancic, 32, founder of cigarsaroundtheworld.com, which he started from his studio apartment in Chicago, Illinois, and turned into a multimillion-dollar business. Bill is a good guy with a great future and has already proven his entrepreneurial skills. He's a careful thinker, serious about his endeavors, and a good bet to achieve the results he seeks.

Omarosa Manigault-Stallworth, 29, a political consultant from Washington, D.C., who worked in the Clinton-Gore administration. Like Madonna, she needs only a first name. Omarosa is the most articulate of the group. She's got a lot of fight in her and self-confidence that will serve her well. If she'd been working on Gore's presidential campaign, he would have won.

Sam Solovey, 27, cofounder of an Internet media company, from Chevy Chase, Maryland. He lasted only until the third episode, but even that seemed like an eternity to some viewers. Sam was the smartest annoying character on TV since Howard Cosell. He is likely to either take a company down in flames or create an IBM. I think he's got a lot of talent, and as long as he learns how to use it correctly he will do great things. I can't believe he proposed marriage on TV. His future wife looks great, but he forgot to ask for the prenup, and I hope he won't ever need one.

Ereka Vitrini, 27, a global marketing manager for Clinique, who learned her business skills working in her family's pizzeria in New York City. Ereka has terrific spirit and a good amount of fortitude. She's not afraid to voice her opinions, and that's crucial.

Nick Warnock, 27, a salesman for Xerox who launched an Italian ice business in Bayonne, New Jersey, and now lives in Los Angeles. Nick is a savvy guy who tries to cover his bases. He is industrious but needs to focus on exactly what is going on around him. His tenacity will see him through.

They were all great, even Sam. What I found interesting was the shifting dynamic of the group and their interplay, with its changing patterns and alliances. That's the way business teams function.

As everyone saw, the women dominated the men at first, and it made some people wonder whether women are superior at business. I believe we're all equal, except in one respect: Women still have to try harder, and they know it. They will do what they have to do to get the job done and will not necessarily be demure about it.

A lot of people were surprised when I decided to lecture the women about the way they were using their sex appeal. They used it successfully at first, but I knew that would not always be the case. It works, and then it doesn't, and I didn't want them to fall into a trap.

All the women on *The Apprentice* flirted with me—consciously or unconsciously. That's to be expected. A sexual dynamic is always present between people, unless you are asexual.

As a result of *The Apprentice,* several of my esteemed colleagues at The Trump Organization have become TV stars. I was joined in the boardroom every week by George Ross and Carolyn Kepcher. They did for *The Apprentice* what they do for me every day—pay attention to the

At Planet Hollywood in Times Square with George Ross and Carolyn Kepcher.

details, see the big picture, and give me excellent advice. When I told them I wanted them to appear on the show with me, unscripted and unrehearsed, they approached it just like any other job assignment, with thorough professionalism and astute attention, and they came across as authentic because of that.

I chose Carolyn, an executive vice president and the director of one of my largest properties, because she's shown a lot of smarts over the years. George, an executive vice president and senior counsel, is a shrewd, tough guy with brains—he doesn't put up with nonsense from anyone.

My executive assistants Rhona Graff and Robin Himmler are also featured regularly, and even though they have high-stress jobs, I think you'll agree they look anything but stressed on TV. My executives Allen Weisselberg, Charlie Reiss, Norma Foerderer, and Tom Downing also made appearances, and Bernie Diamond appears four times. Whenever I make a big hiring decision, these people are involved, so it was only natural for me to include them in choosing the apprentice.

The only person I had to coax into appearing was my vice president and personal assistant, Norma Foerderer. She prefers being "the power behind the throne" and didn't want to be in the limelight, but I finally convinced her.

I've been asked how much the success of *The Apprentice* will mean to my business. My pay per episode, while substantial, does not, for me, mean very much. It is nowhere near what the stars of *Friends* rake in. The real value is in the free advertising and publicity The Trump Organization has been receiving. I can't put a monetary value on that. Before *The Apprentice*, the use of my name on a building was worth untold millions of dollars. That value sure has not gone down. I'm told that *The Apprentice* is the highest-rated show featuring a nonacting businessman in the history of television. When TV viewers think of business in America, a lot of them are going to be thinking about The Trump Organization.

We're already at work on the second season, to premiere in the fall of 2004. For those of you interested in applying and winning, here are the four essential qualities I'm looking for in an apprentice:

1. *An outstanding personality.* Someone who makes everyone feel comfortable. No matter what you're doing in business—selling, buying, negotiating, analyzing, or managing—this may be the most essential trait. You've got to be able to connect with the people you encounter, every hour, every day.
2. *Brains.* Not book brains alone, but street smarts as well. That combination, properly used, is a winner.
3. *Creativity.* The ability to see beyond the obvious, to think unpredictably and imaginatively, to make connections others might not envision. This is perhaps the hardest quality to develop—you've either got it or you don't. But you can be creative in different ways. Jeff Zucker is a creative TV executive. Derek Jeter is a creative shortstop. If they switched jobs, they might not be as creative in their various fields.
4. *Loyalty and trust.* Absolutely required traits. Unlike creativity and brains, any person can possess these qualities, so if you lack them, you have no one to blame but yourself.

Let's suppose, out of the hundreds of thousands of applicants, you're selected. Let's suppose you actually win. You become famous for fifteen minutes (or perhaps more) and bag a $250,000-a-year job at The Trump Organization.

Then what?

I titled this book *How to Get Rich* because whenever I meet people that's usually the first thing they want to know. From reading these pages, I hope you've gained a sense of what it takes, how to live your life in the way most likely to result in a vast fortune. Unless you win the lottery or have a bonanza at one of my casinos, you're not going to get rich purely through luck. You'll have to work for it, and I've tried to show you how.

My ideal goals are success with significance. That's worth more than the money. Being paid is nice. In most cases, it is absolutely necessary, and a good scorecard for success, but it certainly isn't the only one. I didn't do *The Apprentice* for the money, even though it has been very profitable.

It feels great to be in a position to make a difference, and that's what I mean when I say "success with significance."

I hope you become rich. And I hope you use your talent to make some kind of positive change in your immediate world.

Whatever your job is, that's your assignment.

Begin now.

You're hired.

Acknowledgments

This book could not have been written without Meredith McIver, a writer of many talents. She served her apprenticeship with the New York City Ballet, worked on Wall Street, and for the past two years has been an executive assistant at The Trump Organization, stationed at a desk outside my office. As you know, my door is always open, so Meredith has heard everything, and she's taken good notes. She's done a remarkable job of helping me put my thoughts and experiences on paper. I am tremendously grateful to her.

Very little happens in my office without Norma Foerderer, who oversees my schedule and has been instrumental in keeping this book project on track in many ways, especially in the coordination of the photographs.

I want to thank my editor at Random House, Jonathan Karp, who asked me to write this book. I first met Jon in 1997, when he edited *The Art of the Comeback*. He spent a lot of time in my office, and one day I noticed he was staring at the carpet under my desk. Finally, he said, "Donald, what's the deal with the space heater?"

I told him that my feet get cold.

Jon said, "We're in *Trump Tower*. It's *your* building. Can't you do something about that?"

It's important to have an editor who asks the tough questions.

I'm also grateful to many others at Random House who worked long and late hours to produce this book in record time: publisher Gina Centrello; associate publishers Anthony Ziccardi and Elizabeth McGuire; executive director of publicity Carol Schneider; director of publicity Thomas Perry; associate director of publicity Elizabeth Fogarty; editorial assistants Jonathan Jao (who did an excellent job with the photos) and Casey Reivich; art director Gene Mydlowski; managing editor Benjamin Dreyer; production chief Lisa Feuer; design director Carole Lowenstein; production manager Richard Elman; production editor Janet Wygal; copy editor Ginny Carroll; advertising director Magee Finn; rights directors Claire Tisne and Rachel Bernstein; and everyone in the Random House sales force, which is the best in the business.

At The Trump Organization, I am surrounded by home-run, grand-slam people: Matthew Calamari, Allen Weisselberg, George Ross, Bernie Diamond, Jason Greenblatt, Rhona Graff, Tony Morace, Andy Weiss, Don Jr., Jeff, Eric, and many more.

Meredith McIver would like to thank Mark Burnett, Richard Casares, Steve Palitz, the Bosworth Family, George Balanchine, Alain Bernardin, Christophe D'Astier, Peter Irigoin, and Richard Irigoin. To my family, you are the best. To everyone at The Trump Organization, it's an honor to work with you. To my officemates Rhona Graff and Robin Himmler, a special thanks for your support. To Norma Foerderer and Mr. Trump, thank you both for making every day an adventure. To Mr. Trump, you are a writer's delight. I will never be at a loss for ideas. Thank you very much.

Appendix

THE TRUMP ORGANIZATION PROPERTIES

NEW YORK, NEW YORK

Trump Tower

The city's most famous contemporary building and its third most-visited attraction (with in excess of 2.5 million visitors annually), this sixty-eight-story bronze glass and polished brass structure is situated on Fifth Avenue and Fifty-sixth Street. Completed in 1983 by renowned architect Der Scutt, it is one of the tallest residential buildings and concrete structures in Manhattan. It also boasts 170,000 square feet of commercial space and 136,000 square feet of retail space and is a center for business, a mecca of style and high fashion, and an elite sanctuary to some of society's most famous and influential people.

Trump Place (Riverside South)

The pièce de résistance of Donald Trump's real estate empire, Trump Place is a ninety-two-acre property fronting the Hudson River that promises to be the most exciting real estate development in Manhattan since the turn of the century. In June 1994, Mr. Trump entered into a joint venture with four of the largest Hong Kong real estate develop-

Trump Tower right after September 11, 2001.

Trump Tower, February 2004.

Artist's rendition of what Trump Place will look like when completed.

ment firms, which have committed $2.5 billion to implement this project. The project's first five buildings are complete, with a sixth tower under construction. The overall project will feature sixteen buildings containing 5,700 residential units and more than two million square feet of commercial space. The construction of a magnificently landscaped twenty-five-acre public waterfront park has also enhanced this property enormously by providing bicycle paths that link Battery Park in lower Manhattan to upper Manhattan.

Trump International Hotel & Tower
This fifty-two-story mixed-use structure comprises a superluxury hotel, residential tower, and world-famous restaurant (Jean-Georges). Located at the crossroads of Manhattan's West Side on Central Park West and Columbus Circle, it was designed by the renowned architect Philip Johnson and completed in 1997. Trump International has broken all records to date, becoming one of the most successful condominium towers ever built in the United States and pioneering the concept of a condominium hotel. The hotel achieved Mobil Five-Star status in its very first year of operation.

Trump Parc
Sold out since its completion in January 1988, Trump Parc is an elegant condominium located on Central Park South. Trump Parc's 347 residential units provide stunning views of Manhattan's skyline from river to river, as well as unobstructed views of Central Park.

Trump Park Avenue
In 2002, Mr. Trump purchased the fabled Delmonico Hotel, located at Fifty-ninth Street and Park Avenue. It is now being developed, in partnership with General Electric, into a state-of-the-art luxury high-rise condominium.

Breaking ground at Trump Place.

With construction workers at Trump Place.

Trump International Hotel & Tower.

Trump Plaza

This luxurious Upper East Side cooperative, completed in 1984, combines 175 residential units with numerous boutiques and privately owned apartments, each with its own private terrace.

Trump Palace

With a majestic facade that commands an entire block of Third Avenue on the tony Upper East Side of Manhattan, this 283-unit luxury condominium, completed in 1991, is distinguished by an illuminated spire that has become a distinctive landmark in the New York City skyline.

610 Park Avenue

The Trump Organization, in partnership with Colony Capital, restored the former Mayfair Hotel into luxurious residential condominiums. Situated on New York's most prestigious avenue, 610 Park residents enjoy the ultimate in services, including great dining in the legendary four-star Restaurant Daniel. They also have the convenience of the world's most exclusive shops, restaurants, and museums nearby.

The Trump World Tower

At ninety stories, this is the tallest residential building in the world and is uniquely located across from the United Nations headquarters. In addition to its prime location and impressive views of the city, the building contains 376 units, with a state-of-the-art spa and fitness center, a world-class cocktail lounge, and, within the near future, a glamorous restaurant. The building was named Best Residential Building in the World by the International Real Estate Federation in 2003.

The Trump Building at 40 Wall Street

The Trump Building stands proudly in the center of New York's Financial District, near the New York Stock Exchange. Originally built in 1930, the building stands seventy-two stories high and offers a vast

*The Trump World Tower at the
United Nations Plaza.*

*Trump Park Avenue at
Fifty-ninth Street and
Park Avenue.*

1.3 million square feet of interior space. Under Mr. Trump's ownership, it has been restored to all the majesty and splendor it once pos-
sessed.

Trump Pageants

In a unique departure from his forays into real estate, Mr. Trump and
the NBC network entered into a partnership for ownership and broadcast rights for the three largest beauty competitions in the world: the
Miss Universe, Miss USA, and Miss Teen USA pageants.

Trump Model Management

Developed by Mr. Trump, Trump Model Management is a modeling
and talent agency. It is managed by the industry's seasoned movers and
shakers and represents some of the most beautiful faces and exciting
talents in the world. It is one of the ten best modeling agencies in
Manhattan.

Wollman Skating Rink

Located in the middle of Central Park, with incomparable views of the
New York City skyline, this is a world-class (and world-famous) ice
skating rink managed by The Trump Organization.

BEDFORD, NEW YORK

Seven Springs

This lush 215-acre estate is the former home of Katharine Graham,
publisher of *The Washington Post*. The magnificent forty-thousand-
square-foot Georgian mansion was designed by celebrated architect
Charles Platt in 1917 and includes a smaller house called Nonesuch, as
well as two cottages, a ten-car garage, a greenhouse, and barns. Mr.

Trump is currently working with a team of international specialists to design a world-class golf course, club, and spa on this magnificent property.

BRIARCLIFF MANOR, NEW YORK

Trump National Golf Club

Nestled among the hills and valleys of beautiful Westchester County, Trump National Golf Club is a world-class club that boasts a 7,200-yard, par-72 course designed by one of the leading golf course architects, Jim Fazio. Currently under construction on the 207-acre property are eighty-seven luxury golf villas and mid-rise condominium buildings.

BEDMINSTER, NEW JERSEY

Trump National Golf Club, Bedminster

In 2002, Mr. Trump purchased Lamington Farm, in the heart of New Jersey horse country, once the home of automaker John DeLorean. Work is currently under way to build a world-class golf course, designed by Tom Fazio, along with fifteen residential super-mansions. Additional plans for this magnificent 525-acre property include a pool, tennis courts, and converting the twenty-thousand-square-foot Georgian-style main house into a spectacular club-house.

LOS ANGELES, CALIFORNIA

Trump National Golf Club, Los Angeles

In 2002 Mr. Trump also purchased the Ocean Trails Golf Course, a magnificent property that fronts the Pacific Ocean for almost two miles. Designed by legendary golf course architect Pete Dye, it is being refurbished and upgraded by Mr. Trump to the world-class standards of his other courses. Luxury estate homes are also being planned for construction on the three-hundred-acre property.

MIAMI BEACH, FLORIDA

Trump Grande Ocean Resort and Residences

Mr. Trump has entered into a partnership with Dezer Properties for an oceanfront development located between Bal Harbour and Aventura. Upon completion, this project will contain three buildings on eleven acres and nearly one thousand linear feet of uninterrupted beachfront. The Trump International Beach Resort was completed in April 2003, with 372 hotel condominium units, ballrooms, a state-of-the-art business center and twenty thousand square feet of meeting rooms. Currently under construction is the fifty-five-story Trump Palace, a residential condominium tower with 267 units. Construction of the third residential condominium called Trump Royale is expected to start in the fall of 2004. These buildings are the tallest residential towers in South Florida.

ATLANTIC CITY, NEW JERSEY

Trump Taj Mahal Casino Resort

The most luxurious casino-hotel ever built, the Taj Mahal is Atlantic City's foremost gaming facility. Opened on April 2, 1990, it has been awarded the prestigious Mobil Five Star award and the AAA Five Diamond award. It has 125,000 square feet of casino space, making it the largest casino in Atlantic City, as well as 1,250 guest rooms, including 237 exotic suites, eleven restaurants, six lounges, 144,000 square feet of convention space, and the sixty-three-thousand-square-foot Mark G. Etess Arena, which seats six thousand.

Trump Plaza Hotel and Casino

Donald Trump's first foray into gaming, Trump Plaza is a five-star, five-diamond casino-hotel located on Atlantic City's famed Boardwalk, adjacent to the Convention Center. This thirty-one-story, 557-room luxury property features sixty thousand square feet of casino space, eleven restaurants, four lounges, and the 750-seat Cabaret Theatre. It has received worldwide recognition as a favored venue to such mega-events as the World Heavyweight Boxing Championships.

Trump Marina

Formerly Trump's Castle, the newly renovated Trump Marina is located on the beautiful Atlantic City Marina waterway. It is a Mobil Four Star casino hotel. Its twenty-six-story hotel tower contains 725 guest rooms, while the principal public area provides fifty-three thousand square feet of convention and exhibit space, nine restaurants, two lounges, and seventy thousand square feet of casino space.

BUFFINGTON, INDIANA

Trump Casino

This elegant casino-yacht, which opened in June of 1996, is nestled in Buffington Harbor, Indiana, just outside of Chicago. Donald Trump's first gaming venture outside of Atlantic City, it is the largest floating riverboat in the world at an astounding 290 square feet long and 76 feet wide.

PALM SPRINGS, CALIFORNIA

Trump 29 Casino

In 2002, Mr. Trump entered into an agreement with the Twenty-Nine Palms Band of Luiseno Mission Indians to manage the Trump 29 Casino, his first foray into gaming on the West Coast.

The Mar-a-Lago Club, Palm Beach, Florida.

PALM BEACH, FLORIDA

The Mar-a-Lago Club

This famous and historic twenty-acre waterfront estate, formerly owned by Marjorie Merriweather Post and E. F. Hutton, was acquired by Donald Trump in 1985. Designed by the renowned Viennese architect Joseph Urban, Mar-a-Lago was designated a National Landmark by the National Trust for Historic Preservation in 1972. It is the only property to receive this distinction in the state of Florida. It was converted by Mr. Trump in 1995 to a private ultra-luxury club that features a world-class spa, renowned dining, tennis, pool, and private beach. The club also functions as an international meeting place for world leaders in government, finance, business, and the performing and fine arts. In 2003, Mar-a-Lago was named by the American Academy of Hospitality Sciences as "the best private club in the world."

Trump International Golf Club

Designed by the esteemed golf course architect Jim Fazio, Trump International was opened in November 1999 and is already a landmark course that features waterfalls and landscapes unique to the state of Florida. In 2002, it was presented with the Five Star Diamond Award "for achieving the highest standards for the greatest golf course in Florida." A spectacular fifty-five-thousand-square-foot clubhouse was also built and based on the Moorish style of the Mar-a-Lago Club.

CHICAGO, ILLINOIS

Trump International Hotel and Tower, Chicago

Mr. Trump entered into a joint-venture agreement with Hollinger International, Inc., owner of the *Chicago Sun-Times* newspaper, to build a luxury, mixed-use development on the site of the current *Sun-Times* building. Located along the Chicago River, the proposed ninety-story, glass curtain–wall building has been designed by the world-renowned architectural firm of Skidmore Owings and Merrill (SOM). The building will contain approximately 2.2 million square feet, with 470 residential condominium units and 200 hotel condominium units, in addition to 125,000 square feet of retail space, more than a thousand parking spaces, and retail shops and restaurants, along a three-story river walk. Residential and hotel condominium sales commenced in September 2003, and it is anticipated that the project will be completed in 2007 as the fourth-tallest building in Chicago and one of the most luxurious buildings in the world.

INTERNATIONAL
TRUMP PROPERTY DESCRIPTIONS

Trump World I, II, and III, Seoul, Korea

Mr. Trump and his Korean partners have built three superluxury, residential high-rise buildings in the heart of Seoul, showcasing the best finishes, amenities, and services. Mr. Trump and his partners are now building a magnificent four-building complex in Busan, Korea, known as Trump World Centum, which will include more than five hundred residential units.

Trump Island Villas at Canouan Island, the Grenadines

The Trump Organization has joined with an Italian financier, Raffles Hotels, American Airlines, and the Moorings Yacht Charters to create a luxury resort and residential community on 1,200 acres of this Caribbean island, located near the prestigious island of Mustique. The resort will open in June 2004 and will contain a Trump International Golf Club. Ultimately, the island will feature 135 villas consisting of custom-designed estate homes to golf villas.

FUTURE DEVELOPMENTS

Trump International Hotel and Tower, Phoenix

This two-building project on East Camelback Road between Phoenix and Scottsdale (across from the famed Biltmore Hotel and Resort) will include a condominium hotel and residences. Situated near some of the most expensive commercial rentals in the area, the project may contain small retail and office components. The designs and relative sizes of the components are currently being developed. The project is scheduled to begin sales in the third quarter of 2004.

Trump International Beach Club, Fort Lauderdale

Located on AIA in Fort Lauderdale, this superexclusive Trump hotel will be situated halfway between chic South Beach and legendary Palm Beach. The designs and relative sizes of the components are currently being developed. Sales for this project are scheduled to begin in the second quarter of 2004.

Villa Trump International Golf Club, Itatiba, Brazil

Located just outside of São Paulo, it includes 150 golf villas, a twenty-seven-hole Jack Nicklaus signature golf course, a Cipriani boutique hotel, twelve tennis courts, 350 residential lots, a Jack Nicklaus golf academy, a clubhouse, and an events center. It contains 1,659 acres, 800 of which are undeveloped.

Behind the Scenes
at The Trump Organization

TRUMP
Think Like a Billionaire

Everything You Need to Know About Success, Real Estate, and Life

Introduction
Thinking Like a Billionaire

In a world of more than six billion people, there are only 587 billionaires. It's an exclusive club. Would you like to join us?

Of course, the odds against you are about ten million to one. But if you think like a billionaire, those odds shouldn't faze you at all.

Billionaires don't care what the odds are. We don't listen to common sense or do what's conventional or expected. We follow our vision, no matter how crazy or idiotic other people think it is. That's what this book is about—learning how to think like a billionaire. Even if you absorb only ten percent of the wisdom in this book, you'll still have a good shot at becoming a millionaire.

In my previous book, *How to Get Rich,* I shared some of my favorite techniques for running a profitable business and becoming a TV megastar. Consider this new book the second part of an ongoing conversation between you and The Donald—the billionaire's equivalent of those bestselling works of inspiration *Conversations with God* and *Conversations with God, Book 2.*

I'm sure some wise guy in the media is going to accuse me of comparing myself to God, so for the record, I do not think I am God.

I believe in God. If God ever wanted an apartment in Trump Tower, I would immediately offer my best luxury suite at a very special price. I believe God is everywhere and in all of us, and I want every decision I make to reflect well on me when it's time for me to go to that big boardroom in the sky. When I get permanently fired by the ultimate boss, I want the elevator to heaven to go up, not down.

Some of you may think it's wrong to talk about God and business in the same breath, but God has always been central to our way of thinking about capitalism. The Protestant work ethic has thrived for centuries. The pursuit of prosperity is ingrained in our religious culture. The more you have, the more you can give.

Here's something else about God that any billionaire knows: He's in the details, and you need to be there, too. I couldn't run a business any other way. When I'm talking to a contractor, or examining a site, or planning a new development, no detail is too small to consider. I even try to sign as many checks as possible. For me, there's nothing worse than a computer signing checks. When you sign a check yourself, you're seeing what's really going on inside your business, and if people see your signature at the bottom of the check, they know you're watching them, and they screw you less because they have proof that you care about the details.

I learned how to think like a billionaire by watching my father, Fred Trump. He was the greatest man I'll ever know, and the biggest influence on my life.

A lot has been written about my family. A writer named Gwenda Blair spent twelve years on her thorough history, *The Trumps: Three Generations That Built an Empire*. She even traced our lineage back to 1608, when a German lawyer named Hanns Drumpf settled in the town of Kallstadt, forty miles west of the Rhine River. According to Blair, one of my ancestors, a winegrower, changed the family name to

Trump at the end of the 1600s—a good move, I think, since Drumpf Tower doesn't sound nearly as catchy.

My grandfather Friedrich was the first Trump to come to America. Like many entrepreneurs, he ran away from home because he didn't want to work in the family wine business. One of my fellow billionaires, John R. Simplot, left his family farm because he didn't want to spend the rest of his days milking cows. Instead, he became a potato grower and one of the largest suppliers to McDonald's. He earned his billions in french fries. One way to think like a billionaire is to question your surroundings: Don't assume you have to accept the hand you were dealt.

My grandfather was a barber and the owner of several businesses, including a hotel and a restaurant. He moved from New York City to Seattle and eventually to Alaska during the gold rush, where he fed miners at the biggest joint in town, the Arctic Restaurant. Unfortunately, he caught pneumonia and died when my father was just a boy. My father never said much to me about him or about other Trump family history.

Fred C. Trump wasn't the kind of dad who took us to the movies or played catch with us in Central Park. He was better than those fathers. Instead, he'd take me to his building sites in Brooklyn and Queens. He'd say, "Let's make the rounds," and we'd be on our way. He never yelled at me or had to punish me, but he was always strong, and a little remote, until I joined his business. That's when I really got to know him.

I saw how he dealt with contractors and unions, and how he made the most out of every space. My father believed in adding "the extra element" to his properties—he was among the first to build garages into homes in Brooklyn. He could be a showman, too. His deals were front-page news in the Brooklyn newspapers. He advertised regularly and had big openings for his developments. His gift for promotion rubbed off on me, but it was never something we talked about, and to this day, I don't think promotion had much to do with either his success or mine. We succeeded because we learned how to create the best buildings at the best locations with the best zoning. My father showed me how to fight the unions and the politicians in order to get the building done under budget and ahead of schedule. And then, after the building is up and it's a great success, everyone says, "Boy, Donald, that was a great promotion," when promotion had nothing to do with it.

My father always trusted me. He'd been in business for fifty years, but he'd never let anyone else in the company sign his checks until I came to work. He had absolutely no doubt about my ability.

His faith gave me unshakable confidence. Even when I was at my lowest, in the early 1990s, when the real estate market tanked and I was billions in debt and Ivana and her lawyers and a hundred banks were ready to sue my ass off, my father told me he had absolutely no doubt that my business would be fine. He'd say, "You are a killer. You are a king."

My father never wanted to build in Manhattan. He thought it was too expensive. He'd say, "If I can buy a piece of land for a dollar a square foot in Brooklyn, why should I pay a thousand dollars a square foot in Manhattan?" It was a different philosophy, but it worked for him.

I'd been working in the family business for five years when I made the move into Manhattan. Some critics have suggested that my success is the result of family money, but family money didn't get my first Manhattan projects built. I had to raise tens of millions of dollars from investors for those jobs. It wasn't money that my father gave me; it was knowledge—knowledge that became instinctive for me.

When I was in college, I thought about becoming a movie producer, but whenever I talked to a friend about real estate, he would say, "Why would you want to make movies when you already know so much about real estate?" So yes, my father was a millionaire many times over, but if he hadn't shown me how to think about business, I never would have made it into the billionaires club.

I wish I could tell you that the billionaires club meets regularly at Mar-a-Lago, where we gather to analyze our portfolios, make blockbuster deals, eat caviar, and drink vintage wine, but the truth is: I don't drink, I'd rather eat a steak than caviar, and I've met only about twenty of the club members over the years, often on the golf course, where we tend to talk more about our game than our net worth. Still, I've studied fellow billionaires from afar, and I've also read what others have written about us.

In an article for *Forbes* by Matthew Herper, Robert Baron, a psychologist at Rensselaer Polytechnic Institute, said we are persuasive and have strong social skills—that we call upon our charisma to make a sale. In the same article, Kelly Shaver, a professor of psychology at William & Mary College, said we don't care what other people think about us. She said, "They're just happy to go off and do what they're doing."

I agree. My father thought I was nuts to build in Manhattan, but I didn't listen to him because I had my own vision. One of my favorite billionaires is Warren Buffett, who has his own vision, too. He didn't follow the stampede into the dot-com gold rush, even though he was widely criticized for remaining a traditional value investor. Now he once again looks like a genius. One of many things I admire about Warren is that in all of his years as CEO of Berkshire Hathaway, he has never sold one share of stock.

Another student of successful entrepreneurs, Michael Maccoby, a psychoanalyst and consultant, believes that billionaires like Jeff Bezos, Steve Jobs, and Ted Turner are successful in part because they are narcissists who devote their talent with unrelenting focus to achieving their dreams, even if it's sometimes at the expense of those around them. Maccoby's book *The Productive Narcissist* makes a convincing argument that narcissism can be a useful quality if you're trying to start a business. A narcissist does not hear the naysayers. At the Trump Organization, I listen to people, but my vision is my vision.

In *The Natural History of the Rich,* author Richard Conniff put it this way: "Almost all successful alpha personalities display a single-minded determination to impose their vision on the world, an irrational belief in unreasonable goals, bordering at times on lunacy." He quotes a passage from Michael Lewis on entrepreneur Jim Clark in *The New New Thing:* "He was the guy who always won the game of chicken because his opponents suspected he might actually enjoy a head-on collision." I doubt Jim Clark would enjoy that collision, but the fact that he has convinced people he might has a lot to do with his success.

Here are my top ten ways of thinking like a billionaire:

1. Don't take vacations. What's the point? If you're not enjoying your work, you're in the wrong job. Even when I'm playing golf, I'm doing business. I never stop, and I'm usually having fun. Now that my kids are joining the family business, I'm closer to them than I've ever been, and I'm finding out that I love relating to them just the way my father related to me—through a passion for work well done.

By the way, I'm not the only one who doesn't take vacations. My NBC compatriot Jay Leno works just as much as I do, and maybe that's one of the reasons he's stayed on top in the late-night ratings wars.

2. Have a short attention span. Most successful people have very short attention spans. It has a lot to do with imagination. Quite often, I'll be talking to someone and I'll know what they're going to say before they say it. After the first three words are out of their mouth, I can tell what the next forty are going to be, so I try to pick up the pace and move it along. You can get more done faster that way.

3. Don't sleep any more than you have to. I usually sleep about four hours per night. I'm in bed by 1 A.M. and up to read the newspapers at 5 A.M. That's all I need, and it gives me a competitive edge. I have friends who are successful and sleep ten hours a night, and I ask them, "How can you compete against people like me if I sleep only four hours?" It rarely can be done. No matter how brilliant you are, there's not enough time in the day.

You may be wondering: Why do you need a competitive edge? You don't, if you're happy to be an also-ran in life. In *The Natural History of the Rich,* Richard Conniff notes that it's common behavior for moguls to seek dominance. Even such traits as who makes the most eye contact in a conversation can be an indication of who seeks to dominate. Conniff singles me out as an example of someone who achieves dominance through my appearance, by leaving my eyebrows untrimmed in order to intimidate negotiating partners. I'm pleased to note that he doesn't comment on my hair.

4. Don't depend on technology. A lot of it is unnecessary and expensive. I don't have a computer on my desk. I don't use an intercom. When I want someone in my office, I yell. It works a lot better than an intercom, and it's much faster.

I don't even have an ATM card—I've never used one in my life. That's the funny thing about being rich: When I go to restaurants, I rarely have to pay. It's usually on the house. The sad part is that if I needed the money, they would make me pay!

I can understand why some people would appreciate the convenience of ATM cards, but a lot of other tech devices are completely unnecessary and get in the way of human contact. If you have something important to say, look the person in the eye and say it. And if you can't get there, pick up the phone and make sure they hear the sincerity in your voice. E-mail is for wimps.

5. Think of yourself as a one-man army. You're not only the commander in chief, you're the soldier as well. You must plan and execute your plan alone.

People are always comparing business to war and to sports. We do it because these are analogies we immediately understand, not because business is about toughness. It isn't. It's much more important to be smart than tough. I know some very bad businessmen who are brutally tough, but they're not smart people. They want to act like Vince Lombardi, but they don't know how to win. Lombardi would slap his players, even spit in their faces. He'd have three-hundred-pound men virtually crying. He could do that because he won, and you can do that only if you win.

Billionaires like to win. *The Natural History of the Rich* is full of examples of hypercompetitive plutocrats: Larry Ellison racing his yacht from Australia to Tasmania, Steve Fossett flying a balloon around the world, and Dennis Tito paying $20 million for a trip to space on a Russian rocket. "All of them, one way or another, were showing off," Conniff writes. "To put it in the biological context, they were engaging in display behavior. Animals do it all the time, and their displays, like ours, fall loosely into two categories: They show off with fine feathers, and they show off with risky behavior."

I have my own theory, but it's not as scientific: We do it because it's fun. Work hard, play hard, and live to the hilt.

6. It's often to your advantage to be underestimated. You never want people to think you're a loser or a schlepper, but it's not a good idea if they think you're the smartest guy in the room, either. Because I wrote *The Art of the Deal,* everyone is always on guard whenever I negotiate with them. One of the reasons President Reagan was such a successful candidate for office was because rival politicians consistently misjudged him. They assumed an actor wouldn't be able to compete. Through years of insults about his lack of intelligence and political

experience, Reagan would smile and remain genial, and in the end, he always exceeded expectations.

Because I'm too famous to be underestimated—I know that sounds egotistical, but it's true—I'm always impressed by ultrasuccessful people who live great lives in a low-key manner. For example, one of my neighbors in Trump Tower is a man named Joel Anderson. For years, I'd see him in the elevator and say hello, but I didn't know anything about him. One day he called my office and said, "Do you think it would be possible for Mr. Trump to attend my party?" He seemed like a nice guy, with a terrific wife, so I figured I'd pop in for a few minutes. When I got to the party, I was amazed to find myself surrounded by some of the most influential people in New York, including S. I. Newhouse and Anna Wintour. I soon discovered that mild-mannered Joel Anderson is the chairman and CEO of Anderson News, one of the country's largest distributors of newspapers and magazines. He's one of the most powerful and generous people I know. I'd been riding in the elevator with him for years and I never knew who he was.

In *How to Get Rich,* I discussed how important it is to let people know about your accomplishments. I'll always believe that, but there are times when it's even more impressive if people discover your accomplishments without you telling them directly. A few weeks after Joel Anderson's party, I noticed a long and highly positive profile of him in the business section of *The New York Times.* So I want to amend my advice from the previous book: It's often necessary to boast, but it's even better if others do it for you.

7. Success breeds success. The best way to impress people is through results. It's easier for me to do deals now because I've had so many triumphs. You have to create success to impress people in the world of business. If you're young and you haven't had any successes yet, then you have to create the impression of success. It doesn't mat-

ter whether the success is a small one or a big one—you have to start with something and build on it.

8. Friends are good, but family is better. It's better to trust your family than your friends. When I was young, I said to someone who had a fairly big business, "Do you see your brothers and sisters?" The person looked at me and said, "Yes, I do, Donald. I see them in court." That had a big impact on me, and I've always tried to stay close to my brothers and sisters, my children, and my former wives.

9. Treat each decision like a lover. Vast fortunes are accumulated through dozens of decisions a day, thousands a month, and hundreds of thousands in a career. Yet each decision is different and special in its own way. Sometimes you decide immediately—love at first sight. Sometimes you go slowly—the long engagement. Sometimes you gather people in a room and consider various opinions—the equivalent of asking your friends what they think of the person you've been dating. If you treat each decision like a lover—faithfully, respectfully, appropriately—you won't be locked into a rigid system. You'll adapt to the needs of that particular decision. Sometimes you'll think with your head. Other times you'll think with other parts of your body, and that's good. Some of the best business decisions are made out of passion.

Sometimes people are surprised by how quickly I make big decisions, but I've learned to trust my instincts and not to overthink things. I like to compare a decision to a lover because it reminds me to keep in touch with my basic impulses, the drives that excite us, attract us, give us inspiration and energy. We are all drawn to beauty, whether it's the allure of a person or the elegance of a home. Whenever I'm making a creative choice, I try to step back and remember my first shallow reaction. The day I realized it can be smart to be shallow was, for me, a deep experience.

10. Be curious. A successful person is always going to be curious. I don't know why this is true, but it's definitely the case. You have to be alive to your surroundings and hungry to understand your immediate world. Otherwise, you'll lack the perspective to see beyond yourself. One of the great aspects of working on *The Apprentice* has been learning about how network TV works. I recently found out that one of the reasons Thursday nights are so crucial to the networks is because that's when lucrative movie advertisements for the weekend releases are aired. The higher the ratings are on Thursday night, the more the networks can charge their advertisers. And the more they can charge their advertisers, the more they can pay me to save their network! You see? Curiosity pays!

I'll offer a lot more advice on how to think like a billionaire in the following pages. For the first time, I'm sharing practical advice on how to invest in real estate—buying, selling, getting a mortgage, dealing with a broker, renovating, and decorating. I've also put together a consumer guide to the best things in life. You don't have to be a billionaire to afford them, either.

Whenever I give speeches or appear in public, people want to hear about *The Apprentice,* so I'll take you behind the scenes of the first two seasons and describe what it's like to go from prime locations to prime time.

I'll never forget what a thrill the first season's live finale was. We were about to switch from the taped part of the show to the live conclusion, where, without a script, I would spontaneously announce whether I was hiring Kwame or Bill. Right before I went on the air, the brilliant head of NBC, Jeff Zucker, told me he was already receiving instant reports that the audience watching our program was going to be huge. That wasn't exactly what I needed to hear before appearing on live national television, but it turned out to be a truly exhilarating experience.

People have been referring to *The Apprentice* as a "comeback" for me, but I never went away. I was always big. And my buildings just keep getting bigger—and better!

And if you personally are bigger than ever, I've added another new element to this book: "The Mar-a-Lago Diet," a brief guide to the eating habits of billionaires and the people who lunch with them. I'm a frequent follower of the Mar-a-Lago Diet, and even though I'm not going to be considered thin, without this diet, I'd look and feel like a total disaster.

So turn the page and begin reading the only book I'll ever write that will make you rich *and* thin. Perhaps one day you'll join the billionaire's club. I'm sure I'll enjoy your company.

PART I

Real Estate

When people hear the name Trump, they think of two things: wealth and real estate. So while this entire book is dedicated to the creation and enjoyment of wealth, I need to start with the basics. The basics, for me, are all about property. Real estate is at the core of almost every business, and it's certainly at the core of most people's wealth. In order to build your wealth and improve your business smarts, you need to know about real estate.

What follows is some great advice. There are some helpful tips here for first-time apartment renters as well as for multiple-home owners. So read on.

How to Pick a Location

I hate the phrase "location, location, location" because I've seen a lot of idiots ruin good locations and a lot of geniuses make incredible investments out of horrible locations. You could hand over the location for Trump Tower (by far, the best location in New York City), and a moron could run the site into the ground. I guarantee it.

But when it comes to your home, you should always pick a good spot. Spending more on a good location is far smarter than getting a bargain in a bad area. Is it close to work? Is the neighborhood safe, or will you fear for your life as you come and go? Is it close to conveniences such as restaurants, grocery stores, shops, and banks? Do you feel like you belong in the neighborhood, or do you feel out of place? I'm the first to admit that location should be considered seriously when investing in real estate. A lot of picking a location comes down to instinct. You have to believe in the location; otherwise, you'll be making a rotten investment.

Be honest with yourself about the location's proximity to the rest of your life. If you find an apartment or a house or an office you like that puts hours of additional travel into your day, or requires expensive deliveries and services, or prevents people from visiting you, you might as well find somewhere else. I realize that not everyone can live and work in Trump Tower (which certainly works for me), but given the choice, you should find the location that works best for you.

Walk around in the neighborhood. Spend time there. What's the pattern of the day? When does the neighborhood wake up and when does it go to bed? What sort of people are living there and working there? Also, make sure to check it out on the weekends. Some neighborhoods in Manhattan are insanely busy all week and then dead all weekend, and vice versa. What happens if you move into an apartment and realize that there's a nightclub across the street blasting music each and every night or that garbage trucks congregate there after making the rounds in the early morning? You'll either go crazy or move out, neither of which are good options.

The view is important. I don't know anyone who wants to spend their life looking into an air shaft or a brick wall. If you have the option, go for the view. But you have to be careful with a view, particularly if you're paying for it. The current view might look out over a parking facility or an empty lot, but that could change in a week. In cities like New York, buildings seem to be going up at the rate of one per day, so make sure you have a good idea that the view there today will be there tomorrow.

When you're speculating or investing in real estate that will not necessarily serve as your primary home or office, I often advise finding space in a marginal neighborhood, buying or renting at a lower price, and then waiting for the neighborhood to improve. You'll save in taxes, make a meaningful contribution to the redevelopment of an area, and stand to make more money in the long run. If you have the time, the patience, and the fortitude, I recommend it. After all, when I bought up the West Side yards, people thought I was insane, but I've proved them wrong, as my development there can attest. Today that area is one of the most desirable and valuable areas in all of Manhattan.

How to Rent
an Apartment

A lot of people don't take renting an apartment as seriously as they should. I don't understand those people. While renting an apartment is not buying, the place will serve as your home and should be considered carefully. Not only is your home a big part of the way you feel about yourself, it's also a reflection of how others see you. Billionaires, even those who rent their homes, take time when finding places to live, and so should you.

In New York City, an apartment market I know all too well, people often feel lucky to find anything. There's enormous demand, and sometimes hundreds of people will charge through the streets to look at exorbitantly expensive shoe boxes that they all saw listed in *The New York Times*. Most of these people will be prepared—with letters of reference, with bank statements and credit card bills, and with a sense of competition that can be fierce. To play in this apartment market, or any other real estate market, you have to do your homework. Have a clear idea of your financial needs and your living requirements. Going blindly from apartment to apartment will be a waste of everyone's time—particularly your own.

I feel strongly that an apartment should be rented with the help of a good broker. It can be done without one, but to me, that's like taking pills without consulting a doctor or filing a lawsuit without a lawyer. It's possible, but it's stupid. Brokers know the neighborhoods and the specific markets inside and out. They know property values, the pros and cons of certain buildings, the rules and regulations of pricing and rents, and the ins and outs of the actual lease. Brokers are educated and licensed, and there's good reason for that. They will prevent you from making mistakes that will cost you thousands, and in my case, millions, more than the fees that they charge. They will also save you time by filtering out apartments that do not meet your criteria.

But you should never believe everything a broker tells you. The broker is, after all, only there for the commission, as concerned and accommodating as he or she may seem. And when it comes to the commission, whether you're selling, buying, or renting, always negotiate. Sometimes brokers do an amazing job and deserve a high commission, but when you enter the relationship, always negotiate from the start. It's much easier to negotiate the fee at the beginning of a broker relationship. Trying to lowball brokers midway through or at the end of a transaction is poor business form.

If you cannot afford a broker or simply want to go it alone, look in the papers or on bulletin boards. Ask around and walk around. Some of the best New York stories I've heard are about finding apartments that simply came out of nowhere—kind of like those stories about getting a taxi in the pouring rain on New Year's Eve. It can happen, but the odds are lousy. In *When Harry Met Sally*, Billy Crystal reads through the obituaries so he can move in on the apartments of the recently deceased. If you want to go without a broker, maybe try that approach, as morbid as it might sound.

Whether or not you use a broker, find somewhere you'll be happy for a long time. Moving around every couple of years is disruptive and expensive. And most important, figure out what you can afford. It's not a concern for me, but I would never spend more than twenty-five percent of my salary on rent—no matter how fantastic an apartment you have found. Every dollar you pour into rent is a dollar you could be using elsewhere—whether it's for savings, or for utilities, or for enjoying the finer things in life. It's okay to stretch yourself slightly and anticipate that in a few years you may be making more money, but that's not a sure thing—and it's a safe assumption that your rent will increase at the same rate as your salary. Tenants who cannot pay their rent will go nowhere fast—and certainly never make it into the billionaires club.

How to Read
a Classified Ad or Listing

Often people resort to the classified ads or other listings to find apartments and houses for rent. Don't be a fool! In New York, in particular, advertisers will make rat-infested closets sound like the penthouse of Trump Tower. Learn to see through the garbage in the advertisements so you don't waste time looking at apartments that should be bulldozed rather than inhabited. The advertisers should all write novels, since they're clearly so talented at writing fiction.

Pay attention to words like "funky" and "charming," which you can translate as "unlivable" and "run-down." Ads that brag "newly renovated" usually mean that the landlord has simply slapped new knobs on the bathroom cabinets. Other phrases that should make you nervous include "old-world appeal" (read: "dilapidated"), "cozy" (read: "tiny"), and "freshly painted" (read: "There's nothing good to say about the apartment except that it has a fresh coat of paint"). Anything that sounds too good to be true *is*—especially when it comes to apartments.

Also, pay attention to the information that's not provided. If there's no apartment number given, you can bet it's on the first floor (where it's never good to live because of crime and noise), and if there's no square footage provided, it's too embarrassing for the advertiser to mention. Also, if there's no photograph, beware. Even the worst apartments can be made to look palatial on film, so you should be doubly suspicious if a photograph is missing when other apartments in the ad include one.

Houses, apartments, and offices need to be touched and seen before you rent or buy them. Classified ads and listings can point you in the right direction, but it's your responsibility to thoroughly investigate any property you may be considering.

How to Buy a House

The real estate market can be terrifying, which is part of the reason I love it so much. But it can be downright petrifying when it involves what may be your most valuable possession: your home. The market changes every day, sometimes every minute. For home buyers, some of whom will buy one house in a lifetime, trying to time the market perfectly can be a ridiculous waste of time. In ten, twenty, or forty years, any small variations in the price of your house will have amortized into a blip on your financial radar screen.

You have to go with your gut, and if you love a house and you can afford it and your broker assures you that you are paying a fair market price, you're paying the best price. It's as simple as that. When it comes to your home, don't be concerned about spending more than it's worth if you know that you will be there forever and you'll be happy there. Sometimes the emotional price you put on a house may exceed the market price. Buying a home is different from the pure economics of investing in real estate. If you simply cannot afford a house that you love, don't be shy about underbidding; sometimes the seller will surprise you.

Before you start looking for a house, or even figuring out what you can afford to buy, make sure you have money socked away. Brokers and sellers will take you seriously, and you will increase your bargaining power as you're able to increase the size of your down payment. Buying a house is a serious investment, and banks and lenders will be there to help you make that investment.

A typical home buyer will not have access to one hundred percent financing, and you have to be as invested as your lender. The down payment should be your own personal gauge for your commitment to the house. Don't lose sight of the checks and balances because ultimately it will all come down to *your* checks and balances.

While it's good to be mindful of costs when buying a house, don't go overboard. Don't try to save money on necessary items, such as not getting a survey where it might be of value, or relying on people who are not well recommended or not known. Do not attempt to save small amounts of money on items that are important parts of the process. People often stupidly try to save money at a real estate closing, since some adjustments will probably still be made and the negotiations will not have ended. But don't be hardheaded and cheap when it comes to buying a house. It's counterproductive.

Simply put aside some money before you begin the house-buying process (call it your reserve budget), and then legal and financial situations that arise will not be skipped to cut costs. Undermining the purchase of your home from the beginning will only end up haunting you down the line.

How to Get an Appraisal and a Building Inspection

Let's say you find your dream home. A perfect location, perfect architecture, perfect price. Be careful. Always know what you are mortgaging. Don't let your guts trick your brain, and don't rush yourself (or allow your broker—who will always be telling you about the other buyers—to rush you, either). It is better to have researched the opportunity and lose it than to make a mistake by jumping into something you'll come to regret.

The best reality check is the appraisal. The lender will have an appraiser, and in most situations, you will be responsible for paying for the appraisal. The appraisal should not be seen as an annoying expense that will only benefit the lender. The appraisal benefits you as well. Appraisers are professionals, and they will be able to see things that may elude the eye of most home buyers. Ask questions and do your own homework, but at the end of the day, defer to the appraiser. Some of his or her findings might be insulting or surprising, and the truth can hurt, but the appraiser's job is to be objective. A fair appraisal will only help you in the end.

Any number of things—some of which are regulated by the government (such as flood control)—can affect the location. Other factors, such as proximity to high-tension wires, may or may not be so apparent. You're probably not going to wind up buying the Amityville Horror, but you shouldn't expect that every seller will tell you everything unfavorable about the property. You're better off assuming that some things will not be divulged, out of ignorance, forgetfulness, or evasion. If you're confused by what I'm telling you, rent the movie *The Money Pit* to familiarize yourself with the pains of ignoring or forgoing the appraisal.

In the event that a structure is being purchased with mortgage funds, most probably you should also have a building inspector examine the premises. A building inspection is often required, but you should always require it for yourself. A knowledgeable, licensed inspector-engineer can detect whether the heating unit is functioning properly, whether the air-conditioning is sufficient, whether a sump pump is needed, and so on. Think of a building inspection as an X ray; the inspector will be able to see through the entire house and identify any systemic problems. For instance, what sort of materials were used for a house's piping? Galvanized? Brass? Copper? Synthetic? Galvanized pipes rust and don't last as long as brass pipes, which don't last as long as copper pipes, which don't last as long as synthetic pipes. Only a building inspector will be able to see this level of detail within a house or apartment.

If the inspector makes you nervous or you sense that he or she is working too quickly, find someone else. The inspection is too important to be careless about it.

Sometimes the problems inspectors find are fixable at a reasonable cost, but other times they find things that cannot be fixed without major renovations or even a teardown. The inspector will provide an objective, independent report that may or may not affect the value of the home, but either way, you can request price adjustments based on the inspection.

Another quick tip: Some investors make the dumb mistake of assuming that new constructions do not require building inspections.

Wrong! New constructions often have the largest problems, particularly if the build-out and contracting were sloppy. In addition to structural, plumbing, and electrical woes, new constructions can be vexed by mold infestation and other problems typically associated with longer-standing buildings.

How to Sell a House

If you are selling your home and there is no or little activity, or activity but no offers, you should revisit the price. The real estate market is volatile, and prices change daily. I always keep in mind the saying "Old listings, like old soldiers, never die—they just fade away" when it comes to pricing. Also, don't worry about competition; count on it—you will save yourself a lot of time. Competition may even help you by drawing in prospective buyers within the same market.

If you know your property is valuable, remain patient. As long as you're realistic about its value, there will always be a buyer eventually. Mar-a-Lago was sitting there a long time before I saw it and decided to move on that magnificent site. I had the right vision for it, and the timing was right for me—and, ultimately, for the seller as well.

Just make sure what you have to offer *is* the best, and you need not worry. If you have a broker, make sure he or she understands what the value of the property is to *you*. But don't be too bullheaded if your broker thinks the property is worth far less than you do. The broker should be the expert, and you're paying him or her not only for service but for advice.

Your broker, if he or she is good at the job, will strategically advertise the property's sale. A lot of interest is not necessarily always a good thing; be wary of a broker who fails to screen applicants and lets the whole world traipse through your house. Good brokers will screen applicants for prequalification, negotiate on your behalf for the best price, and facilitate the legal and financial processes. You will be paying the broker a substantial fee (usually on the order of six percent and sometimes higher), so he or she is working for you and should be working hard for that commission.

Some people try to sell houses without brokers—not a strategy I would recommend. But if you're feeling up to it, by all means, be my guest. If you want to be your own broker, then the best piece of advice I have is: Act like a broker. To do so will require a lot of guts, a lot of brains, and a lot of patience.

An article by Lynnley Browning entitled "The Sweet and Sour of 'For Sale by Owner,'" in the June 6, 2004, edition of *The New York Times*, made it clear just how difficult (but also how money-saving) selling your own home can be. You should find her article and maybe pick up some books to help you along the way. You will have to educate yourself on title searches, legal forms, and the pricing market; you will also have to learn your state's disclosure laws to avoid being sued if the ceiling caves in or mold takes over after you have left. It all sounds like a headache to me, which is why I've always recommended using a broker.

How to Find a Good Office

Location is probably the most important concern when it comes to finding a good office. Traveling for meetings, delivering goods and services, and attracting customers and clients can be a hassle if you have a poor location. You, your customers, and your employees have to be happy and productive in that space, and cutting costs and choosing poor office space is a fast way to kill your business.

Think about the space you will need, hopefully with enough room for some expansion without requiring you to move within the too near future. If you can find raw space on the fringe of your desired location, this strategy could prove lucrative to you in the future. It may require more up-front time and planning on your part, but it can have enormous financial and professional benefits. Being ahead of the pack is the best place to be.

It's also important that you find an office in a building that's well maintained and well run. Is the landlord notorious for not fixing the heat? Are the elevators operating efficiently and the bathrooms cleaned regularly? No one I know wants to spend time in an office—either working there or just doing business there—that's unattractive, uncomfortable, and inhospitable.

Where you work and what that space looks like are just as important as where you live, if not more. Give it the same thought, and you
will be thankful you did. I've been in the same offices at Trump Tower
for over twenty years. The location and the space work as beautifully
today as they did twenty years ago. It's not dumb luck, though. I knew
exactly where I would be today twenty years ago.

How to Deal with a Broker

Why have a novice try to understand the value of a great piece of art? Choose your broker as you would an art dealer—which is to say, judiciously. And as with many things, timing is crucial to success. Stay on top of things, and make sure you and your broker are honest with each other at each step in the process. A good broker will listen and respond to your concerns. If the broker takes days to return your phone calls or runs late to meetings, borrow my line and simply say, "You're fired!" There are countless other brokers who deserve your business. You're the customer, after all.

The best brokers know that whatever is good for you will be good for them. They make money only when you finally make a transaction, so the smart ones won't waste time trying to sell or rent something just for the sake of a commission. My advice is to find a reputable, established broker who has shown a substantial growth index over a number of years in the area in which you desire to live. As in all matters of life, brokers specialize. Why waste time with a broker who only knows high-end retail real estate when you're looking for an affordable one-bedroom apartment?

The best brokers are psychologists, or at least they are incredibly insightful. It's their job to figure out what's best for you, but in order for you to help them figure what is best for you, you have to be up-front and honest with them. Don't be embarrassed about telling them that you can't afford something or that you don't like a particular space. Experienced brokers tell me they can usually sense the people who are serious by their first two questions, and those are tip-offs on how to proceed.

Don't ever follow the advice of any broker who is pushy. That should be the indication for you to become wary. It isn't necessary for brokers to behave that way, and if they do, they are best left alone. I know some terrific brokers who are low-key, sincere, and genuinely interested in your well-being.

Susan James, who runs the sales office at Trump International Hotel and Tower, is one of the most elegant people you will ever meet, and her elegance isn't an act to get her into your good graces. She remains friends with her clients for many years after they are happily ensconced in their apartments. She is clear about what she is presenting to you before, during, and after. That's the mark of a great broker.

Find a great broker and your chances of finding or selling the right place at the right price will be improved by about one hundred percent. The fee you pay will be one of the best investments you ever make.

How to Hire an Attorney

In some areas, attorneys are not ordinarily involved in real estate closings. In other areas, they absolutely need to be involved. If the cost is reasonable, hire one, even if the situation seems simple. I never, ever sign a contract without consulting an attorney, and I work with contracts all day long. Real property can involve complicated legal concepts, some of which date back to feudalism. If you feel that the situation is simple and you cannot afford to pay standard rates, most attorneys will negotiate their fees. And if the situation turns complicated and a larger fee materializes, you shouldn't complain. You should consider yourself lucky, since you have probably avoided some problems not otherwise foreseen.

How do you a get a good attorney, if you do not already know one you can trust? Call any bar association, as they usually have referral services. Do *not* ask your mortgage broker to refer an attorney. Though brokers always know many attorneys, there can be a built-in conflict of interest if the sale deserves to be aborted. The lawyer might be reluctant to recommend terminating the deal, since the person who recommended him or her will then lose a commission. You're better off getting an independent recommendation for a lawyer who practices primarily in the area of the kind of real estate in discussion—someone who has a good reputation in the eyes of people you know and trust.

How to Get the Best Mortgage

Even billionaires need to borrow money now and then, and I've learned a lot about mortgages over the years. The first step is to know what you are mortgaging. I know that sounds obvious, but it's amazing to me how often people will seek a mortgage for something they clearly don't know the value of.

Numerous books have been written on how to get the best mortgage. Much of the advice is good, and much of it is common sense, and much of it is never properly acted upon. You can probably find a dozen books in your public library on mortgages, but what you really need to understand is how officers at banks and insurance companies think about loans, property, and you. Lenders can often make the most money off of idiots, so be sure to educate yourself before you see them.

Like buying a property, applying for a mortgage works best when you have options. Shop around, ask questions, and always bargain. There are countless choices in the mortgage market. The trick is finding the mortgage that works best for you—for your bank account, for your salary, and for your future plans. A mortgage is a product—like the house or the car that you're buying with it—so you should know its ins and outs before "purchasing" it. Drive a hard bargain and don't be afraid to walk away.

Loan officers can be schizophrenic, offering different rates and deals from one minute to the next. Never, ever accept a first offer, and always ask for better terms. Negotiate or be eaten alive! If you receive a better deal from Lender A, always go back to Lender B and see if they can match it. After all, each lender is peddling the same product—money—so it doesn't matter where it's coming from. Mortgages are designed to be haggled over, and not to do so is the equivalent of burning money in the street.

If you are buying or mortgaging a house or a multifamily dwelling, you have to know what the financials are. Certainly the mortgage company will have to know. Here are some recommendations:

1. Seek accounting advice. Your lawyer and mortgage broker can be of help, too.

2. Know the tax history of the property and also any foreseeable tax hikes. Good indicators of an impending tax increase include the need for a new school, a pending reassessment, a busted sewage system, or unpaid liabilities. Once you have taken on the burden of a mortgage, the last thing you'll need is a huge tax bill.

3. Look for hidden costs. There always are some, and they can sink you if you're not careful. Sound, comprehensive cost analysis is crucial. For instance, what if the building cannot be insured at ordinary rates? How do costs for heating, water, and extermination change throughout the year? Try to anticipate any scenarios that will put you in the thick of financial jeopardy.

At the end of the day, your mortgage company will want to know what you know. The mortgage company is there to help you. If the mortgage company isn't happy with a certain situation attached to the property, you should not be happy with it, either. Most likely, they have more experience than you and have seen other properties turn into nightmares once mortgaged.

Also remember that mortgage companies often sell their mortgages to other corporations, banks, insurance companies, or Fannie Mae; the people who are dealing with you initially may not be the same people you will be sending your monthly check to. For that matter, you may very well get notices to send your monthly check to different parties over a number of years.

Ordinarily, you will be personally responsible for any home mortgage, and there is a good chance that you will be required to place a personal guarantee on any investment mortgages. If you guarantee a mortgage, you could find yourself paying on a guarantee, even if you have prepared yourself thoroughly. Guarantees can be called upon due to the ups and downs of the market, weather-related catastrophes, and all sorts of insurance-related issues.

The subject of title insurance, which you should have to protect yourself against such frauds as forgery in a previous deed and other malfeasance, is also one you should discuss carefully with your attorney. Don't get caught unawares.

Real estate can afford great opportunities through mortgaging, leverage, and possibly even absentee management, but don't bet on it. Like anything else, it requires caution, devotion, hard work, and some luck. In truth, there is nothing complicated about mortgaging properties, but care and study are required.

Anyone who has seen those commercials on TV in the middle of the night where individuals claim to have retired to Hawaii on the basis of real estate purchased, sold, or rented should realize that the people who sell these courses make more money from selling the courses than they do from selling any real estate or mortgaging. Those infomercials never tell you about the mountain of problems that can be associated with the ownership of real estate.

How to Pick a Mortgage Broker

A good way to get a mortgage is to pass the buck to somebody else. Shopping around and comparing mortgages can be time-consuming, so it may save you time to pay someone to do your shopping for you. Get a mortgage broker, but get a good one. These people are engaged daily in the world of mortgages, which means that they have to know where to get the best rates, who is offering the best conditions, and generally, where it's advantageous to apply.

In the long run, you will probably pay less for everything if you get a good mortgage broker, since the broker will know what kind of hidden charges there are and steer you clear of various problems. Not only that, but mortgage companies want to keep in the good graces of anyone who is in the habit of referring business to them. There are certainly technical considerations, such as the length of the mortgage, whether guarantees are involved, conditions of default, and all kinds of other things that a mortgage broker and a good attorney will inform you about.

Ask your real estate broker to recommend a mortgage broker,

or get a referral from friends, colleagues, and neighbors who have recently taken on mortgages. Like your real estate broker or your attorney, the mortgage broker should be someone you feel comfortable working with—and someone you know will not sideline your best interests in favor of his or her own financial considerations.

How to Pick an Interest Rate and a Down Payment

Interest rates are not the mystery they're cracked up to be, but before you get into any real estate venture, you must educate yourself about them. I always think of interest rates simply as the "cost of money." The interest rate is like a yearly membership fee or a utility bill; it's the amount you're paying to use the mortgage per year. It's like a golf membership to an exclusive club where you're the only one with the keys to the clubhouse.

You should note that some institutions will try to trick you with adjustable interest rates so that your fees will bounce around, depending on the economy. If you're adverse to change and want to minimize your risk, I would recommend working with fixed rates. Interest rates have been sagging for the last twenty-odd years, and there's good reason to believe that they will only be going up in the short term. Mortgage holders with adjustable rates may be forced to foreclose if the payments become too big. If this setup scares you (and it should), lock in a rate that you know you'll be able to afford for the length of the mortgage.

When choosing an actual rate, if it's too good to be true, beware. Rates, truth be told, should actually not be the most important consideration, though certainly they need to be considered. To get the best rate today, there are all kinds of services and information available that can tell you what the various banks are charging. The Internet has exploded with information (but be careful, as not all of it is accurate). Newspapers often chart interest rates as well.

If you get a rate that is much lower than what is out there on the market, you might be looking for trouble. The company might not be around by the time you want to close the mortgage, or you might be charged outrageous fees for a closing. For any mortgage, the lender will also charge assorted fees, and it's wise to make sure you're not getting taken for a ride. A good rule to remember: The lower the interest rate, the higher the possible fees. Read the fine print. Look for a low rate, but remember that the lowest rate may end up costing you the most.

When it comes to a down payment, it should be determined in large part by your budget. A lower down payment will result in higher mortgage payments, and vice versa. Depending on where you live, the down payment will hover around twenty percent of the total loan. In New York City, where the competition for real estate is fierce, the percentages tend to be a lot higher. If you're a good negotiator and want to free up as much of your money as possible, you should try to get as low a down payment as possible.

How and When to Renovate

If you're going to mortgage a property that you already own, make sure it is in good condition. For a multifamily building, attention should be given to all kinds of things, such as the condition of the roof, stairways, elevators, storage areas, boiler room, and everything else. Suffice it to say, if the building is not in good condition, an experienced mortgage officer is not going to want to lend money on it. Nor will a bank lend you money on a structure if they do not believe you are going to preserve and protect their collateral. Why should they?

If you're about to mortgage your property, you should never make repairs just for cosmetic purposes. Make good, solid repairs and then sell the property or mortgage it for a lot more money. Fix the kitchen; redo the bathroom; put on a fresh coat of paint. My father used to say that every property ought to be sold in "mint condition." He said it to me all the time. We all know what it means, and it's some of the best advice he ever gave me. After all, a $15 can of paint can add $1,000 to the value of your property; $1,000 in landscaping can add $10,000; and $10,000 in remodeling can add $100,000. You get the idea.

In addition to renovating before selling a property, you may choose to renovate after buying or over the years while you're living or working somewhere to make the space more livable or workable. Renovation equals devotion. It can be expensive and time-consuming, so it's crucial that you figure out whether or not renovations will be worthwhile before committing to them. Renovation is worth it only if your heart and your checkbook are in it. If they're not, it will turn out to be one enormous hassle after another. After all, renovating can often be more difficult than building from scratch.

I have always found that the trickiest part of renovations is matching the original ingredients, which isn't always easy. Sometimes just finding them can require a lot of investigative work. I have an employee at Mar-a-Lago who spends his whole week, every week, just keeping up with the tile work on the premises. There are something like thirty-six thousand Spanish tiles at Mar-a-Lago, most of which date back to the fifteenth century. I know it might sound ridiculous, but the tiles alone require this kind of attention, and so they get it. You can't just let an investment like that deteriorate. Be prepared for this kind of devotion when you begin serious renovations.

The Mar-a-Lago Club is a classic example of smart renovation. In addition to historic merit and exquisite beauty, Mar-a-Lago has been a phenomenal investment—made even more priceless by the hard work that my staff and I have devoted to it. It's more than real estate or an investment; it's a piece of art that requires endless, painstaking work—work that's not only financially rewarding but somehow spiritually uplifting as well. I make sure everything done there is top-notch, because Mar-a-Lago is up there with Venetian palaces in terms of craftsmanship and beauty. It deserves the best.

The ceiling, the flooring, the walls, the chandeliers, the mirrors—you have to be insane about the details or the whole enterprise will fail. For instance, I've spent a good eight months choosing the right chairs for the ballroom being built at Mar-a-Lago. The ballroom is seventeen thousand square feet in area, so the chairs will be a big part of the room. I have seen probably hundreds of them by now. They have to be

just right or the effect will be lessened, if not spoiled. The gilt on them has to be compatible with the entire room, and their shape and comfort must be considered as well. You should be as attentive to details as I am, no matter what the scale of your project.

This point should be obvious, but I'll state it anyway: Never, never do serious renovations on a property that you're renting, or begin negotiating for renovations on a property before your mortgage closes. To do so is financially destructive and an absolute waste of time.

How to Landscape

Once you have found your home or your office, hire a reputable landscape firm to help you. It will add incredible value to the property. Trump Tower is one of the most visited buildings in New York City, and part of the attraction is the trees that decorate the building. If you've never been to New York, Trump Tower should be your first stop. It's breathtaking.

It's amazing. Trees, bushes, rocks, and flowers can turn the most mundane buildings into works of art. Landscaping can add value to a building far above the cost of labor and materials. If you can't afford a landscaper, do it yourself. I always joke that landscaping on your own is a win-win; it's cheap *and* good for your health.

If you hate physical labor, like I do, you'll hire someone. The trick is finding someone with your taste who can work within your budget and within your schedule. Remember that the cheapest is not always the best. As with contractors, shoddy work will need to be redone or, even worse, corrected, and that can be a disaster. When choosing a landscaper, find a firm with a good reputation by asking your neighbors or other business owners for recommendations.

Also, try to visit some sites where the landscaper has previously done work. If the work is shoddy, you'll know right away to find someone else. You can also check on the equipment that the landscaper is using. If the equipment is busted, the service will most likely be busted, too.

And finally, make sure the work that they're doing will last for years with minimal maintenance. No one wants to have to replant every year. A landscaper can do incredible work, but if it looks worn and dead within six months, you will have thrown your money away.

Of course, it helps to have a lot of money and clout. When I'm building and landscaping golf courses, I love to buy beautiful trees. Sometimes, though, those trees aren't in nurseries; sometimes they are in a person's backyard. I'll be driving down the highway, see a great tree, and ask my limo driver to pull over. I'll knock on the door. Usually, a woman will answer the door, and I'll say, "Hi, lady. I'd love to buy your tree." She'll say, "Oh my god! It's Donald Trump! I can't believe this is happening!" And then I'll tell her that I'm building a golf course nearby, like the one I'm building in Los Angeles right along the Pacific Ocean. Usually, I'll get the tree. I've bought a lot of great trees that way, and those trees can be found all over the country at my golf courses. Money can't buy happiness, but it sure as hell can buy some great trees.

How to Decorate Interiors

I feel the same way about interior decorators that I feel about real estate brokers. They are worth every penny. If you know your tastes, hire a professional who can help you fine-tune those tastes and work with you to create the perfect environment for your work or for your home.

If you see a space you like—whether it's a living space or a restaurant or an office—ask questions. Who was the architect? Who decorated it? Like hiring a broker or a contractor, hiring the right decorator works by word of mouth and by finding someone with your sensibilities. Make sure the designer has your best interests in mind, not merely their own. It's their job to know your tastes, whether innately or otherwise, and to find the best way to display them.

Most people incorrectly think that interior decorators are a wasteful extravagance, but believe me, they will save you time and money. Interior decorating is not as simple as walking into a furniture store and pointing at a couple of pieces. Good interior decorators have a talent for spatial configuration, choosing colors and materials, and, most important, negotiating. The best interior decorators have that rare mix of artistic talent and business smarts.

Even something as simple as choosing a carpet can require days and days of flipping through sample books. I can't think of anything more boring. Instead, good interior decorators will scour warehouses, antique shops, and furniture showrooms for you, and then come to you with a plan, including fabric, carpet, and paint samples, as well as layouts and themes. With the best interior decorators, you just sit there and say, "Ah, that's perfect. I never would have thought of that."

Most decorators work on commission (anywhere from ten to fifteen percent, and sometimes as high as twenty or twenty-five percent). Instead of grumbling about the commission, look on the bright side. Not only do decorators save you time (and in the end, money, since you won't make as many mistakes), but dealers and warehouses always extend decorators discounts not available to the average consumer. They can pass those savings on to you. Simple math tells you that it's better to pay a commission on a sofa that's marked down to a professional discount of fifty percent than on the full price. For instance, if a decorator finds a $2,000 sofa that she can buy at a discount for $1,000, at a commission of twenty percent, you'll be paying $1,200 for that sofa. Even an idiot can see what's a better deal. And of course, more expensive tastes result in even bigger savings. Still, negotiate the commission down.

When you are working with a decorator, make sure you ask to see all of the invoices. Decorators are by nature honest people, but you should be double-checking regardless. It's okay to question them on certain expenditures, but don't haggle too much, because high-quality materials cost money. High-quality interiors last for years and years, so cutting corners will only lead to disrepair and an unattractive interior that you will have to live with—or change, at even more expense.

Once I hired a decorator whose portfolio of work had impressed me. I was busy at the time and didn't spend a great deal of time with the designer or watching the progress of his work. I just assumed the work would be on par with the portfolio. The results were a nightmare. I tried to live with the work, but after one month I couldn't stand it anymore and everything was taken out. I had to start all over. It cost me a small fortune, but it did teach me a lesson I learned once and have never had to repeat: First, find the right person, and second, monitor his or her progress.

How to Deal with Contractors

If you think real estate brokers and interior decorators make you nervous, you should spend a day with me when I'm working with contractors. They are like racehorses—they can be as lazy as all get out, and then they can race to the finish line and surprise you. There's not much in between. They can really be difficult to handle, but if you prepare yourself, you'll have a much better experience working with them. Always remember that they will try to get away with as much as they possibly can. If you call them on it, they'll shape up. They're a strange bunch—and I won't be offending anyone by saying that, because they know it as well as I do.

Some of them can work wonders and will do so eventually. Some of them won't work wonders ever, which you will also find out eventually. That's why it's good to pick contractors you already know or who have a good record on their past jobs. If you're new to the business of hiring contractors, ask neighbors, friends, and colleagues about contractors they've worked with. Nine out of ten will tell you horror stories, and if they don't, get the contractor's name and put it to use.

Always get references from contractors. Ask the contractor to give you ten names of other jobs they have done within the last year. Jobs that they did four or five years ago are not good measures; the jobs need to be recent. And don't ask for just two names; ask for the full ten. It's easy to make two parties happy, but only a great contractor can make ten parties happy.

Once you've hired a contractor and negotiated a budget, my best advice for you is to be tough on them. If you're not, they'll think you're soft and a pushover. You have to make your expectations clear. Be clear and up front about timing and the inflexibility of your budget. If you need the job finished by a certain time, hold the contractors to that date. If you keep an eye on their work and act as knowledgeable as possible, you increase the chances that the contractors will respect you and get something done.

I knew some contractors who took two months to finish renovating a single shower because they had so many "emergencies" at home that they couldn't seem to get anything done. The poor couple believed every sob story and would even give the contractors homemade cookies, brownies, and lasagna for their unfortunate friends and families. These contractors gained about ten pounds each, and not until the couple figured out what was going on did they manage to finish the shower—in less than two days. It's amazing—and sometimes criminal—what goes on in the world of contractors.

How to Make Sure Your Property Appreciates in Value

Appreciate your property, and your property will appreciate for you. If I visit one of my buildings, and I see something out of place—something that only the most discerning of eyes would be able to spot—I make sure it's fixed immediately. Chipped paint, an upholstery stain, a missing lightbulb—if you do not stay on top of the maintenance, the property will deteriorate quickly. Small problems multiply.

You owe it to yourself and to your community to make your property the best it can be. All that work and devotion are combined into a single manifestation of creativity, energy, economics, and talent. A great building is an emblem of the time and people that produced it. It represents the economics and the spirit of the era in which it was built. Buildings can be enormous contributions to society that will remain long after our time here and, if built right, will garner more and more value as time goes by.

So not only is it a crucial step to becoming a billionaire, but guaranteeing that your property appreciates in value is also a civic responsibility. I am a committed philanthropist to many charities, but perhaps my greatest gifts have been the buildings and properties that I have bestowed on various communities. Increasing the value of a single property has a ripple effect in the community around it. All of the buildings that bear the Trump name have made their environs more valuable—not just economically but culturally as well.

Beyond the steps you can take to increase the value of your property (landscaping, interior decoration, renovation), you also need to work with your neighbors to make sure they have the same goals as you. My advice: Join or form a neighborhood association. Neighborhood associations help control crime and traffic, maintain parks and other recreation spaces, and monitor the efficiency of services such as litter pickup and recycling.

You're only as good as your surroundings. You can have the best Brioni suit in the entire world, but if it's paired with some crappy shoes and an awful tie, the Brioni suit is pretty much worthless. It's the same for properties. I often see a nice house alongside another house that's badly maintained—it hasn't been painted, the grass is uncut, a broken-down car is rusting in front of it. That's a huge negative for a homeowner, so you have to work with your neighbors to keep up your investment.

Also, if you see the value of your property being threatened, write letters to your politicians. Just the other day I wrote a letter to Mayor Bloomberg about the deplorable conditions on Fifth Avenue in Manhattan. The street vendors are ruining the street's image. They claim to be veterans so they can receive exemptions to peddle trinkets and souvenirs, but only a few of them actually are veterans. Do you see street vendors on the Avenue Montaigne in Paris? I don't think so.

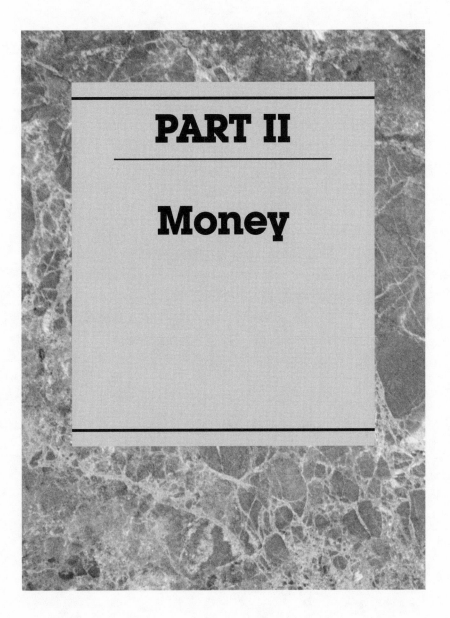

PART II

Money

When you have a lot of money, it can cause misery. But I'd rather have that kind of misery than the misery without it.

Money may not grow from trees, but it does grow from talent, hard work, and brains. I have a talent for making money; some people don't. But part of my "talent" is my drive and my work ethic, so even if you don't have the genetic makeup to be a billionaire, you can still work hard and maybe, if you're lucky and smart, you can be a millionaire. Maybe you can even be a billionaire.

I won't deny that some people are luckier than others. That's a simple fact of life. But you can create luck. I remember one night, when I was billions of dollars in debt and the media that had at one point called me brilliant was now making me out to be a total dope, I had to be at a dinner party that I wanted to skip in the worst way. I just didn't feel up to it, but something inside me made me get up and go.

At the dinner that night, I ended up sitting next to one of many bankers. It was one of the luckiest nights of my life. He gave me some great advice and pointed me in a new direction. The rest is history. So when it comes to money, even if you're broke or in debt, your luck can change. You have to work hard to make that luck change, so keep reading to learn how to do just that.

How to Be a Good Investor

Good investing requires financial intelligence. Billionaires are often blessed with a high financial IQ. Most of them could be considered financial geniuses. But your financial IQ is not a fixed number, and you can improve it each and every day. My financial IQ is constantly improving as I watch over my many businesses and my staff. I work hard to make sure that they remain assets, not liabilities, and you should look at your holdings in the same way.

Having a degree from Wharton and a lifetime of investing experience, I will explain a few things for those who haven't been blessed with such advantages. Finance and business are a complex mix of components that embrace a large spectrum of enterprises. I think of it the way an artist thinks about technique. You need to have a basic technique before you can apply it to different media such as drawing, or sculpture, or painting. As a builder, I use my financial technique as a basic blueprint for increasingly complex transactions. Over the years, those blueprints have become larger and more complicated—and also more profitable.

Good investors are good students. It's as simple as that. I spend hours each day reading the financial media (*The Wall Street Journal, Forbes, BusinessWeek, Fortune, The New York Times, Financial Times*). I also read a lot of books and other magazines; you never know where your next great idea is going to come from. You should be on top of all the news within your industry and, beyond that, all local, national, and global news as well. Ignorance in current affairs can go a long way toward destroying your credibility—and your bank account.

People always ask what I like to watch on television. Typically, I only watch television that I know will improve my financial IQ. My one indulgence when it comes to television is sports. For news and financial advice, of course, I watch *The Apprentice,* but I also watch the CNBC business report, Larry King, Bill O'Reilly, the *Today* show, and Fox Cable. Whatever you watch or read, study something every day. It's essential that you keep your mind open and alert.

And if you're young, don't think you don't have the experience to come up with good investment ideas. I had some of my best ideas when I was twenty-two years old. When you're that young, you don't censor yourself as much, and ideas that you may have will not be clouded by your business experiences. Genius is the ability to assemble in new forms what already exists, and sometimes the youngest people are the greatest geniuses.

If you're still in school, pay attention. Education is a money machine. If you're long gone from school, consider enrolling in a financial education class. Some financial courses can be dry, but I always made them more interesting by applying the principles immediately to some project, either imaginary or real, that I could work through in my mind. That way, I was already getting real life experience while I was still in school.

How to Follow
Market Indicators

A savvy investor is a sponge for information. You have to read the news-papers, watch the news, and listen to the world carefully as it spins around you. You have to follow the market each and every day—and not just your own holdings, but globally. It's a huge task, and it takes years of practice to be able to synthesize information in the way the best investors do. Though recent events in finance have given us businesspeople a bad name, most of us are highly educated and hardworking. Most of us are not money-grubbers, as the media would have you believe.

Good investors use market indicators for two reasons: (1) to evaluate how they have done in the past, and (2) to make better predictions about how the market will perform in the future. If the Dow Jones or Nasdaq or the S&P always seems to be trouncing your own portfolio, then con-sider making changes in your investments or turning your money over to a money manager. If, instead, you're always ahead of most market indi-cators, you can start to watch for trends. If the Nasdaq rallies, how does that affect the bond market? If housing starts are down one month, what effect does that have on lumber prices or mortgage rates? The market is a crazy, interconnected monster, and you have to know how a change in one part will affect the whole beast—otherwise, it will clobber you.

How to Divide Up
Your Portfolio

If you are in a position to have a portfolio (even if it's just $10,000), it's a good idea to consult with experts. It's a tricky business, and the experts, though not magicians, can do a much better job than you at managing money. They spend all day tracking the markets, so trust them. A lot of idiots went crazy over dot-coms and start-ups, thinking they could make millions, and most of them lost everything.

I consider myself a savvy investor with billions to prove it, but even I wouldn't dare to strategize about my portfolio by myself. The fees that the experts charge will be zilch compared to the money you can make, especially if you find a trusted investor on your behalf. It's worth it. Your money can work for you if you put it in the right hands.

Sometimes the more money you pay a money manager, the more money he or she will make for you; don't be wooed by cheap advice, because your money may not go anywhere. Some advisers charge a fee as a percentage of profits; others charge by the hour or per meeting. Make sure that whomever you decide to use is honest and up front about the services that he or she will be providing you.

To find a trusted, competent financial adviser, I would consult people who live and work in the same area you do—and that may be in the same income bracket. Working with someone whose primary client base is in a vastly different bracket is not the best course to take. The National Association of Personal Financial Advisors is a good source of listings. They can be reached by phone at 800-366-2732 or online at www.napfa.org. If you feel nervous about an adviser, you can check to see whether others have complained, or make a complaint yourself, with the Certified Financial Planner Board of Standards (CFPBS). You can contact the CFPBS through its website at www.cfp.net or by calling 888-237-6275.

If you're stubborn and refuse to hire someone to work with your money, go for it—but work to minimize your risk with a bunch of different investments. If you put all of your money into one stock or one building or one venture and then it crashes, you're broke. Plain and simple. I'm probably guilty of not having a diverse enough portfolio—after all, it's almost all real estate. But I have teams of people working for me, and I know from years of experience how to protect myself when the markets get rough.

Determining the right mix of cash, bonds, and stocks for your portfolio does not have to be tricky if you follow the formula that Eric Sacher, a financial guru within my organization, recommends. Start with one hundred percent of your assets; most likely you will be devoting this pot to a mixture of cash, bonds, and stocks. Take the one hundred percent as the number 100 and then subtract your age. Eric recommends that you devote your age as a percentage to cash and bonds and the remaining amount to stocks. That way, as you age, you minimize your exposure to stocks, which can be a lot riskier and a lot more volatile than bonds.

For example, let's say you're thirty years old, and you have $100,000 to invest. By Eric's formula, you would subtract 30 from

100 to arrive at the following allocation: $70,000 (or seventy percent) to stocks and $30,000 (or thirty percent) to bonds and cash. Each year, as you grow older, make changes to minimize your vulnerability to stocks by moving money into cash and bonds.

Obviously, you will need to consider other factors as well, such as market conditions and interest rates. In a hot stock market, you could consider elevating your stock allocation, and in a high-interest environment, I would recommend raising your bond and cash allocation. With this basic guideline to follow, an individual looking to invest some cash should be able to do so in a reasonable, and hopefully lucrative, manner.

You also have to invest with your own personal financial needs in mind. If you'll need your savings for a down payment or to pay for college in the short term, do not pay a lot of broker fees to lock away your money. Instead buy certificates of deposit (CDs) or another investment vehicle that will keep your money liquid and safe.

The worst thing you can do is be timid and let your money just sit in your savings account. It's pure waste. Your money should be at work at all times. You should think of your money as your staff; you wouldn't let your staff sit around, so don't let your money sit around, either. Even in the worst economy, there is no excuse for putting money under the bed.

How to Buy Stocks and Bonds

I am a firm believer that unless you have the inside scoop or a great investment adviser, the average investor is usually at a disadvantage. Therefore, three points of advice:

1. Do your homework before you invest. A dumb investor is a dead investor.
2. Hire an adviser if you can afford one, and always research what you are buying. Don't go for the hot tip or quick hit. Those types of investments usually end up in the trash can.
3. Buy companies only when you understand what they do. It is always easy to go with the herd and buy what everyone else is buying, but remember what happened to most of the dot-coms you bought? Stick to what you know.

Stocks and bonds are a dangerous game, so if you're in the market for them, my advice is to be judicious. They are the gambler's gamble. You'll win sometimes, and you'll lose sometimes. Remember that the house has the advantage, and I would be more comfortable gambling in one of my casinos than I would on Wall Street. After all, if a company falls apart, the stockholders and the bondholders are typically last in line at the junkyard. In my casinos, you'll be a lot more comfortable—and you'll probably win a bit more as well.

If stocks are irresistible to you, then always invest in ones that you understand. I understand real estate—the nitty-gritty terms of the deals but also the nearly indescribable forces that make the real estate market tick. I don't understand biotechnology or computers or lumber, so I'm not going to throw my money at those industries. If you're already gambling, why play a game where you don't even understand the rules? If, on the other hand, there are companies and industries you know, take your roll and go.

When picking stocks and bonds, the bottom line should be the people involved. There are some great companies with some great products, but if a klutz comes on to run the show, the company is doomed. If a pharmaceutical company develops a pill that extends life by a hundred years and everyone goes nuts, the company will still fail if a loser is in charge. So pick your stocks like you would pick your surgeon. You're not going to have an incompetent operating on you, so don't have an incompetent tending to your money.

And then look closely at the numbers. The company should be growing by leaps and bounds each year. If a company's profits have been growing by only a small amount per year—or even losing money—ditch the stock or bond and invest in something else. Since the risks of the stock and bond markets are so enormous, you should be playing only if the rewards outweigh the risk. And always remember that the proof is in the pudding. CEOs will make promise after promise about future performance, but if the results haven't been delivered before, don't expect them to be delivered next time. Sell the stock or bond and move on.

How to Spot a Fraud

There's a simple rule here: If it seems too good to be true, it is. That rule should weed out a lot of "opportunities" immediately. The world is filled with scoundrels looking to make a dishonest buck, and when it comes to your money, you have to protect it from them. When making investments, particularly with unknown parties or in untested industries, make sure you do your homework. If you're prudent and cautious, you won't be swindled.

Often, charlatans will try to rip investors off by advertising a "new venture" that's dressed up in smart-sounding rhetoric and promises that are too good to be true. Just because you don't understand something doesn't make it a good investment.

Some people come up with the craziest investment opportunities. The other day I heard a rumor that pharmaceutical companies may try to develop a pill that would make cheating men and women monogamous. Sort of the opposite of Viagra. Some scientists studied voles, and they gave promiscuous male voles a special hormone shot that stopped them from straying. If humans took this kind of hormone, a cheating spouse could say to his or her spouse, "Oops. I forgot to take my medicine today."

But all joking aside, don't trust anyone who needs your money for a new venture. The words "new venture" sound to me like a loan that will never get paid back. That's my advice, even if the new venture is for a monogamy pill. They want your money, pure and simple, so they'll have a chance to make money. If you aren't entrepreneurial enough to create the venture, I'd recommend finding a safer way to invest.

How to Pinch Pennies

When *Spy* magazine started years ago, they decided to do a "Who Is the Cheapest Millionaire?" test. They sent checks in amounts from fifty cents to five dollars to a list of millionaires throughout the country. I received a check for fifty cents, and we at the Trump Organization deposited it. They may call that cheap; I call it watching the bottom line. The higher you climb on the list of billionaires, the cheaper people become. Every dollar counts in business, and for that matter, every dime. Penny-pinching? You bet. I'm all for it.

Penny-pinching is the opposite of being wasteful. I have never liked waste, whether it's time, effort, or money. I think I inherited this attitude from my parents, who were careful with everything, particularly money. I still don't like to overspend for anything, and I will always take the time to compare prices, whether I'm buying a car or toothpaste.

As I said before, I always sign my checks, so I know where my money's going. In the same spirit, I also always try to read my bills to make sure I'm not being overcharged. There is human (and now computer) error everywhere—at restaurants, at the phone company, at the grocery store, at hotels—and you'd be surprised by how much this human error can cost you. Don't be obsessive about it, but check through your bills from time to time.

You should also always feel comfortable bargaining for goods and services. I do it all the time, and I'm one of the richest men on earth. Even in high-end shops, I bargain. After all, the more you're paying for something, the more the seller should be able to shave off the price. I hate paying retail, and it makes me cringe when I see other people doing it. I've walked into stores and offered $2,000 for a $10,000 item. It can be embarrassing for me (especially since everyone knows that I'm Trump and that I'm wealthy), but you'd be amazed at the discounts you can get if you simply ask. You do have to be willing to walk away, but after you've walked away a few times, the price will come down. It's moronic to be too proud to save money.

Another way to pinch pennies is to avoid the brand names when it's necessary. I obviously buy brand names when the brand is tied to a product's quality. Golf equipment, jewelry, and clothing are good examples of brand as a signifier of quality. But aspirin is aspirin, shampoo is shampoo, and cereal is cereal, so don't throw away your money on packaging and advertising.

I understand that penny-pinching can have a negative connotation—as in "miserly"—but when you calculate how much ten cents on a price can matter if you multiply it by a hundred thousand or a million, the value of ten cents becomes clear. For instance, let's say I have to buy one hundred thousand lightbulbs for all of the buildings that I own and maintain each year. If I manage to save ten cents on each lightbulb, that's a savings of $10,000 per year! That's $10,000 I can put toward another building or another investment or donate to a cause that needs the money more than I do.

Pay attention to the small numbers in your finances, such as percentages and cents. Numbers that seem trivial add up and have enormous implications. My parents hammered frugality into me at an early age, and it's the most important money-management skill a person can use. Call it penny-pinching if you want to; I call it financial smarts.

How to Decide
How Much Risk to Assume
When Investing

It all comes down to one simple question: How much money can you stand to lose? That's how much risk you should assume. If you can't afford to lose it, play it safe. It's common sense, and it doesn't require a degree in finance to figure out.

You should never fall in love with your investments. If you do, you're in big trouble. Even if I think one of my buildings or resorts is absolutely the most spectacular place in the world (and most of the time they are), I still know when it's smart for me to move on to something else or keep it within my portfolio. It all comes down to your guts and your brains.

You need to watch the bottom line. Allen Weisselberg, my chief financial officer, has to be one of the toughest people in business when it comes to money. When I was having some financial problems in the early 1990s, I called Allen into my office and told him there would be tough times ahead. The banks were about to cut off our funding. Allen said, "No problem," and went back to his office, where he proceeded to renegotiate almost every payment from that point forward. He did whatever was necessary to protect the bottom line—and refused to succumb to the pressures of risk.

Now he's negotiating with bankers on deals worth hundreds of millions of dollars, and he's so tough that most banks would rather I negotiate the deal than him. He's a loyal employee, and he's the ultimate master at playing the cards of business.

To be a visionary and to be a billionaire, you have to chase impossibilities. Few ever get rich easily. So if you find yourself in a situation that you think is nearly impossible, ask yourself once more whether bailing is really the right decision. You never want to walk away and then see someone less deserving walk off with the pot.

For instance, I recently announced that my building at 40 Wall Street is up for sale for $400 million. That's an enormous price, and it's been a brilliant deal. I bought it in 1995 for only $1 million. It's a seventy-two-story 1929 landmark building, and now, sadly, the tallest building in the financial district. When I bought the building, it was completely empty, and I took on some enormous risk. People had given up on the financial district, and many said that my investment would be a failure. I stood by it. Today it's completely full, and I'll be selling it for at least four hundred times what I paid for it. Deal making doesn't get any better than that.

How to Stay on Top
of Your Finances

Periodically, I ask my financial department for what I call my financial "small shot." This report reflects, among other financial data, my cash balances, investments, sales of condominium units, and so forth. If I didn't check up on it regularly, I would be in big financial trouble, and I would have no one to blame but myself. You should pull yours together once in a while, too.

Keep track of your various positions, and when you see a trend you don't like, change it! Don't assume that your stocks are performing well or that your house is appreciating in value or that your business is growing just because someone tells you it is. Always look at the numbers yourself. If things turn grim, you're the one left holding the checkbook.

One day back in the late 1980s, Jeff McConney, my controller, prepared my small shot and brought it to me. I looked down at it and immediately told Jeff, "You're fired." I told him I didn't want excuses and I thought he was doing a lousy job managing my cash. Although I am a multibillionaire and I head a multibillion-dollar organization, every dollar spent by this company comes out of my pocket. The point I was making to Jeff was that even though various payments always need to be made, always question invoices and never accept a contractor's first bid. Negotiate! Negotiate! Or get out. Jeff got the message and has been with me for seventeen years and is doing a terrific job. He looks out for my bottom line as if the money were his own.

Whether you have someone managing your bottom line or you're doing it yourself, money, like anything, takes maintenance and planning to grow. Don't ignore it, because if you do, you're going to lose it.

How to Motivate Yourself Financially

I've met some brilliant businesspeople in my time, but some of them will never be billionaires because they never act on those brilliant ideas. Twenty percent of your priorities will give you eighty percent of your productivity. You should always focus your time, energy, and efforts on the top twenty percent of your priorities; that's a four-to-one return on your investment. So if you have a great idea, no matter how much work you know it will require, get going. Don't just sit there. There's nothing more criminal and self-destructive than having a great idea and then putting it off. As the saying goes, a slow starter is always the fastest finisher.

I once knew a guy who had terrific ideas, would talk them up at hurricane force, and then go off and putter away at something else. He would lose his momentum before he even got going. What's the point? He was the personification of the term "windbag," and I see and hear a lot of them every day. Maybe they're just entertaining themselves, and in that case they should be charging admission, because it's the only way they'll ever make a cent. Get a move on. Being rich isn't a passive state. Ultimately, time is more valuable than money, because if you run out of money, you can start over again. But when you've run out of time, there's no starting over.

How to Manage Debt

Debt needs to be managed, and the only person who can manage your debt is you. I always tell myself that I can put the leverage on or I can take the leverage off. I'm entitled to do either. Don't let your debt scare you into not doing anything. It should only invigorate you to work harder.

When I went through tough times financially, I used debt as leverage. I loved leverage, and leverage makes a lot of businesses both profitable and possible. But love of leverage when the market crashes is what ultimately eats you alive. I know the perils of too much debt better than anyone else, so believe me when I tell you that excessive debt is best avoided. I'm a much more conservative person now in terms of debt, and I would advise you to be conservative as well.

Debt can be managed if you thoroughly plan for contingencies and mishaps. Know the terms, the penalties, and the defaults associated with your debt. And if you do have debt, make sure you're using it proactively. Don't take on debt for regular expenses; debt should be used only to finance ventures and projects that will have a return to you. People with excessive credit card debt, for which the terms may be ridiculously inflated, are committing financial suicide.

If you do find yourself in debt, assess the full extent of the situation. How much debt are you in? How much are you paying each month to maintain that debt? What steps will you take to rid yourself of that debt?

Cut your expenses, shop for a refinancing tool that will allow you to maintain your debt at a lower interest rate, and make your minimum payments to avoid bad credit. If those steps don't work, then consult an expert in debt reduction. There may be alternatives that are not obvious to you.

How to Save and Pay
for College

The best time to start saving for your children's education is the day they are born, if not before. Good education isn't cheap, and it's crucial to guarantee that your children will have a fair shot in the world. Start a college savings account immediately.

If you are paying for your own education, look into grants and scholarships. There are a lot of them, and as a result of the high costs of education today, you may still be required to be creative in finding a way to make money while going to school. Don't gripe about having to work during school. It will be better for you in the long run, not only for your finances but for your character. You will graduate with a top-drawer education and work experience to boot.

It's also wise to consider from an early age what professions pay well, and plan accordingly. Physical professions—sports and so forth—are always risky and usually short-term in comparison to the length of a doctor's career or a lawyer's. You should also encourage your children (or yourself) to be honest about what makes them (or you) tick.

People often ignore their talents and opt for careers that don't suit them. That way only leads to failure. People should always be encouraged to follow their dreams (my children have) but realize that a lot of time and money can be wasted chasing dreams that just weren't meant to come true.

How to Plan for Retirement

Aging is the absolute pits. I hate it. There's nothing good about it. But there's nothing any of us can do. We all have a credit card that's been given to us by God, but that credit card has an expiration date that's fixed and firm. If we don't use that credit card properly, we have no one to blame but ourselves.

Part of aging, unfortunately, is planning for retirement. Social Security is in big trouble, and anyone who's relying on it to get them through retirement is in bigger trouble than Social Security itself. You need to plan ahead; otherwise, getting older will be all the more miserable.

There are many smart, inexpensive ways to save for retirement. As your retirement draws closer, put together an annual budget and try to determine if there are any areas in your spending where you could trim the fat. Directing more and more of your discretionary income into savings is the first step.

If you're still working, make sure to take advantage of your employer's retirement planning options. Every worker should have a 401(k) plan, and if your company does not provide one, demand it. The 401(k) allows you to take a portion of your pretax income (up to

$13,000 in deferrals per year, for most employees) and set it aside in a retirement account. It's beautiful. You lower your taxable income (and possibly your tax rate), and the government is essentially giving you money to save. There are no excuses for not participating in a 401(k). The earlier, the better. You should also make yearly contributions to a Roth IRA, an account funded by post-tax income but sheltered from capital gains taxes later down the road.

Also, study all of your existing assets to make sure that the current mix meets your near- and longer-term goals. For example, do you have too much money in stocks, or do you own multiple homes? If so, move money away from stocks and convert more and more of your holdings to safer, more liquid assets.

Once you have streamlined your investments and carefully evaluated your current budget, set up an investment and expenditure strategy to cover your remaining life. You can allocate your portfolio according to both the time frame and the amount of risk you are willing to shoulder. Bonds, CDs, and Treasury bills become the most appropriate investment vehicles for retirees or those facing retirement.

If you plan carefully (and from as young an age as possible), your retirement should be everything it's meant to be. But while you may have pulled away from work, one area you can never stop working on in life is your money. In fact, retirees need to work extra hard to guarantee that they will be solvent and financially secure until death comes a-knockin'.

How to Plan Your Estate

We're all going to die. Money can't stop that. In fact, money can't do anything about it. One thing you'll need to do is plan how your money will live on after you're long gone.

People often criticize me, saying that my success is due to the financial gifts my father passed down to me. That's absolutely untrue. It's true that I owe everything to my father, but not because of the money he gave me—it's because of the education and the practical skills he imparted to me. I plan to do the same for my children, but I absolutely refuse to allow them to live solely off inheritance. They have to make their own way in the world, and they're well aware of that.

Few activities in life match the thrill of creating wealth from one's own labors and then putting that wealth to work to seek out new challenges. Conversely, there is little in life more unrewarding than wealth that consumes its owner or sits idle and unproductive. It's my feeling that dumping huge amounts of money on your children without properly educating them about how to put that money to work—or how to make money on their own—is the worst thing a parent can do. It's negligent.

I have many friends who, through brilliance, accident of birth, or just dumb luck, have achieved great wealth. But in my dealings with them, I often come away with the distinct feeling that their wealth is more of a yoke around their necks than a benefit. They often seem to lack the courage, determination, and perhaps the talent to, on the one hand, put their wealth to work for them and, on the other hand, use the money they have actively and responsibly.

For me, wealth should not be treated as a precious work of art to be hung on a wall and admired from time to time or locked away in a vault. Rather, for me, wealth is a vehicle with which to achieve clearly defined goals. My wealth is in a perpetual kinetic state. I use it as a tool to fix what in my many business ventures may need fixing and to create new opportunities, new challenges, and, when I do it right (which, I am delighted to say, seems to be most of the time), additional wealth.

But as much as I enjoy making money, wealth carries significant social responsibility. Although my businesses and properties employ thousands of people and therefore inherently benefit society through the incomes my employees earn, I believe that some portion of personal wealth must also be used to help those who are in need, to reward good work, and to encourage better work and higher productivity in the greater community. In that way, we all benefit.

So, when planning your estate, you have two responsibilities (three, if you consider the coffers of Uncle Sam to be your "responsibility"):

1. Not to burden your children with undeserved wealth that could paralyze them, preventing them from working hard and achieving their own measures of success
2. To make a legacy for yourself that revolves around charitable giving

You should consult a lawyer who specializes in estate planning. That lawyer will take you through the legalistic and tax concerns that will empower your estate to do the most good. Then the rest is up to you.

Sit down, with your spouse if appropriate, and draw up a list of priorities. How much do your children need or deserve? Are there members of your extended family who could benefit from a gift from you? Should your bequests be tied to certain benchmarks or limited to certain uses? Which charities do you regard as worthy?

Your estate should be the last great business deal you make. Think of your estate as an investment in the future—a future that hopefully you'll be watching from up in the clouds. Make sure that whatever choices you make, you'll be seeing the greatest return on your investment. Part of thinking like a billionaire is thinking about those billions when you'll be gone.

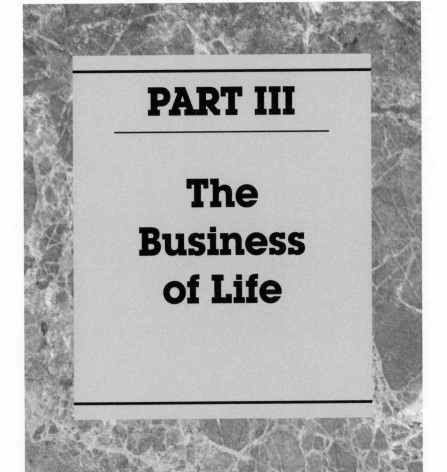

PART III

The Business of Life

Whether you're a homemaker or a schoolteacher, a lawyer or a doctor, a news anchor or an aerobics instructor, you are conducting business each and every day. There's no such thing as *personal* and *work* business; it's simply your business, twenty-four hours per day. You are your own storefront, your own manager, and your own brand, so don't screw it up by making bad business decisions in life.

Don't ask other people questions you should be asking yourself. Billionaires think for themselves, stopping to review themselves and to check their motivations at each step of the way. We've all seen on *The Apprentice* that the sixteen contestants wanted to learn something. They wanted a mentor. There is nothing wrong with that, but a mentor's job is to teach someone to be independent and to learn to think that way as well. Sometimes getting the boot can be both the lesson and a boost in the right direction. But it will save time if you can go for your own blind spot before someone else gets to it first.

If you want the best, you'd better *be* the best—in all aspects of business.

How to Love Your Job

Billionaires love their jobs—not because their jobs make them wealthy, but because they wouldn't have become so wealthy doing something that they hated. You have to love what you're doing, because then it won't seem like work to you and you will bring the necessary energy to profit from it. That passion alone will take care of ninety percent of any problems with any job.

Here's another trick: Always pretend that you're working for yourself. You'll do a wonderful job in that case. It's simple, but it works. If you're finding that you don't love your job or that you're not doing a good job, demand a meeting with your boss immediately. If the situation doesn't improve, fire yourself (and your boss) and go do something else.

I never want someone working for me who doesn't want to be there, and in the same way, you shouldn't want to be there, either. Life's too short and work's too important to stick around in a situation that isn't working.

While you should strive to love your job, you should always expect the shit to hit the fan every day. It will prepare you in the best way to face every business day, and it will also keep you on your game.

Once you know you love your job, never stop and never give up. If you have a concrete wall in front of you, you must go through it. Life is difficult no matter what, but hard work and perseverance make it a lot easier.

How to Promote Yourself

I'm always amazed when people tell me I'm a master promoter. I've never thought of myself as a good promoter. I think people get confused. They think I'm successful because I'm a great promoter rather than the reverse, which is that I am successful, and a certain amount of fame has stemmed from that. I get a lot of promotional credit because my buildings are the best. The buildings make me a good promoter, not the other way around.

Promotion comes naturally from doing what you're good at. I'm good at building buildings, and that's how I promote myself—as the best builder of buildings. And everyone agrees. Neil Ostergren, a great guy who used to run the Hospitality Sales and Marketing Association, polled bigwigs in business to see what names came to mind when they thought of real estate. Mine easily came out on top.

I'm not a fan of promoting yourself, but I do think it's important to promote an image of yourself each and every day. It's part of having a sense of self and a sense of purpose. Without a sense of self or a sense of purpose, you can never think like a billionaire. So if you're good at something—and it doesn't matter what that something is (it could be tap dancing or palm reading, for all I care)—people will recognize you for it. And then people will come to you to promote you, not the other way around. Don't worry about actively promoting yourself. If you deserve to be promoted, you will be.

How to Behave
in a Meeting

In meetings you have to be innovative and break things up. Otherwise, meetings will slowly kill you with time. I can't stand long, pointless meetings. I need people to be concise because I always have about a thousand better things I could be doing with my time. Nothing stifles creativity more—and thus, good business more—than long agendas and endless rigmarole. Meetings, like all business matters, require a certain sense of hustle.

In the 1990s I remember a meeting in the big boardroom with bankers, lawyers, and members of my team, and it was late at night. We were trying to work some things out, and things weren't exactly great for me financially at that time. I looked around the room and saw a group of tired guys with their ties loosened and their sleeves rolled up, drinking coffee, and trying to keep going.

Instead of letting the meeting drag on into the night, I decided to jump ahead a few years. I started talking about the new deals I would soon be involved in. At first I received bewildered looks from everyone, but then the heaviness dissipated and we all got a fresh start with the meeting. That's an example of looking at the solution, not the problem, and it works.

Whether you're in a meeting taking notes or running it, your behavior should be at all times attuned to the matter at hand. Grandstanding or talking just to hear yourself talk are counterproductive and bound to get you fired. You should have an agenda—even if it's just in the back of your own head—and be prepared to gather and spread the necessary information in as short a time as possible. Idle chatter and banter are appropriate during the first few minutes, but after that, you're wasting everyone's time.

When you're at a meeting, monitor your behavior and work at being an observer—of yourself and of others. Try not to get angry, unless it's absolutely necessary or uncontrollable. Anger often indicates a lack of intelligence. I can remember when things could get under my skin, and when I look back, it was because I didn't have the intelligence to see them for what they were as quickly as I can now. Pay attention to your anger: Sometimes it's warranted, and sometimes it will only get in the way.

How to Organize
Your Office

I don't keep a particularly neat office, because I have so many things going on at once. I have an enormous desk and a big round table, and both are usually covered with current projects that need my attention. There is order to the apparent chaos, however, and I'd rather be effective than just tidy.

One journalist recently spent an afternoon at the Trump Organization in Trump Tower, and he commented that most of the offices were messy, but he also noticed that the teamwork was impressive, as was the energy level. We get a lot accomplished every day, and that's our bottom line. So it's not about how you organize your office but how you organize the team who works in and around that office.

How to Dress and Groom for Work

Always remember: Dress for the job you want, not the job you have. I can't stand to see the way some people dress for work these days. It's criminal. If anyone comes into my office in sneakers, or ripped clothing, or attire that looks like it belongs in a nightclub, I just can't take him or her seriously. People want to do business with people who look good, and if you look like crap, you're not going anywhere.

Clothes make the man and the woman, and if you want to be successful in life, you should start with your wardrobe. Clothing does not have to cost a fortune, but you should invest in some high-quality items that you can rotate throughout your week. It takes money to make money, and clothing is always a good investment.

People these days groom themselves even worse than they dress: dirty fingernails, stained clothing, bad breath, bad haircuts, scuffed shoes, and out-of-control facial hair. Good grooming doesn't cost money; it just costs you a little time each day. You need to check yourself in the mirror to make sure you're proud of what you're seeing there. If you appear unkempt, your business will be unkempt, too.

People ask me what happened to my signature red power ties. Nothing. I still have them; I just like going the gamut now. After I wore red ties, I noticed that everyone else started to wear them, too. I also happen to be a little superstitious. For example, I had been thinking that red ties brought me luck, so I kept wearing them. Then one day when I was wearing a big, bright red tie, I got creamed in a court decision. After that, I decided no more red ties for a while. I've joined the color spectrum, and I'm glad I did.

How to Balance Work and Pleasure

If, during the workweek, all you can think about is how many hours and minutes there are until the weekend, you'll never be a billionaire. You'll never even be a millionaire, most likely. Billionaires never wish away the minutes; life's just too good to wish it away. I hate the phrase "TGIF," and if you want to think like me, you should hate it, too.

Sometimes my weekends are even busier than my Monday-to-Friday routine. I often get some of my best work done during the weekends, when the phones die down and the fax machine stops whirring. For instance, a couple of weekends ago I carried the Olympic torch in New York City for a portion of its route as it traveled to Athens. It was an incredible honor to be a part of such an amazing tradition, and I'm proud of all the work New York City is doing currently to bring the Olympics here in 2012. That same day I also had to do three shoots for *The Apprentice* and attend a black-tie event—all on a Saturday. In between all of that activity, I managed to review some updates on my properties and make several important phone calls. I know some of those things sound like good fun—and they were—but they're also work, and I remain as committed to my job on the weekend as I do on a weekday.

Success requires work seven days per week. If you're interested in balancing work and pleasure, stop trying to balance them. Instead, make your work more pleasurable. For billionaires, work and pleasure are one and the same. Even when I'm golfing, a hobby that gives me immeasurable pleasure, I'm studying the course. If it's my own course, I'm looking for ways to improve it, and if I'm playing as a guest on another course, I'm looking for ideas and inspiration that I can adopt and use as my own.

How to Balance Work and Romance

Believe it or not, I'm a romantic guy. If there isn't any romance in my life, then I don't have much incentive to be the best that I can be. That's one reason I love women. They're great motivators. I think any honest man would agree. Romantic pursuits should motivate you to be the best, to keep growing and learning. They should be the basis from which you make a lot of your decisions in life.

So when it comes to balancing work and romance, I'm not a believer. There should be no balance. Romance should simply propel you to work harder. To me, work is as important as breathing; it's something I do automatically. I have an inherent work ethic that will never diminish. In the same way, my love for women—especially Melania—is an inherent part of me and the work that I do.

These two hungers, for work and for romance, work together in successful people. To me, both are full-out endeavors, endeavors that depend on each other and should never get in the way of one another. I give to both everything I've got, and the effort, in the long run, is always worth it.

How to Impress Anyone in Business

Here are some time-tested rules for anyone working in business that will help you impress people and thus make money:

1. Be on time. Punctuality is essential. You should never tolerate late arrivals and missed deadlines for yourself or from anyone else.
2. Do your homework. Wasting other people's time due to poor planning and thoughtlessness will only leave a *bad* impression.
3. Make a mental dossier on people. Before meeting people for the first time, do some research on them. People will be flattered if you reference a deal you know they've done or a charity they're involved in.
4. Remember people's names and small details about them. Use both in conversation. People love to hear their names and their stories said out loud.
5. Be honest. Most people can smell a lie and will appreciate honesty, even if it's not exactly what they want to be hearing.
6. Let other people talk. Any business conversation should be two-sided.

7. Be self-deprecating and disarming. Don't be a bulldozer in business; save your hardest edge for when you need it most.

Some people might think billionaires don't have to impress anyone, but most of us still live by these rules. Your manners, like your money, need to be maintained at all times.

How to Balance Money and Marriage

Don't let anyone do major surgery on your wallet. In other words, get a prenup. "M" may be for "money," but "DJT" is for prenuptial agreements. Oftentimes lawyers will recommend against a prenup because they'll be able to get a lot more money later on if you don't have one.

Everyone goes into a marriage thinking that it will last forever. But over fifty percent of the time, marriages don't work out. And when there's money and real estate and stocks and lots of personal possessions involved, it can get messy—fast! Tremendous bitter battles. A lot of my friends have gone through terrible divorces, and they always say that divorce can be the worst business deal imaginable. And I'm not just talking about men; women can be equally ruined financially without a prenup. There's nothing romantic or beautiful about a prenup, but it's better than having a sleazy lawyer do it for you or dealing with endless court proceedings. I've had two prenups, and without them I probably wouldn't be writing a book about thinking like a billionaire today.

Business is complicated and so are relationships, so the best way to avoid chaos is to have a prenuptial agreement. It's common sense. You should never ignore the power that money has to destroy relationships.

It is often the glue that brings people together and likewise the wedge that can drive them apart. Work with a lawyer to draft a prenup that will protect both you and your spouse-to-be.

People who don't agree with me should take a close look at the dynamics of a couple who experience a shift in power due to money. Both men and women, but men in particular, often struggle to adjust to situations where the woman earns more than the man does. It might be about pride, or control, or ego. It can be a difficult adjustment, even with couples who proclaim to be equals in all aspects of life. Many relationships crumble in this scenario.

Talking about money in a relationship is important, because taking care of your finances is equal to taking care of your health. It has to do with your well-being as people and as a couple. I've heard people say, "Oh, we don't talk about money," as if it's a swear word or something. This stigma is asinine. It's like enjoying being illiterate. Your financial statement is your report card. If you've worked hard for an A, don't let anyone downgrade your mark to a D for dumbbell. That's my advice.

How to Be Married

A good marriage is like negotiating an important deal: You have to consider all the factors, thoughtfully and thoroughly. If you were investing a large part of yourself and your fortune into a venture, believe me, you'd make sure you thought about it for a long time first. That's how I see marriage. It's serious, and it's important. I don't approach it any more haphazardly than I do a very important deal. In fact, considering the amount of deals I've made compared to the number of marriages I've had, I'd say I'm quite cautious about marriage. You should be, too.

I'm a bit older and certainly wiser now, and marrying Melania is a big decision, but not at all surprising. We have gotten along very well for some years now, and the comfort zone is definitely there, and we also have a lot of fun together. Enjoying someone's company is a big step in the right direction for marriage, and even though that sounds obvious, I've seen some slam-bang rotten marriages take place between two people who simply don't enjoy each other's company.

I believe strongly in the concept of "the woman behind the man," or vice versa. I have been with Melania for five years, and they have been the best five years of my life, not only personally but in business—

I am the biggest and best developer in New York; my show, *The Apprentice,* went to number one and was nominated for four Emmys; my book *How to Get Rich* became the number one business book of the year (by far); my ninety-second-a-day radio show became the number one biggest launch of a new show in the history of radio (over three hundred stations), and so on. So I figured I better marry the woman who stood behind me (and in front of me) during this amazing and crazy period—and fast!

How to Make Good Friends

First, have something in common. I am good friends with Regis Philbin because he is a positive guy, and therefore I always enjoy his company. I, too, am a positive type of guy, and I prefer to see the good things in life, so we have a great time together. That's one recipe for a good friendship: simple and solid.

Consider my friendship with Richard LeFrak. He called me the other day when I was in the middle of an important meeting, but he's too good a friend for me not to take his call. He's just the best of the best. We were joking around together, and I told him that I was looking out for him because I was keeping an eye on some scaffolding work being done on his building that I can see from my office windows. If the workers start slacking or the work looks shoddy, you can bet I'll be dialing Richard in a second—and he would expect me to.

We spoke for a couple more minutes; he asked about my shooting schedule for *The Apprentice,* and I asked about his health. He asked me about my children, and I asked after his. He has two amazing sons, and one of them, Harry, is a true dynamo who will go on to great heights. Attending to that sort of detail is necessary to maintain good friendships. You have to *invest* yourself in the details of your friends' lives. Otherwise, there's just no bond between you.

And then there's the old saying "To have a friend, be a friend." Well, sometimes. I've been around some selfish people, and their idea of a friend is for you to be everything they want you to be. The minute you step out of the role they've designed for you, watch out! You're a bad friend!

It helps if your friends have a level of confidence equal to yours, which will eradicate any envy or jealousy they might otherwise have. I am a successful man, and I've seen a lot of ill-concealed envy toward me because of my accomplishments. I quickly have to assess those who are sincere and those who aren't because I've met so many of the latter. It's not a condemnation but a part of human nature that I'm well aware of by now.

Steve Wynn, the successful Las Vegas hotel impresario, is a friend. We have had some tremendous ups and downs with each other, but somehow it seems to work, and we always seem to end up together. Steve called me when he was thinking of changing the name of his hotel in Las Vegas (which will be a great success, by the way) from Le Reve to Wynn. I told him to do it. Now we are both fighting HBO, using the same lawyer, Barry Langberg, as HBO is attempting to do an awful movie on a battle we had in Atlantic City. I hope HBO will be smart enough to make corrections before a lot of money is spent doing battle over it.

I know many successful people who only want to be with people who are not successful—it makes them feel better about themselves. I have one very successful and well-known friend who boasts loudly that he will only hang out with losers. (How would you like to be one of them?) I, on the other hand, don't discriminate—I like (and dislike) all sorts of people—winners, losers, and those in the middle!

How to Know Whether Someone Is Loyal

It's taken me a long time to figure out how to recognize whether someone's loyal or not. I suppose it takes some bad mistakes to learn this valuable lesson. I'm not sure it can be taught. These days, I have a better sense of people and their motivations, and most of my friends and colleagues have proved loyal to me.

A lot of people envy billionaires and successful people, so I have to be mindful of that every time I approach a new relationship. The people in my life who recognize the high price I have paid to be where I am—in stress, in hard work, and even in failure—are the loyal ones. I always try to surround myself with people who would stand by me if tomorrow I woke up a pauper.

The best time to test whether or not somebody is loyal is when things are going horribly for you. When I was having trouble in the early nineties, I learned a lot about loyalty because there were people I thought would be totally loyal to me who weren't. And then, of course, there were people I thought would be disloyal, and they were great. When you're successful, people will kiss your ass and clamber to be around you. When things aren't going so well, loyalty and disloyalty surface naturally. I don't like to test people, and I've learned that people will prove themselves to be what they are sooner or later.

By the way, almost all of the people who were not loyal to me in the early nineties have called me since then to try to get together. My response to them is very simple: F____ you! One thing I have learned in life is that if someone is disloyal to you once, they will be disloyal to you again.

I had a friend in New York who would call me all the time and who was a lot of fun to be with. He is a very successful businessman (I think!). After years of being his friend and doing him favors, a problem came up for me that he was in a position to solve easily. He claimed that he didn't have the power over the situation that I thought he had (which was nonsense) and did not come through for me. I believe he didn't even try very hard. Needless to say, he is no longer a friend.

Stuff

Billionaires are not defined simply by the size of their holdings but also by the quality of their stuff. There's no point in being a billionaire if you cannot enjoy those billions.

To have the best, you have to know the best. Thinking like a billionaire means recognizing the best and enjoying the best. Of course, it takes practice. Can you confidently name the top five jewelers in the world? The best champagne? The best, most exclusive real estate? The most highly rated restaurants? The top art dealers? If not, you've got a long way to go to be a billionaire. But don't feel bad, because I don't know all the answers—other than the real estate ones—either!

It's nice that people think Dom Perignon is a good champagne, because it is. But it isn't the best. When I hear people bragging about drinking it, it's an automatic tip-off that they're not clued in. Always remember that the most famous doesn't always equal the best.

The best is a quest. Elevate your tastes; don't stagnate in the mediocre-to-good category. It will end up categorizing you. If an expert were to review your pantry or your wardrobe or your travel itineraries, how do you think you'd rate? How can you aim for the best if you don't know what you're aiming for? But at the same time, always remember that some of the richest and most successful people, like Warren Buffett (or, before his death, the great Sam Walton), live very simple lives. Sam drove to work in an old Chevrolet every day—I love it!

If you want to truly *be* rich, recognize the virtue of making your own choices versus doing what is expected or what everyone else is doing. If wine makes you ill, don't drink it just because you think it makes you seem sophisticated or worldly. That's preposterous. If you do like wine, learn about it, and if you don't, find something else to spend your money on. I often see people who supposedly love wine making stupid choices. It's a giveaway that they don't know what they're doing, and on several levels. Much as we don't like to admit it, we are often judged by our choices, even minor ones.

Luxury is what takes us from the ordinary to the extraordinary. Here's a Donald Trump "consumer guide" for the best luxuries around:

The Best Car: My favorite car is a Mercedes. I've had one for a long time, and it's reliable, elegant, and sturdy all at once. I have no complaints about my Mercedes. It's never disappointed me. The cars are not temperamental, and they make my life easier. Mercedes cars are also great because they are classy without being ostentatious. I also have a Ferrari, a Lamborghini, and a bunch of other cars in different places.

The Best Suit: I wear Brioni suits, which I buy off the rack. Some people think it's best to have custom-tailored clothing. I don't recommend it unless you have an oddly shaped body, and unless you have a great deal of time.

The Best Cuff Links: The best cuff links are the TRUMP five-star diamond cuff links that Joe Cinque of the Five Star Diamond Awards gave to me. I keep some on hand to give to people as gifts, and they are great-looking. I also wear solid gold cuff links from time to time, but I have to say, I prefer Joe's TRUMP cuff links.

The Best Shirts: I've worn some great shirts over the years, but I now favor Brioni (the same brand as my favorite suits). Brioni shirts are fitted so they feel and look great. I used to have a favorite dry cleaner, located in Atlantic City, but I've mellowed a bit and I can handle the dry cleaners in New York City just fine now. Actually, once you get a good shirt, who really notices anyway?

The Best Ties: Brioni and Hermès make the best ties. And I must say, as I keep mentioning Brioni, that they graciously supply me with my clothing for *The Apprentice*.

The Best Shoes: I love a variety of high-end shoes. I can remember when I thought some good shoes were great until I found some *really* great shoes. The price was substantially greater, too, but after wearing them, I can't go back to the others. I also find that they last for a much longer period of time, so that the real cost is actually less.

The Best Jewelry: I go to Graff, Harry Winston, Asprey, Tiffany, and Fred Leighton for jewelry. Asprey has been around since the eighteenth century, and their jewelry makes the most beautiful woman look even better. In addition to gems, Asprey is also famous for their silver, leather, porcelain, and crystal. Asprey's flagship store is in the Trump Tower, so I can slip in there whenever I want, almost always to buy something for Melania. You can buy a gift for anyone there, and the salespeople are excellent. Winston and Graff have, I believe, the best diamonds in the world.

The Best Golf Equipment: If you're new to the game, you don't have to invest a lot of money to buy a decent set of clubs. Cary

Stephan, the golf pro at the Trump National Golf Club, tells me that only good golfers can tell the difference between good and bad clubs. It is important to buy a set of clubs designed with your frame and your weight in mind. Seniors need different clubs than juniors, men need different clubs than women, and so on.

If you're a decent golfer, definitely go for the modern technology. Get every advantage you can. The new equipment totally outperforms the old stuff. I have always liked Callaway, while Lee Rinker, head professional at Trump International Golf Club in Palm Beach, prefers TaylorMade. Good players can use forged irons, but the average person should use a perimeter-weighted iron. Also, make sure the shaft flex matches your swing speed.

The newest balls, particularly the ones made by Titleist and Callaway, are fantastic as well. These balls go forever when hit off a tee but still have great feel in the short game. It's like having two balls for the price of one.

The Best Furniture: The best furniture doesn't have a brand name. Furniture is as diverse as it comes, but I've noticed the brand names aren't consistent to one level of quality or taste. I never like all the pieces by one designer, and sometimes I'll find one incredible piece in a collection that otherwise leaves me uninspired. That's why I take so long to decide about certain pieces. One badly chosen item can ruin an entire room. Furniture is as important as lighting to a room, about which I'm equally demanding.

I admire Mies van der Rohe very much, but I don't like sitting in his chairs. Furniture should be elegant, but it also needs to be comfortable. Whoever or whatever manufacturer can provide that combination will get my business.

The Best Antiques: These come from high-end antique dealers. Collecting antiques is up there with collecting art, and I go for the most reputable dealer I can find. Sometimes there's a fine line between good-looking junk and the real thing, and a dealer will spare you wasted time and scams.

The Best Credit Card: The best credit cards are Visa and American Express. I even did a commercial for Visa, and American Express is a great tenant of mine at 40 Wall Street.

The Best Shampoo: The best shampoo is Head & Shoulders.

The Best Book: I have two: *The Art of the Deal* and *How to Get Rich*, both by Donald J. Trump.

The Best Movie: My favorite movie of all time is *Citizen Kane*.

The Best Album: There's so much great music. For me, I'd have to say it's a toss-up between Frank Sinatra, Tony Bennett, and Elton John. I never get tired of listening to them and probably never will. Frank Sinatra's favorite singer was Tony Bennett, so those two sort of go together. Any album by any of them is bound to be fantastic. And besides that, Tony lives in one of my buildings.

In Trump Tower, we play a variety of music—anything from renditions of "Moon River" to versions of Rachmaninoff's famous piano concertos. Some people call it cheesy, but others love it, and so do I. If you love a certain kind of music, don't let other people's tastes influence your own. Whatever's the best for you is the best. Never forget that. And by the way, I also love Eminem.

The Best Broadway Show: My favorite Broadway show is *Evita* by Andrew Lloyd Webber, starring Patti LuPone. I saw it six times, mostly with Ivana. *Evita* is not on Broadway right now, but I'm hopeful that they'll bring it back. Also, *The Phantom of the Opera* was great!

The Best Painting: The best painting is the finger painting of a house by my daughter Tiffany. Nothing else comes close.

The Best Ice Cream: Cherry Vanilla by Häagen-Dazs is by far my favorite flavor, and I've tried a lot of them, as I'm an ice-cream fan from way back. When I open my own ice-cream parlor in Trump Tower, maybe we'll give Häagen-Dazs a run for its money.

The Best Hamburger: I have two answers for this one. I like McDonald's hamburgers and the DT Burger as served at the Trump Grill in Trump Tower. The DT Burger is definitely more deluxe, but I've been a loyal McDonald's customer and even did a major ad for them.

Places

Billionaires tend to be well traveled and cultured. You should be, too. There's no excuse for staying home; the world's too fantastic to miss out on it. I wish I could travel more, but I am having too much fun at home. When you do decide to travel, always pack the word "elite." It's a great word. It's a great place to be, too. If you want to think like a billionaire, elite should never be a destination that's too far away. But don't confuse "elite" with "expensive." Elite is much more about a frame of mind, about curiosity and experience and appetite. Even if you haven't got tons of money yet, why not prepare yourself for when you do?

How to Travel in Style
Even If You Don't Have
Your Own Jet

You don't need your own jet or your own yacht to travel in style. Traveling in style usually takes cash—lots of it. But beyond cash, traveling in style requires a certain mind-set—a mind-set that you can develop for free.

The first trick is to go to places where you will be comfortable. It's impossible to travel in style if you're fearing for your life, or the temperature is unbearable, or you can't eat anything because it will all make you sick. Don't run off to crummy places because you've found a good deal. One day in the south of France will be far more restive and rewarding than a whole summer spent in a hellhole. Use your head when making travel plans. It's okay to look for a good deal, but you sometimes have to spend money to enjoy yourself. Not to do so is a waste of money and can be dangerous.

I make a habit of only traveling to places with running water and good amenities. I don't have a calling to the great outdoors, unlike both of my sons. I've never felt I needed to climb mountains or ride rapids down a river. Why try to climb Mount Everest when you can see it perfectly well on television or in a book? I always say, "Don't challenge nature, because ultimately, nature will win." You're far better off in a hotel.

So while I'm not an expert in off-road, rugged travel, I know what I'm talking about when it comes to hotels and resorts. Here are some tips for when you travel—and when you want to travel like I do:

1. Never check your luggage. That's a cardinal rule. Checked luggage is lost luggage. If you have an important meeting, you will not have time to shop for a new set of clothing.
2. Stay in a nice hotel. People's perception of you is influenced by the quality of the hotel you're staying in. If you're trying to sell yourself or your business, others will not perceive you as a deal maker if you're staying at the Fleabag Inn.
3. Get your suits pressed. It should be one of the first things you do after you arrive at your hotel. Most hotels will offer complimentary pressing, so there's no excuse for leaving a hotel looking like your suit's been crumpled in the bottom of a suitcase for days.
4. Bring golf clothing. You never know when you'll be called upon for an impromptu round of golf. You can rent clubs, but clothing and shoes that fit are harder to come by.
5. Always arrange your transportation from the airport to your hotel before your plane takes off. You can waste a lot of time and money stuck at the airport with a beat-up taxi as your only option. Plan ahead.
6. Have your assistant call the hotel in advance to let the manager know of your arrival. Good managers at good hotels know the comings and goings of each guest, and if they are alerted to your arrival, you're bound to get better service.

How to Be Treated Like Royalty in a Hotel

The best way to be treated like royalty in a hotel is to tip well. Tip the bellhop who brings up your luggage, tip the concierge when he or she makes your restaurant reservation, and tip the waitstaff when they deliver your room service. If you tip liberally, the hotel workers will watch your back. When you need a reservation at the best restaurant to impress a client or you need a car five minutes ago, hotel workers will absolutely bend over backward for you if they know that you'll take care of them.

The best way to judge a hotel is on cleanliness. That's huge. If you walk into a hotel room and it's dirty, check out. Run, actually. A hotel's rooms should be immaculate. If you've taken my advice and opted for a top-notch hotel, you're paying top dollar for what should be top service, so never tolerate mess or filth.

Veterans of hotels always know to ask for an upgrade and always know to negotiate their rates. You might get one or the other, and there's no shame in trying; there's shame only in not doing so. If you're staying multiple nights or over a weekend, your chances of an upgrade or a rate reduction are even greater.

If you get to your room and you hate what you find, complain. Don't be shy. Ask for the manager (don't complain directly to the bell-hop), and I assure you that he or she will try his or her best to help you. You could get a new room or an upgrade. If the hotel's booked, you might be able to get the price reduced. Too many people are too shy to complain. Neither you nor the hotel staff members want your stay to be unpleasant.

And finally, expect the staff to be pleasant, smiling, and aggressively hospitable. You can be grumpy and tired, especially if you've just come off a red-eye flight or out of a long meeting, but the staff should be as accommodating and as polite as possible. If not, you're at the wrong hotel.

How to Get the Best Service at a Restaurant

Get to know the restaurant's owner, the maitre d', the waiters, and anyone else associated with the restaurant. Some of my favorite people in New York are restaurateurs: Jean-Georges Vongerichten, who's the genius behind Jean Georges in the Trump International Hotel; Sirio Maccioni, who runs Le Cirque; and Giuseppe Cipriani. I know how demanding they are of themselves as far as quality and innovation go. They're artists and craftsmen when it comes to cooking and hospitality. There are only a few people in the world in their league. And they never let a customer down. There are a lot of traditional businessmen in New York who could learn a lot about business from watching Sirio, Jean-Georges, and Giuseppe.

If you can't afford the best restaurants, the same advice works anywhere. I'm building a golf course in Bedminster, New Jersey, and whenever I'm there, I always try to visit Bedminster Pizza. It's about three minutes away from the golf club, and it's the best pizza I've ever had. The men who work there, some of whom barely speak English, treat me like a king. Great service is available at every level of the food chain. You just need to know how to find it.

Another trick is to treat the waiters and the restaurant owners as you would treat the host of a dinner or a party. Always remember that even though you may be paying for your meal, you're still a guest of the restaurant. If you act like a guest, you'll be treated like one—sometimes like the guest of honor.

How to Improve
Your Golf Game

If you play a lot of golf, your game will improve with time. Cary Stephan, the golf pro at the Trump National Golf Club in Briarcliff Manor, New York, feels that good golfers need to put in two to three hours per week of practice—whether it's on the putting green, or playing rounds, or at the driving range. Serious golfers looking to improve their game should also devote an hour a week to instruction. Golf, like everything else in life, requires dedication.

The rest is pure talent. I recently played golf with Annika Sorenstam, the Swedish golf champion, at the Trump National Golf Club at Briarcliff Manor. Hard as I try to be fair about the fairer sex, I still don't like being outdriven by a woman. After playing with Annika, I have to say that I'm happy I'm in the real estate business. I did, however, ask her how she does what she does so well. Her answer reminded me of Babe Ruth's: "I just do it." Basically, she works hard, but she's got great talent.

I was recently asked whether I see golf as a business or as a pleasure. I had to say that I find even more pleasure in building great golf courses than in playing the game. There is something so aesthetically pleasing about bringing a golf course to life. In fact, I feel guilty now if I'm playing golf at Winged Foot, which is a great course, because if I'm playing there, it's for pleasure only, not business. On my own courses, I can play and work at the same time, as I'm scouting the course for any problems I might see or possible improvements to make. I'm doing two things at once that way.

How to Find
Great Vacation Resorts

To zero in on a great vacation resort, ask people where they've been lately and ask for a firsthand account. Joe Cinque travels constantly, and he always gives me an honest opinion of where and what's the best. If he speaks highly of a place, I put it on my mental list of destinations. Sometimes I'll flip through magazine articles and photographs, especially a beautiful publication such as *Elite Traveler*. I know that Douglas Gollan, the president and editor in chief, does a lot of the research himself. His tastes are sophisticated and discerning. I caught up with Doug recently at the Beverly Hills Hotel, and his immediate agenda included Dubai, South America, Geneva, Paris, and other European cities. He can always provide you with a list of the hottest destinations, as does his magazine.

But I am fortunate not to have to travel far to find one of the most beautiful places on earth, which is the Mar-a-Lago Club in Palm Beach, Florida. Melania loves it there more than anyplace, and she spent years going to the south of France, Portofino, Lake Como, and other beautiful places in Europe. She prefers Mar-a-Lago to them all, and so do I.

Etiquette

HOW TO TIP

Tipping, unless service is absolutely reprehensible, is mandatory. You should always tip waitstaff at least fifteen percent, if not twenty percent. I always make a point of tipping the maître d' or the sommelier if it's appropriate. If you make a habit of certain restaurants, you'll be increasingly less welcome and will receive shoddy service if you don't pay up.

In other aspects of daily life, tipping can confuse people, but I always say, "More is more." I know I'm an advocate for penny-pinching, but you have to think of service workers as your colleagues in the business of life. Service jobs are never easy, and service workers can be some of the more tolerant, professional, and polite people working today. Learn from them.

You should always give at least a couple of dollars (and, in some cases, a lot more) to valets, skycaps, restroom attendants, door attendants, bellhops, coat checks, the concierge, and housekeepers. If someone goes out of their way for you or makes your life easier in any way, tip them a lot more. I think a sure indication of a loser is someone who can't tip adequately.

HOW TO ATTEND A PARTY

I can remember the times when I was not invited to as many parties as I am today. Today I am overwhelmed with invitations. I'm wanted places—sometimes for five or six events per night—but I don't go to many of them.

When I was younger and less known, I avoided parties where I might be considered a fringe member of those on the invitation list. It's never a good idea to be at a party where you're not welcome, and if you are invited somewhere, don't show up too early and don't leave too late. I'm always amazed to see a party that's emptying with three or four oblivious partygoers just not wanting to leave. Also, drinking too much or behaving inappropriately is a one-way ticket to the Z-list.

If you're going to talk about something at a party, make sure you know what you're talking about. I was recently at a party where I was subjected to listening to a woman who let us know exactly how much she didn't know about owning a yacht by trying to tell everyone how much she did know about it. Unfortunately for her, quite a few of us there had owned yachts, myself included. We were polite and let it slide, but we all knew this know-it-all was trying to impress the wrong people. If she had known what she was talking about, she would have known that the second-greatest day of a man's life is the day he buys a yacht, but the *greatest* day of a man's life is the day he sells it.

HOW TO BEGIN AND END
A CONVERSATION

Interested is interesting. If you remember that simple rule, you should have no trouble making conversation. I'm gregarious by nature, but a simple key for those who are more introverted is to be curious. Ask questions that will make the other person talk. After all, most people love to hear themselves talk, so if you're shy, let the other party do the work.

Most people are fascinating if you ask the right questions, and small talk can be one of the best ways to educate yourself. Rarely does a day go by in which I don't have five to ten conversations that change the way I see the world.

You can end a conversation quickly if you don't mind being blunt. Other ways are to stop talking, move away a bit, pretend you see someone you know across the room, or just say, "Enjoy your evening. Nice talking to you." The phone is easier because you can simply hang up.

I enjoy most conversations I engage in, especially with contractors, and since I usually have a lot of people to talk to, most people are considerate and don't bog me down. Those who do will get the message, and if they don't, I just tell them I have to move on. No one enjoys being rude, but on occasion you need to be—otherwise, you'll spend your entire life trapped in pointless conversations and small talk.

HOW TO GIVE A GOOD GIFT

Never just pick something generic. It's a waste of money, and the gesture will be forgotten in a second. Strategic gift giving should be thoughtful and appropriate. It should reflect the recipient's interests or your relationship with the person. Gift giving takes time and careful planning. Don't plan on buying a gift on your way to see someone. If you're clueless when it comes to shopping, ask a trusted personal assistant or a friend to help you—especially when you're shopping for the opposite sex.

I keep up with catalogs from Bergdorf, Tiffany, Louis Vuitton, and other fine stores, so I'll know what's new and what's out there. Occasionally, as I walk through a place, I'll see something that catches my eye and will buy it on the spot.

HOW TO CORRECT SOMEONE

I'm a New Yorker, so I tell it like it is. Be up front and direct with people, and they will return the favor. But sometimes, in more sensitive social situations, you have to consider the source and let it slide.

In business and in life, I've heard people say things that are so out-rageously incorrect that I don't feel it's worth my energy to say any-thing. Sometimes it's easy to just say, "You might want to check into that. I heard differently," and leave it at that.

If you can avoid an altercation, do so, since most of them aren't worth your time and energy. I have to set a lot of things straight every day at work, and doing this during social hours is a total turnoff. I'd rather walk away and let other people waste their time. People will, hopefully, correct themselves eventually.

HOW TO CRITICIZE SOMEONE

It's best to avoid criticizing anyone. Compliments work better, and sometimes silence is the best form of criticism available. I've known people who have said bad things to and about me who cannot take criticism themselves. Most people are one-way streets, and it's better not to spend your time dodging head-on traffic. If you stay silent, peo-ple will eventually make fools of themselves without your help at all. It's revenge the easy way.

HOW TO SAY NO

Learning how to say no is crucial to thinking like a billionaire. We are faced with a barrage of requests each and every day—for time, for money, and for favors. We have to learn to say no most of the time, occasionally to some worthy causes and some great opportunities.

When it comes to saying no in the context of a deal, I learned a valuable lesson from one of my lawyers: Distill the information pre-sented to you. Lawyers are pros at distilling complex information, and it's a skill worth cultivating. As you read over the terms of a deal or a contract, translate the language by using the phrase "in other words . . ." and then paraphrase the rest.

You will begin to see the tricky ways in which language can be used. If you can distill the language into simpler terms, you'll be able to see how the deal will reward you and also what it will require of you. Once you have the pluses and minuses straight in your head, saying no (if necessary) will be a lot easier.

Frankly—and this advice might strike you as strange—accept it when people are not nice to you. I like it when people are not nice because they're easier to control. It's much more difficult to be tough with someone who is nice. If they're nasty, saying no is a cinch.

PART IV

Slices of the Billionaire's Life

I could continue giving you advice about how to think like a billionaire, but I've always felt that the best way to teach someone is by example. Following are some excellent examples of a billionaire's mind at work.

Columbia University

Last year I wrote a critical letter to Lee Bollinger, the president of Columbia University and the former president of the University of Michigan. As a committed real estate developer in New York City, I feel that it's my responsibility to look out for some of the cultural institutions in town, and Columbia University is one of New York City's greatest treasures. Part of Bollinger's mission is to expand the size of the university—not just its academic offerings but also its campus—and I couldn't agree with that mission more.

But it came to the attention of the real estate community that Bollinger was interested in buying up land in Harlem, the university's neighborhood. To my shock, Bollinger at that time controlled approximately forty percent of the seventeen acres he was looking for. Take a lesson from Bollinger's mistake: Never, never tip your hand about your desire to own something, particularly real estate, before you make a deal. You'll only end up paying through the nose. Bollinger will have to pay a premium on the remaining sixty percent of the property because the owners now know how much he wants it. That's simply bad business practice, and if I were on Columbia's board of trustees, I would tell Bollinger, "You're fired!"

Not only is this scenario an example of bad strategy, but Bollinger is also buying in the wrong location. Al Lerner, a close friend of mine who, sadly, passed away from cancer, was on Columbia's board for some time, and he had a fantastic vision. He thought Columbia should have occupied fifteen magnificent acres of unobstructed land from 59th to 62nd Streets fronting both West End Avenue and the Hudson River. It would have brought part of the Columbia campus into the heart of Manhattan and made the campus more accessible to New Yorkers. As it is now, Columbia is in a horrible location, and thanks to Bollinger, it will stay that way forever. Columbia deserves the best location, not the worst. By the way, I own the land that Columbia should be buying.

The United Nations Mess

Only an incompetent could create and continue the mess, or I should say *messes*, at the United Nations. Kofi Annan, the secretary general of the United Nations, has created a fiasco out of one of the world's most valuable institutions.

Let me give you some background on what's going on at the UN. Not so very long ago, I had a meeting with a high-ranking official of the United Nations regarding the possible renovation and restoration of the UN complex in New York City. After studying the details of the renovation, and with the constraint that there be no relocation of any employees during this reconstruction, I knew I could accomplish exactly what the United Nations wanted in two years and at the cost of $400 million. They had originally approached me because they could not believe I'd built Trump World Tower at the United Nations Plaza for only $300 million, but it was true. If you know what you're doing, you can get things done at the right price and the right way.

Then, without hearing from the United Nations on my proposal, I read that they had hired someone to do exactly what they had asked of me. This other party would renovate and restore the United

Nations complex but was demanding a seven-year completion schedule at the cost of $1.5 billion.

It does not take a genius to recognize the enormous difference in these proposals—several years and $1.5 billion, or $1.1 billion more than I would spend for a job that would not be as good as mine. It makes me wonder: Who is in charge at the United Nations? Could they be as incompetent in world affairs as they are at simple numbers? Does anyone else find this situation as alarming as I do?

While the fundamental premise of the United Nations is wonderful, perhaps we need to reevaluate its current function. It started out so well. What has happened? With these enormous oversights in the area of finance, perhaps we need to start worrying.

The Statue of Liberty

Paris has the Eiffel Tower, Rome has the Coliseum, and we've got the Statue of Liberty. To me, it's the icon of New York, and it moves me to see it up close, even to see photographs of it, and to think about what it symbolizes. I often imagine the boats full of immigrants who have sailed into New York Harbor with that amazing statue to greet them. It still stands proudly today.

Despite our sometimes strained political relations, we should not forget that this landmark was a gift from the country of France—the France of liberty, equality, and fraternity. The French recognized our quest as Americans and gave us this incredible symbol in appreciation for what America represents. I think that the recent divide between France and the United States is a tragedy. We would have felt as bad for them if the Eiffel Tower or La Defense had been destroyed as they felt for us when the Towers came down on September 11.

For one of the opening scenes for the second season of *The Apprentice,* Mark Burnett and his crew took me to the Statue of Liberty. As we approached Lady Liberty, I was taken back to my youth when I was told I was fortunate to be in America, that I had opportunities other people in the world could only dream about. And here

I am, a major player in the greatest city of this incredible country, and I realize once again how amazingly lucky I have been.

With the parents I had and this country as my backbone, anything was possible. I operated on that premise of possibility, and I'm walking, talking proof of the American Dream. For me, the American Dream is not just a dream; it's a reality.

Breakfast at the Waldorf

I like going to the Waldorf, especially when I'm receiving an award. Recently, the International Radio and Television Society had a breakfast for me, the casts from *Queer Eye for the Straight Guy* and *Sex and the City,* producer Michael Patrick King, Bob Schieffer of *Face the Nation,* and Herb Scannell of Nickelodeon Networks. Jeff Zucker of NBC was also there to announce that while it took five guys to save Bravo, it only took one—me—to save NBC. Then Bob Wright, chairman and CEO of NBC, took the stage to introduce me.

It was an honor to receive the award, because, as Bob Schieffer mentioned, we have a responsibility in the television and radio industry to try to make media intelligent. That's our approach with *The Apprentice,* and to be recognized for my contribution feels great. As our culture changes, so must our television, or it would lose relevance. In addition to providing entertainment, radio and television have increasingly become powerful tools for educational enlightenment. I keep this in mind for both my radio and my television programs.

As power breakfasts go, that one was up there with the best, and we all agreed to keep up the good work.

Ten Amazing Minutes

Steve Wynn recently called and told me he was about to bid on a great painting, a Vermeer. The auction was taking place at Sotheby's in London, and Steve asked me to listen in on the bidding process. It was very interesting, especially for someone like me who has never been a big buyer of paintings. Steve loves this Vermeer painting, and usually, what Steve wants, he gets.

The bidding began at $10 million and quickly escalated to $24 million when Steve entered the fray. People began to drop out, and finally, it was just Steve and one other bidder until Steve ended up winning at $30 million. It was a really amazing ten minutes, and Steve now has a painting by an artist whose work will probably never go to market again. I look forward to seeing it!

People Magazine and
What People Do

Ann Moore, the chairman and CEO of Time, Inc., invited me to speak to a *People* magazine management meeting—"to share a few secrets on your leadership success," as she put it. My speaking fee is typically $250,000, but because *People* magazine has always treated me well, I decided to do Ann a favor. I opened the lunch meeting with the observation that they'd left me out of their latest issue, "The 50 Most Beautiful People," but after setting that straight, we were off to a good time.

I began by discussing the power of the media. When Jean Georges, the wonderful restaurant in the Trump International Hotel and Tower, first opened, I told chef Jean-Georges Vongerichten that I absolutely hated the interior design and didn't even want to eat there because of it. He said, "Mr. Trump, I want people to notice the food, not the decor." I thought that was one of the greatest lines of pure bullshit I'd ever heard and told him so. Then *The New York Times* wrote an absolute rave review of the food, giving the restaurant its highest rating, and suddenly, I thought the room looked pretty good after all. The newspaper's analysis and praise of the restaurant completely changed my mind. That's power.

I continue to alienate members of the press on occasion, but on the whole, I like them. I know their jobs aren't easy. That day, facing a room of attractive and attentive publishing types, I mentioned that while they may be lovely young women and sharp-looking young men, they couldn't fool me. I know they're vicious. I deal with vicious people every day, but most of the time, they *look* vicious. These people appeared well polished, but I told them I know they're out to get me. The room laughed.

The media represents great power. As someone who has received a lot of attention from the media, I know that its power to make someone recognizable is unbelievable. I had always been relatively well known, but it was nothing compared to my fame now. Even six-year-olds walk up to me on the street and shout "You're fired!," and elderly men in their Rolls-Royces in Palm Beach will roll down their windows to yell at me as they drive by. I thought I was famous before, but I was wrong. *Now* I'm famous.

In order to comply with Ann's wish that this be a business meeting, I spent a few minutes talking about success—and gave the audience some advice on how to find it for themselves. Then, as I suspected, I discovered that the only thing they were interested in was *The Apprentice*. I don't mind answering these questions, but the level of interest always surprises me.

With this crowd, however, I also asked questions about the show. What did they like about it? Should I expand my inner circle of advisers? What task pertinent to magazine publishing would they come up with for the candidates? And so forth. One person asked me what had been the biggest surprise to me about the show. I answered that the biggest surprise had been the show's success. Ninety-five percent of new TV shows don't make it. Those aren't odds I like, and it's a good thing I didn't know that going in or I never would have signed on in the first place.

As I was discussing *The Apprentice,* I also mentioned that prior to the show's success, I remembered standing with Melania behind a guy who was also waiting to get into the NBC Upfront event at Lincoln Center last year. I mentioned to Melania that he was a great-looking guy. It turned out to be Rob Lowe. He also had a new TV show coming up, and I remembered thinking that I really didn't want to go up against someone who looked like that. I'd never make it. Unfortunately, his show didn't make it, and mine made it big. So you never know what will work.

I also told the audience that I thought certain kinds of people shouldn't be on *The Apprentice,* such as Sam and Omarosa, who were loose cannons as far as I was concerned—but that's part of the entertainment factor. If we'd had sixteen intelligent, polished, and productive people from the audience as candidates, it might not have been as interesting a mix. That's what Mark Burnett and his team do so well— they put together a group in which the common denominators may be intelligence and ambition, but with enough variety to be entertaining, and maybe create some sparks along the way. Disasters can be more interesting than smooth sailing. So much for my casting instincts, but these are things we learn along the way. If it were up to me, I'd choose sixteen supermodels—not good!

I ended the conversation by bringing the topic back to business. I mentioned that whomever I choose as the winner on *The Apprentice* will always be chosen from strictly a business, not an entertainment, viewpoint. I don't want someone who is entertaining; I want someone who knows what he or she is doing. After all, my own life is entertaining enough.

In Praise of Audacity

I agreed to give a speech in New York City to seven hundred people from Sanofi-Synthelabo, Inc., a pharmaceutical company, for Patti Giles. Patti is a terrific businesswoman, and she and the Sanofi group had all been at my Mar-a-Lago Club for a dinner a few months earlier, so I wanted to welcome them to my city.

I know from experience that this group is hardworking—I had invited some of the team to play golf with me at the Trump International Golf Club in Palm Beach, and they all declined. Every single one of them turned me down! However, I realized that these people had their priorities straight. They love their work, are responsible to the positions they hold, and are completely focused.

Over the course of my speech, I told them that if you can't dream about new products, they will never happen. I also pointed out how important it is to set their own standards. That will ensure that they remain innovators in their field. I already know how disciplined they are, so I am stressing their creativity and urging them to go against the tide.

In summing up, I told them what I've said before, but these are points worth repeating if you are intent on big success:

1. Think big.
2. Stay focused.
3. Be paranoid (keep your guard up).
4. Be passionate.
5. Don't ever give up.
6. Love what you are doing.

To be a winner, you must think like a winner. Try it. You'll be surprised. And before long, you might be thinking like a billionaire.

Pageants

As the saying goes, Miss America is the girl who lives next door. Miss USA is the girl you *wished* lived next door. To diversify my investments, I entered into a partnership for ownership and broadcast rights with the NBC network for the three largest beauty competitions in the world: the Miss Universe, Miss USA, and Miss Teen USA pageants.

Few people are aware of the large audience that pageants have worldwide or of the weight they carry internationally. Their value to the economies of the countries that host them is enormous, and the bidding for them is a competitive and serious business.

While millions around the world tune in each year to see a new titleholder crowned, few people realize just what the year entails for each young woman. All three (Miss USA, Miss Universe, and Miss Teen USA) become bona fide full-time employees of the Miss Universe Organization and immediately put their lives on hold for a year to relocate to New York. They all move into a three-bedroom luxury suite in my Trump Place development.

Whether or not you enjoy beauty pageants, they serve a purpose aside from the celebration of beautiful young women. The importance of good works is at the center of the pageantry, and these women are using their gifts in incredible ways. In that sense, the pageants provide an excellent lesson for everyone. Marco de la Cruz, who works as a motivational coach in Los Angeles, told me how impressed he was with the contestants of the Miss USA pageant after working with them for a few weeks. He said that what might be perceived as a sexist or narcissistic event was much more, due to the social conscience the contestants displayed. He felt the pageant was a form of empowerment for women. I agree. What they will all be able to accomplish after this pageant is staggering. The pageant already aids the Make-A-Wish Foundation, breast cancer research, and AIDS research, and each contestant devotes a serious amount of time to a specific cause. Marco also noted the steady progression of confidence developing in each young woman as the weeks progressed. All in all, a good score.

The ratings for the Miss USA pageant this year were the highest they have been in ten years. The event took place in the glamorous and beautiful city of Los Angeles, and the contestants visited Universal Studios, Santa Monica Pier, the *Queen Mary,* and Hollywood. The show itself was held at the Kodak Theatre, home of the Academy Awards, and was covered by Billy Bush and Nancy O'Dell for *Access Hollywood.* The afterparty and the lines to get in reminded me of Studio 54 in its heyday.

After Miss USA is crowned and the credits have rolled, she flies immediately to her new river-view Trump residence in New York, where she will spend her reign pursuing professional goals and making appearances on behalf of our charitable partners. No other pageant system in the world is set up this way. Every other beauty queen stays home until she's called to make an appearance. When not traveling around the world, our titleholders spend every week volunteering during the day and attending A-list events at night.

As Miss USA 2004, Shandi Finnessey is an official spokesperson for breast and ovarian cancer awareness. She will assist in raising millions of dollars on behalf of these organizations. The benchmark is enormously high, as Miss USA 2003, twenty-four-year-old Susie Castillo, helped raise $28 million for the same cause. Shandi happens to be a gorgeous blonde who is working toward her doctorate in counseling, and she is an advocate for mentally challenged children. Shandi has traveled to Korea with the USO to entertain troops and will travel later in the year to the Middle East.

When a woman becomes Miss Universe, her world is turned upside down. Before Jennifer Hawkins, Miss Universe 2004, left her home in Australia for the pageant in Quito, Ecuador, she was able to be in Sydney without being recognized. Now, having been featured on the cover of every magazine and newspaper Down Under, and having been the subject of several television shows, she has become an instant celebrity. In her new role as a spokesperson for HIV and AIDS awareness, Jennifer has been a moderator at the International AIDS Conference in Bangkok, and she will spend the year meeting world leaders focused on this terrible pandemic. She is also one of the most beautiful women I have ever seen.

Tami Farrell, the nineteen-year-old Miss Teen USA 2004, hails from a farm in Phoenix, Oregon. She has spent the year as an advocate for DARE! and other teen-related causes. Prior to the pageant, she had never left Oregon; now she has traveled all over the United States in addition to a first-class trip to London and Berlin.

When they are not globe-trotting, these three beauties are roommates, which can sometimes be more traumatic than the *Apprentice* apartment. Bill Rancic never had to worry about a misplaced $100,000 tiara.

The Mar-a-Lago Diet

You can't just think like a billionaire; you have to eat like one, too. Whether you have a world-class chef preparing all of your meals a simple hot plate, always remember: You are what you eat.

Gary Gregson, the executive chef of the Mar-a-Lago Club and the Trump International Golf Course, has worked for me for nine years, and he's one of the top chefs in the world. His job is to make sure that all of our guests eat well during their stay. The guests include national and local politicians, television personalities, movie stars, musicians, and the wealthiest of the wealthy. Gary's job is demanding, but he's an absolute pro.

Gary used to keep a list of all the notables who have been entertained at the Mar-a-Lago Club, but the list got too long. There are just too many people who want to experience Mar-a-Lago.

What keeps them coming back? Gary tells me that it's his food, and I'm inclined to believe him.

You may not believe me, but I keep to a somewhat strict diet—a diet that Gary invented for me. We call it the Mar-a-Lago Diet, and if I didn't adhere to it from time to time, my waistline would be an absolute disaster. I'll admit that I go for the occasional DT Burger, or ice cream, or pizza, but for the most part, I watch what I eat.

How do you go about getting started on the Mar-a-Lago Diet? Visiting the Mar-a-Lago Club is a good start, but you can also try it at home.

Gary developed the Mar-a-Lago Diet with me in mind. He tells me that it has a lot in common with some other popular diets out there right now, but the Mar-a-Lago Diet is more sustainable and far more realistic. And it works. A former Miss Universe who had gained some weight stayed at Mar-a-Lago, and after a couple of weeks she was back in pageant shape.

Gary believes it's ridiculous to think you can enjoy life without carbohydrates and sugar. Everyone's avoiding bread, pasta, rice, and potatoes these days. Next month people will probably be swearing off fruits and vegetables. You have to satisfy your appetite and stay balanced. It's as simple as that.

The Mar-a-Lago Diet is not what you can't eat but what you can—and should—eat to stay thin. Part of the Mar-a-Lago Diet is always fulfilling your cravings as they develop, as ridiculous as those cravings may be. Gary's motto may as well be: "Want caviar on your Dover sole? No worries! What about caviar on your scrambled eggs? Even better!"

Breakfast might consist of an egg-white omelet with spinach, tomatoes, and a little feta cheese, a small cup of tropical fruit, and a mimosa made with freshly squeezed orange juice.

Lunch could be a small portion of tilapia and steamed vegetables with fresh herbs and extra virgin olive oil, served with yogurt sauce on the side, iced tea with lemon, and fresh blueberries for dessert.

Dinner depends on whom you are dining with. If you're eating alone or with your spouse, you can cut back a bit. When you're dining with guests and friends, you should indulge a bit more. One of my favorite meals at Mar-a-Lago is lemongrass-infused salmon with scallion pancakes. I also enjoy the yellow-heirloom-tomato gazpacho, with summer squash, and lingonberry sorbet, which is out of this world. I tend to be a little more partial to meals that include Caesar salad, meat loaf, strip steak, or roast chicken, and you should adjust your diet based upon your own tastes.

With immediate family and close friends, there tend to be larger portions and multiple courses. Pan-seared foie gras with spiced pumpkin bread and wild Maine blueberries followed by mango soup with shallot flan is one of Gary's classics. He also serves Parmesan-crusted sea bass with celeriac potatoes, bok choi, and sauce beurre blanc. To finish the meal, even if you're on the Mar-a-Lago Diet, Gary often provides a selection of minuscule desserts or an incredible Grand Marnier soufflé.

If you're a drinker (which I'm not), enjoy a glass of fine wine, but don't overindulge in alcohol. It can be a high-calorie and dangerous habit.

I once asked Gary to tally up the food orders during the busiest part of Mar-a-Lago's season. Apparently, it's not unusual for the club to purchase one hundred pounds of Florida stone crab, forty pounds of fresh grade-A foie gras, twelve points of high-grade caviar (osetra, beluga, or sevruga), and four hundred pounds of sea bass—each week! And, of course, all of these foods work within the Mar-a-Lago Diet.

To summarize the Mar-a-Lago Diet:

1. It has to be served in a fantastic setting.
2. It has to look fantastic.
3. It has to taste incredible.
4. It cannot make you gain weight.

If you eat the best foods and watch your waistline, you'll begin to look and feel great in no time.

Saturday Night Live

One day in late March 2004, Jeff Zucker, the brilliant president of NBC, called to make an appointment to see me at my office. I knew something big must be up for him to pay a personal visit. He said, "I'd like to see you." So he arrived at my office and said, "Donald, do me a favor. Host *Saturday Night Live*."

I like and respect Jeff a great deal, and we'd been experiencing a tremendous success with *The Apprentice,* so I couldn't say no.

I'd like to say that I showed up a few hours before the show on Saturday, April 3, tried on some costumes, learned a few lines, and then did the show live with the help of the hilarious *Saturday Night Live* regulars. As with *The Apprentice,* that wasn't the case. It took up a few days of my time—a few days well worth it, as experiences go.

Saturday Night Live is a legendary show, and being asked to be the host was a great honor. Considering its twenty-nine-year history, I was walking into something big and something new to me: comedy skits, a monologue, a face-to-face with someone who imitates me for a living, a chicken number. Were they joking? Yes, and quite well.

Here's how the show came together that week:

PREPARATION

On Tuesday, I met with Lorne Michaels's terrific team of seventeen writers, led by Tina Fey. They pitched ideas and asked questions. We chatted for about one hour. How much could they get in one hour? Plenty, as it turned out.

On Wednesday, the writers had various sketches completed, which they presented to me in a series of read-throughs. Some of these writers have been at *SNL* for over a decade, five are new this year, and one was new that week. The job of an *SNL* writer is tough. There's no fooling around. Lorne Michaels and Marci Klein certainly know what they're doing.

After a variety of sketches were finished, they narrowed them down to approximately twelve skits considered viable for the show. This process took about three hours, and then I was free to go back to my office.

On Thursday, we read through the chosen sketches, where I interacted with members of the *SNL* team and got a feel for the format of the show.

On Friday, we had our first full day, which started at 1:30 P.M. and ended at 10:30 P.M. We blocked and did run-throughs of the skits on undressed sets on the *SNL* stage. That space is historic; it was originally Toscanini's recording studio and was built on springs to avoid the rumble of the subways underneath the NBC building. It has about seven thousand square feet of workable space, which isn't a lot, considering what the show accomplishes every week.

In the first skit, I played a hippie in a business meeting about the worldwide marketing of bongs. After three quick run-throughs, I realized that I was dreading having to wear the long blond wig they'd picked out for me. Luckily, this skit would be cut during dress rehearsal. I hate messing up my hair for any reason, even for *SNL*.

On the way to the next skit, I stopped and chatted with Greg

Tull, who has worked at *SNL* as head of props for twenty-five years. He's also a fellow graduate of the New York Military Academy. He reassured me when he told me I was doing a great job so far—a vote of confidence I trusted, as he's watched countless rehearsals over the years.

The second skit involved my so-called latest romance novel, *Erotic Moonlight Confessions*. The protagonist, Ronald Strump, lives in a famous skyscraper in the penthouse apartment with citywide views. Convinced it will be a bestseller, I happen to be the narrator. As it turned out, this favored sketch of mine (short and easy) would also be cut after dress rehearsal.

We took a short break, so I returned to my dressing room, passing the pretzel and potato chip bins, and made a few phone calls and checked in with the office. The very talented Jim Dowd of NBC showed up to give me a tour of the control room. I had gotten to know Jim while working on *The Apprentice*—he doesn't stop. *Saturday Night Live* is a big operation, and everyone involved is a pro.

Back on the set, Stone Phillips of *Dateline* stopped by to visit. He had been down at my Mar-a-Lago Club in Florida over the past weekend doing a story. Then Lorne Michaels came in to say hello. The set was buzzing with activity, and through the windows above the audience bleachers, we could see the NBC tour participants watching us. They waved and gave me the "You're fired!" gesture. Just what I needed: some votes of confidence. Fortunately, they hadn't seen enough yet to pass judgment, so I waved back.

Then I had some rehearsals, one with Finesse Mitchell for a lawyer-client skit that included the Harlem Globetrotters, and another with Darrell Hammond, the brilliant impersonator who can nail just about everyone from Bill Clinton to Regis Philbin to me. The skit was titled "The Prince and the Pauper," and it required a costume change mid-scene that the writers were still trying to nail down.

By then it was 6 P.M. and we were on dinner break. Jeff Richmond came in with a keyboard to go over some lyrics with me for the "Boardroom Band" scene. It only took about five minutes. Andrew, an accommodating page at *SNL,* brought in a steak for me from the Palm. It arrived with plastic utensils. I made a stab at it, but Andrew ran up to Lorne's office to find some silverware for me. I found some golf to watch on TV and relaxed for a while.

A bit later, I signed a dollar bill for the Friday Raffle, an *SNL* tradition. This raffle is a big event, announced by drumrolls on the set, and the crew tried to pull one on me by announcing my name as the winner. However, I already knew the buzz around there. It turned out that Lonnie in wardrobe was the winner.

So it was back to the set for the "Boardroom Band" scene, the most complicated scene for me, as I had to play the keyboard, sing, and remember some complex lines and lyrics. Where was Billy Joel when I needed him?

We did the "Chicken Wings" number (involving Trump's House of Wings), which seemed to be popular right from the start. I kept thinking, "How do I get myself into these things?" I had nixed the chicken outfit, but I did see a strange-looking yellow suit around the set, which had me worried.

We took a break, and Lorne visited me for a while. Carolyn Kepcher arrived to run through her scene. She was relieved to know her lines were limited. Scripts aren't her thing, either.

I went back out to practice the opening monologue. The monologue had to be the most difficult part of the show. I would come out onstage, address millions of people, and hope to be funny. I asked the set builders, "How'd I ever get into this? I should be building, like you. I can relate to you guys." We practiced the monologue a couple of times, with Darrell as my "understudy" and with Jimmy Fallon playing Jeff Zucker. We got some good laughs, and then we called it a night. It was already 11:00 P.M. by then.

THE LIVE SHOW

We had a 1 P.M. call, and I was there on time. Saturday would be another rehearsal on dressed sets and a semi–dress rehearsal. We made changes as we went along, so I had to play close attention all day long.

Not surprisingly, that pastel yellow suit showed up in my dressing room. I tried it on and asked myself a few questions—specifically, "What the hell am I doing here?" Chris Kelly, the stage manager, offered me the neon Chicken Wings sign for my office in Trump Tower as a souvenir. My memories would be vivid enough, but it was thoughtful of him.

We ran through the show, which included three encounters with Star Jones of the TV show *The View*. Star was played by Kenan Thompson. I also visited the set of *Live with Regis and Kelly*, as played by Darrell Hammond and Amy Poehler. I liked all the skits but realized that only certain ones would make the live show.

The *Saturday Night Live* setup is theatrical in concept: If the show works for a live audience of three hundred people, it will work for national TV. The dress rehearsal audience is the focus group for the live show. The skits with the best audience response remain in the live show; the others are cut. The dress rehearsal ran from 8 to 10 P.M., and the live show began at 11:30 P.M. Not until after the dress rehearsal would we know the content or the running order of the live show.

We had a dinner break, and I decided to visit the NBC canteen. What a great setup, with all kinds of entrées and salads and seven or eight desserts and puddings. I got some great chicken and mashed potatoes that I took back to my dressing room. Matthew Calamari came to visit and ended up joining me for dinner. George Ross and Carolyn Kepcher also arrived for dress rehearsal, so they visited for a while, too.

Steve Higgins of the *Saturday Night Live* team came in to go over some writing issues, as skits were still being fine-tuned. I heard the guest band, Toots and the Maytals, practicing out on the set. They sounded terrific, and I went out to listen to them for a while. My daughter Ivanka had told me how great they are, and she was right. The music relaxed me, and surprisingly, I was not at all nervous.

At that point, the fantastic Sharon Sinclair, a makeup artist, took me to get ready for the dress rehearsal, and by 8 P.M. the show had begun before a live audience. I had a few friends and colleagues there, so I knew that I could count on a few free laughs. One half hour of the show would be cut, and I was curious to see what would go and what would stay.

Unfortunately, some of my favorite skits were cut: the Finesse Mitchell tour de force, the audio version of my new romance novel, and a couple of close encounters with Star Jones, but all in all, it would still be a great show.

Melania, Don, Jr., Ivanka, Eric, John Myers, John Mack, and some of my best friends had arrived, and their presence was a big comfort, considering what I was about to do. Then the music started up, and it was showtime—live, this time, in front of the world.

The live show was an hour and a half long, a total whirlwind. We had small portable dressing areas set up on the set for fast changes, and an experienced team of dressers, led by Donna Richards, made sure I was ready for each scene. Did I ever think I'd be the star of a hit television series? No. Did I ever think I'd be the host of *SNL*? Not in a million years.

After the show, I signed some photos for the crew, including one that will hang in the hallowed halls of *Saturday Night Live* for all time. It was a night to remember. Both Lorne Michaels and Jeff Zucker seemed pleased with the show, and I thanked them for a wonderful experience.

We all left for the aftershow party. For the record—and this may *be* a record—I got home at 6 A.M. on Sunday. Just in time to get up and read my newspapers and start a new day . . . and to top it all, the ratings turned out to be great!

A Week in the Life

It's become a tradition for me to include a chapter in my books about a typical week in my life. Readers always tell me they like these sections the best, and I don't want to disappoint anyone. Here's a snapshot of this spring, before the second season of *The Apprentice* took over my life. There are some good examples buried within showing how I think about my time, my business, and the people who surround me.

MONDAY

8:30 A.M. I have a meeting with Matthew Calamari, executive vice president, and Norma Foerderer, vice president, about Trump Ice, my new bottled water, and about the YOU'RE FIRED! T-shirts, which we can't keep in stock due to high demand. As problems go, it's a nice one to have. After seeing the popularity of bottled water, I decided to join the competition with my own. It's certainly an interesting market.

During our meeting, Steve Riggio of Barnes & Noble calls in, so I talk to him for a while. He had ordered a huge quantity of my last book, *How to Get Rich,* and called to say he was glad he did. Steve and Len, his brother, have done a great job with Barnes & Noble.

9:00 A.M.   I do a short video in the conference room for Rich Handler's son, Max. It's for a school project. Afterward, he comes into my office, and we give him a tour. I hope he gets a good report card. He will be a winner.

9:15 A.M.   We have a Trump Tower board meeting in the large conference room. Larry Twill is present, as is Sonja Talesnik from my staff, among others. These meetings are important to me, and I never neglect them. That's Lesson Number One in property management. We cover a lot of territory at these meetings: the operations of the buildings—personnel, security, maintenance, construction—as well as the ongoing sales and leasing status of the units. Eric Sacher, of my accounting department, prepares a financial status report of the building, and we discuss improvements and upgrades, such as renovations of hallways and anything that will provide our tenants with the best surroundings.

10:00 A.M.   I call Paul Spengler, of Pebble Beach, to talk about stone walls. Paul's a great guy and full of good advice.

10:15 A.M.   Rhona comes in to tell me that Chris Matthews is ready for our scheduled interview. We're both on time, and it's done quickly and efficiently. Chris is the kind of guy I like playing hardball with.

10:45 A.M.   We all watch Don, Jr., on CNN/Finance. He mentions how he's the original apprentice, and how his interest in our business and working with me have been a natural progression for him. He comes across as focused and intelligent, which he is, and mentions how much he's enjoyed overseeing the redevelopment of Trump Park Avenue. He's done a great job, I might add. This building is the former Delmonico Hotel, a famed hotel that once hosted Ed Sullivan and the Beatles. It's not only beautiful but historic as well.

11:00 A.M. I make and take calls from Scott Butera, Jon Tutolo of Trump Model Management, and Ashley Cooper of Trump National Golf Club in Bedminster, New Jersey. They have positive updates for me, so it's smooth sailing so far. I also take calls from Tony Veneziano, Ray Royce, Jay Neveloff, and Phil Ruffin. These guys all get to the point quickly. It's a pleasure doing business with them.

11:45 A.M. My development team comes in for a meeting, which includes Charlie Reiss, Don, Jr., Russell Flicker, and Jill Cremer. We spend a few moments congratulating Russell on the birth of his daughter Molly over the weekend. Being a father is a great honor, and I'm happy for him. My team is on target on their projects, and Canouan Island is going to be a piece of paradise in no time. Canouan is off the island of Mustique, and it will be the new definition of the word "elite."

Canouan Island was brought to my attention by this team, and it will not only rival Bali in beauty and amenities, it will be much more accessible. We will have an eighteen-hole championship golf course, designed by Jim Fazio and Trump Island Villas, that will consist of luxury villas and estate properties set on one thousand acres of lush mountainous terrain overlooking the ocean. It will also have a European-style casino, Trump Club Privee. This island will be my first venture in the Caribbean, and we are all excited about it.

12:30 P.M. I take a call from Paula Shugart about the upcoming Miss Universe pageant in Quito, Ecuador. This event will be big, and we're going over all the details. The Miss USA pageant broke records this year, and we expect the Miss Universe contest to do even better. People couldn't believe I actually went into the beauty pageant business to make money, but it turns out I have, and we've had great success with them. Beautiful women can be a great attraction.

I ask Rhona to order some pizza for lunch, and I call Regis Philbin to chat. I also spend some time reviewing some reports on my properties. Since the final episode of the first season of *The Apprentice*, I've actually had time to devote myself fully to my properties. I like being a TV star, but I'm a builder at heart and always will be. I told Katie Couric on a recent appearance on the *Today* show that she wouldn't have to see me again for a few months, after I nearly became a regular on their morning lineup. I began calling the *Today* show the *Yesterday, Today, and Tomorrow* show to my staff.

1:00 P.M. I call Mike van der Goes, director of Trump National Golf Course in Los Angeles, for an update. This course is becoming an unbelievable beauty, thanks to Pete Dye's expertise and Mike's daily care. I visited recently on a trip to Los Angeles and can't wait to play when the course opens.

A friend calls in who had recently visited Paris and went to the Lido. In the show, an airplane arrives as a special effect, and the French people seated at the next table exclaimed, "Regardez! Doe-nald Trump est arrivé!" and then proceeded to discuss *The Apprentice*. Apparently, they receive tapes of the episodes from American friends. Guess I'm world-famous.

I get a call about the *Apprentice* sign that had hung in front of Trump Tower until the final episode. It's no longer there, but it caused some media attention, as the city almost fined me for it. The amount of money and tourism *The Apprentice* has generated for the city of New York doesn't seem to matter to city officials. Should I be surprised?

I call Melania to see what time I need to be ready tonight. We're going to the Costume Ball at the Metropolitan Museum of Art, which is a fabulous event in New York City, especially since I don't have to wear a costume. This reminds me of something, and I call Anna Wintour at *Vogue* magazine. She is fantastic!

1:30 P.M.   I call Carolyn Kepcher for an update on activities at Trump National Golf Club at Briarcliff Manor. It should be a great season. Even with all her *Apprentice*-related duties, she's remained as effective and efficient as ever as an executive vice president. She could be categorized as a wonder woman, considering her executive activities, being a regular on a hit TV series, and being the mother of two children. She handles it all.

I take a call from Paul Davis, CEO at Trump Place. He's another gem. He has an enormous property to watch over, and with his amazing talent, I can be assured it's in good hands. This property is not only a property to me but a community. Visit the pier sometime at twilight, and you will have yourself a New York experience to remember.

I go over the lyric sheets for the Katie Couric benefit aboard the *Queen Mary 2* coming up in New York City. I'll be accompanied by Harry Connick, Jr. Since I've already done some singing on *Saturday Night Live,* this event shouldn't be too hard. It should be a great night. I hope Harry can keep up with me. However, according to this script, he fires me. Life, as we all know, isn't fair.

Jay Bienstock and Kevin Harris of Mark Burnett Productions are back in town. They come in to review assignments for the second season of *The Apprentice*. I can't discuss these with you now, but it looks like we're in for another exciting series. I have a comfortable rapport with all of Mark's people, and it's a productive meeting. We'll be shooting an intro scene at the Statue of Liberty next week, provided we can get clearance in these days of heightened security.

2:30 P.M. I return several calls that came in during the meeting. We are still debating which ballroom chair design we will use out at Palos Verdes, home of Trump National Golf Club/Los Angeles, and several chairs have been brought in and lined up in my office to view and think about. There's a spectacular ballroom at the clubhouse for formal events. I'll keep the chairs in my office for a few days to see how they "sit" with me. The wrong chairs will ruin the entire room. In fact, I'd better see a few more, and I ask that a total of eight styles be brought in. This ballroom has apparently become the number one choice for weddings, and it is booked far, far in advance.

Norma keeps my calendar straight, which has become an even greater challenge these days than ever before. She comes in to update me about the week's important events, board meetings, and so forth. She also tells me of humorous calls. This morning we had an Al Pacino impersonator call to talk to me, a call that almost got to my office until "Al" asked one of my assistants for her phone number. And we received another check for $250,000 from someone who will pay to work here, a phenomenon that has occurred several times in the past few months. If we thought we received a lot of mail and calls before *The Apprentice,* we were right, we did. But we now have ten times that amount, and we are doing our best to keep up with it. However, if it takes a longer time to hear back from us, you'll know why.

3:00 P.M. Jason Greenblatt comes in to go over a few things, and Bernie Diamond, general counsel, comes in to discuss licensing issues. My legal team is kept extremely busy, and they are conscientious about keeping me informed. Even George Ross, with his commitment of time to *The Apprentice,* has managed to keep up with all the new developments we've encountered as we deal with territory more familiar to a production company than a property management organization. I think we've all enjoyed the new challenges, and no one here can ever complain of boredom.

Dan Roth of *Fortune* magazine calls in to discuss the positive buzz his cover article about me has generated. The article is titled "The Trophy Life: You Think Donald Trump's Hit Reality Show Is a Circus? Spend a Few Weeks Watching Him Work." People are always surprised at how hard I work, which I have to say surprises me, because I don't consider it work—but rather fun.

3:30 P.M. Jeff Zucker of NBC calls, and we discuss the incredible ratings the final episode of *The Apprentice* generated. Close to forty-one million viewers watched. These were stunning numbers for a new show or an old show, and I'm proud of that. If I'm going to do something, no matter what it is, I want it to be great. There have been nearly one million applications received for the second season of *The Apprentice,* which is close to five times more than for the first season. NBC and I are looking forward to the new season.

A reporter calls in to verify that on *Larry King Live* I offered to pay for Troy's education. Troy was on *The Apprentice* and has a lot of smarts but not much formal education. He is a good example of someone who deserves the best, which includes great schooling. Guys like Troy make America great.

3:45 P.M. The next call is a good one. This contractor is so full of it that I hang up on him. Until he comes to his senses, which I think will take at least a few days, considering what I've just heard, I won't be taking his calls. Instead, I call Ron Baron for some levity.

4:00 P.M. My pilot, Mike Donovan, calls in. The most important thing to consider when you have your own 727 is the right pilot to go with it, and I have been very lucky to have Mike.

What is it about Mondays? Here's another contractor who is totally out of his mind. If today were April Fool's Day, I could manage these idiot calls, but it isn't, and this next call also gets a well-deserved slam into the receiver.

Costas Kondylis, a man with brains and elegance, calls, which is a relief from the last few phone calls. We go over some details and discuss the impending Olympics in Athens. Costas is from Greece and has great insights into Greek culture. One reason I like to read Greek philosophers, as I mentioned in my last book, is because of Costas's influence.

I call Tiffany in California. I saw her recently when I attended the Miss USA pageant at the Kodak Theatre in Hollywood. Rick and Kathy Hilton also attended with us, as did Roberto del Hoyo of the Beverly Hills Hotel.

John Spitalny of Bear Stearns calls. We play golf together and enjoy discussing a lot of different things. John gives finance another dimension entirely when he starts in on something. He's an example of someone who applies comprehensive knowledge to specific scenarios. He's an expert of the highest level. He keeps an open mind to everything, and if you ask him a question, he'll find a way to answer you on the level you can relate to most readily.

I call John Stark, another great guy, and take a call from Joe Cinque of the Five Star Diamond Hospitality Awards. We discuss one of our favorite places, the Beverly Hills Hotel, and what makes it so special, which is basically everything. It's a full and total class act. Joe is adamant in his praise for my Mar-a-Lago Club in Palm Beach, which is fine with me. We discuss the new ballroom at Mar-a-Lago, which is close to being finished.

We also discuss the fact that our receptionist at the Trump Organization, Georgette Malone, has returned today after recovering from a vicious attack by a pit bull. Doctors were able to save her fingers and hands, but it's been a long process. We are all happy to have her back in almost one piece. Allow me a few words of advice: Don't keep pit bulls for pets. After seeing what happened to Georgette, I will never forget it, and neither will any of us here.

I take a few calls regarding different properties, and then talk to Elaine Diratz about events at the Trump World Tower. Since people saw the penthouse on an episode of *The Apprentice,* this building has become a hot property. There's a huge waiting list of people wanting to buy!

Tom Downing, general manager of Trump International Hotel and Tower, calls in. Tom was also featured on *The Apprentice* in the semifinal round of interviews, and he's an important member of our organization. We'll be filming a task assignment for the upcoming season of *The Apprentice* at Jean Georges, the restaurant is located in the hotel. Running a great hotel is demanding, but under Tom's leadership, the hotel has been consistently lauded by critics and guests.

4:30 P.M. Allen Weisselberg, my CFO, comes in for a meeting, and then I show him some carpet swatches and ask his opinion. I like to get as many opinions as I can before making a decision. I also ask him about the chairs I'm considering. Rhona comes in, and I ask her opinion as well. These chairs aren't quite right, and I realize that I'll have to ask to see some more.

5:00 P.M.   I review some photographs of developments and read a pile of faxes that have come in. We have several fax machines, and they never stop. Then I review a stack of letters. I like to read the ones from students. Some schools have written about each episode of *The Apprentice* and what they have learned from it.

In one class in Illinois, Troy is the most popular candidate, followed by Kwame, and they think New York City looks like a lot of fun. They have sent in twenty-eight handwritten reviews, and while I may not agree with everything they say, I will say I admire their penmanship. I cannot respond to all of them except to thank them for their time and thoughtful comments.

5:30 P.M.   I sign a book for Alex Rodriguez, better known as A-Rod, when he comes to our offices for a visit. I take him around and enjoy seeing the surprised expressions on everyone's faces. We peek into a meeting in the large conference room, and everyone does a double take. He's hard to miss, and it's a great way to end a Monday. I had met A-Rod before, as he is looking at an apartment in Trump Park Avenue. He is a great guy and a great player.

6:00 P.M.   Robin tells me that one of the crazy contractors I spoke to earlier has called back yet again. They can all forget about it today. Enough is enough. I take some faxes and documents and head upstairs.

TUESDAY

8:45 A.M.   I have a meeting with Steve Kantor of Credit Suisse First Boston and Brian Harris, Peter Smith, and Matthew Kirsch of UBS. I like these guys, and our meetings are never a problem. I've always gotten along with bankers, and I appreciate their perspective. People sometimes ask me about the best way to deal with bankers. I always tell them to give them the respect they deserve. That's the best way.

9:30 A.M.   I have a Diet Coke and read an article wherein I am called "the Elvis of Business." I'll take it as a compliment. Rhona comes in to give me my messages, and I ask her to return some calls.

I look over some photos from the final episode of *The Apprentice* and from the party we had here at Trump Tower afterward. It was a media circus, but we all had fun. I never thought it would take one hour to walk a hundred feet, but it did. My beautiful sister Maryanne attended but could take only about fifteen minutes of it before slipping out. I find a great photo of her with Norma. I ask Rhona to send it to her.

10:00 A.M.   We watch Mike van der Goes, director of Trump National Golf Course/Los Angeles, being interviewed on Fox TV about his job having been offered as one of two choices for *The Apprentice* finalist. Mike had been advised of this possibility, and I have to say I was relieved when Bill Rancic chose the Chicago tower as his project, since Mike is doing such a great job. He also gave a terrific live interview. Fortunately, Mike has many qualifications, including being an accomplished golfer, so we would have been able to find a suitable position for him within our organization without any problem. Versatility is always a benefit for everyone, but we're glad Mike is where he is.

Helmut Schroeder, who manages some properties for me in New Jersey, comes in for a visit, so we chat for a while, and Robin comes in to advise me that Paula Shugart and our new Miss USA, Shandi Finnessey, of Missouri, are here to see me. I'd picked Shandi as my first choice during the pageant in Los Angeles, and I was right. She's a beauty.

Tom Barrack calls in. Tom is one of the smartest real estate investors in the United States. He is looking to invest in my ninety-story building in Chicago. He heads the Colony Capital Fund, and I built a building at 610 Park Avenue with Tom. It's been a terrific success. Not only is Tom a brilliant investor, he is also a great friend.

10:30 A.M. Our mysterious Al Pacino impersonator calls in again. Whoever he is, he's pretty good, but not good enough. We finally get rid of him. I really doubt that Al Pacino is anxious to apply as a candidate for *The Apprentice*. We call Al's office and let them know someone is impersonating him.

11:00 A.M. Norma comes in to advise me of the funeral service for Estée Lauder, who recently passed on. She was one of the most remarkable people I have ever known, and I am sorry she's gone. She left a beautiful heritage, and she will never be forgotten. Her "little business," as she referred to the cosmetics line she founded, controls forty-five percent of the cosmetics market in U.S. department stores. She had an idea and went with it. She was one of the great salespeople of all time and a great example for all businesspeople.

Steve Florio of Condé Nast calls, and then I watch the cut of the new commercial I filmed last week for Visa. It gets a big laugh from my staff. I hope the TV audience likes it as much as they do. At first I thought it might not be so good for my image to be seen in a Dumpster scrounging around for my credit card, but I like to expand my range whenever possible, and fortunately, this is only a role. I do, however, think Visa is a great card to have, or I wouldn't endorse it, especially at this extreme.

I take a call from Random House about my new book and tell them I've been able to find the time to work on it. I like writing books, and if I like something, I can find the time for it. They seem to take my word for it, considering I've got a good sales record. We had two book signings last week, at Grand Central and at the Borders on Wall Street. The turnout was amazing. I enjoyed meeting the people who showed up.

11:30 A.M.   You'd think it was still Monday, since another contractor just called me. If you think I make up this stuff about them, you're wrong. And I'm not out to get them. It's just that facts are facts, and what they present me is another story entirely. I cool down before I blow up by looking out the window and wondering whether I should call Darrell Hammond of *Saturday Night Live* to fill in for me for a while.

Kevin Harris comes up to take me down to the set for the new season of *The Apprentice*. The boardroom was left intact, but the living quarters have been redone. It looks terrific.

12:00 noon.   I go with Brian Baudreau to a meeting at Trump World Tower at the UN Plaza. We also go to the sales office and meet with Elaine Diratz. I absolutely love this building. Once I walked all the way up—ninety floors—just to get the feel of it when it was completed. That wasn't an unusual occurrence with my buildings—it happens from time to time.

Brian, who has been with me for seventeen years, will be moving to Las Vegas this summer to be the owner's representative for my new tower there. Brian has been with me long enough to have a terrific eye and insights into everything and everyone, and I'm pleased to make him an executive.

1:00 P.M.   Back in the office, I see Robin eating a great-looking chef's salad from the Trump Food Court downstairs and ask her to order one for me. I start returning calls that came in from my daughter Ivanka, Rick Hilton, and others. Next month is an important event: Ivanka will be graduating from Wharton. Someone once commented that while getting into Wharton isn't easy, getting out is even harder. She got great marks, and I am extremely proud of her.

1:30 P.M. I take a call from Bob Wright. We're on for dinner next week with his beautiful wife, Suzanne. I feel lucky to enjoy the people I do business with, and Bob's a perfect example. We discuss Jeff Zucker's comment in *The New York Times:* "It turns out that the next *Friends* was not a half-hour scripted comedy. It was *The Apprentice.*"

I take a call from Mark Burnett to review the possible task assignments that have been developed so far for the new season of *The Apprentice.* I've learned that some ideas sound great but don't translate too well onto the screen. For example, writing a presentation might seem like a good assignment until you realize it's passive, there's not enough action, and it would be boring to film and for the audience to watch. Since we are filming in an exciting place like New York City, locations are also important considerations. The details are myriad concerning this show.

2:00 P.M. Don, Jr., and Andy Weiss come in for a meeting. They make a good team, and they're both great workers. I'm not sure which of the two has the messiest office, though; it could be a tie.

Laura Cordovano calls in from Trump Park Avenue sales. All is going well there, and I decide to call Susan James at the Trump International Hotel and Tower sales office. I like to check up on every property myself. Sounds like smooth sailing all around. Great properties can make life in the real estate industry a lot more fun for everyone involved. Great markets aren't bad, either.

Bernd Lembke of the Mar-a-Lago Club calls to brief me about the ballroom proceedings and other work being done on that property. We discuss the moldings around the mirrors, and I'll check them out for myself next weekend.

2:30 P.M. Verne Gay, the television critic of *Newsday,* calls. In one of his stories, he said amazingly nice things about me, including the fact that I'm "the greatest star in the history of reality TV."

Boxing promoter Don King calls. Don is a real character whom I have known for a long time. He is a big believer in "the look," and every time he sees me, he starts shouting, with his magnificent voice, "Don, you have the look! You have the look!" Well, I agree that Don also has "the look." The look certainly does mean something!

I speak to Herbert Muschamp of *The New York Times,* who is doing a review of one of my buildings. Herbert has been very nice to me over the years, and I hope he continues to be, but regardless, he is a truly talented architecture critic and a really great guy.

3:00 P.M. Bill Rancic, winner of the first season of *The Apprentice,* is here to visit. My staff greets him warmly, and he makes the rounds of the office to meet all of his new colleagues. I think he'll fit in nicely, and we're happy to have him aboard. We have a meeting in my office with Charlie Reiss, Russell Flicker, and Don, Jr.; Charlie oversees the Trump Tower Chicago development. Bill is handling everything well and does not seem to be daunted by the heavy pressure to do a good job. I have to say, his focus is impressive, and I hope it stays that way.

3:45 P.M. I make a call to my good friend John Myers of GE. His son was wounded in Iraq, and I want to know how he is doing.

John Burke and Scott Butera come in for a meeting, and we are interrupted by a fire drill. Since September 11, I find that people no longer complain very much about the once-inconvenient fire drills. They're very important. John is an executive vice president and treasurer, and Scott is the director of corporate finance and strategic development. Scott is a great young talent who will soon be heading the casino company. We discuss casino operations and refinancing, specifically the Credit Suisse First Boston investment in the proposed recapitalization of the casino companies. It is very interesting.

4:30 P.M. Robert Morgenthau, one of the greatest of the greats, calls. His dedicated work for the Police Athletic League has been ongoing for forty years now, and he is one of the most respected prosecutors in the history of the American justice system. We will be honoring him at the annual PAL Superstar Dinner at the Pierre Hotel in June, and I am pleased to be the chairman of this event. We are looking to raise $1.7 million for PAL, a record. Bill Clinton will be the presenter.

Bill Carter of *The New York Times* calls to ask me questions about *The Apprentice*. Bill is a very talented and respected television reporter who was the first to point out that it was not merely the success of *The Apprentice* on Thursday nights that was so impressive, but in particular its tremendous success when it was rerun on Wednesday nights and many times on CNBC. Bill felt that without all of these weekly reruns, the numbers on Thursday nights would have been even better, if that is possible.

Rick Reilly of *Sports Illustrated* calls, but I don't take his call. I've heard some negative reviews of Rick Reilly's reporting, and after reading his chapter on me in his book *Who's Your Caddy?*, I would have to say I agree with the critics. I totally disagreed with many of

Reilly's statements in the chapter on me, and the claim that I go around calling people "baby" is just ridiculous. The rest is too trivial to mention, but even though Rick, for the purpose of his book, was supposed to be my caddy, I talked him into a match with me. Rick is a good golfer, a five handicap, but he had a bad day. We played with no strokes, and at the end of nine holes he was nine down, and at the end of eighteen holes he was fourteen down. Rick told me it was the worst beating he had ever had, and I told him there was no way he would mention this in his book. He said, "No, Donald, I will indeed mention it. I got creamed." I again reiterated that "you will never say how badly you lost." In the end, he made reference to losing but nothing like what really happened that day. Only the caddies and my staff know for sure. Well, at least Rick said that Trump National Golf Club in Westchester is a great course. I have a feeling I won't be playing with Rick again.

During the course of our round, Reilly spent a lot of time talking about *Sports Illustrated,* ESPN, and his new contract. I thought he was playing one against the other. I told him he should stay with *Sports Illustrated* out of loyalty. I said, "Don't be a pig, and stay with the people that got you there—it's a little thing called loyalty." He ended up signing with *Sports Illustrated.*

I decide to take a walk down the hall and visit Jeff McConney and Eric Sacher. On the way, I see George Ross, so we have a short conversation and he tells me that eating lunch downstairs at the Trump Grill can sometimes be a lively event now that people recognize him from the show. George can handle it, and sometimes he even smiles at people.

I receive a copy of an article by writer and editor Patricia Baldwin, who interviewed me for *Private Clubs* magazine. She begins the article with a quote from baseball Hall of Famer Dizzy Dean: "It ain't braggin' if you can back it up." Her conclusion: I'm not a braggart, just incredibly good at my job. Patricia spent a day with me while I visited my golf course in Palos Verdes, California.

5:15 P.M.　I take a look around my office and realize I should try to downsize some of the piles of paper, so Norma comes in and we start sorting and sifting. We end up with shorter piles, but more of them. It's a start. I can actually see people on the other side of my desk now. Norma tells me that since her appearance on the show, people have stopped her on the street and in restaurants, and even on the bus, for an autograph. Our lives have definitely changed.

I get a call from Bob Kraft, who owns the New England Patriots. When Bob bought the Patriots, they were a disaster, and now they're the best team in football and the Super Bowl champions. Bob is an extraordinary man who has done an extraordinary job, and he has the best quarterback in football, Tom Brady, who is also a friend of mine.

I review the faxes of the afternoon, decide whether or not I have time to accept public speaking engagements, and look through photographs for a magazine request. Considering that taping for the new season of *The Apprentice* will start up in less than ten days, we have to be careful about the time I have for activities not directly involved with my business at the Trump Organization. I'm not playing hard to get; I just have to keep my priorities in order. Norma knows how to handle my schedule and decline invitations thoughtfully, and that's one reason why she's a great gatekeeper.

My son Eric calls. He'll be attending Ivanka's graduation next month, along with everyone else in the family.

6:00 P.M.   Jay Bienstock and Kevin Harris come by to go over some more ideas for the *Apprentice* tasks. This step is an important part of the show, and I like being actively involved with the decisions. Also, it helps that I am a native New Yorker and know the territory well. We spend an hour or so going over a lot of details and thinking through a few possibilities.

7:00 P.M.   George Steinbrenner calls. No matter who I might be with, if they hear George is on the phone they are impressed—he is a true winner, and he is always like a jolt of adrenalin. I love George and his winning way!

I'm ready for a busy night in New York City, so I call it a day and go home.

WEDNESDAY

8:00 A.M.   I decided to come down a little early today to catch up on some of my mail. Here's a letter from a high school student in Wichita, Kansas, who writes: "Although your story of business success is inspiring, I have another, more unusual reason for making you my hero: You live richly. Although it may sound strange, I'm tired of the people that truly do something to earn their fortune sitting around on it without using it. Finally, in you we have found a man that lives richly." That's a nice comment though actually, I lead a much more simple life than people would believe—but I don't want to disappoint this young man.

Here's a letter from a guy who remembers my father helping him change a flat tire when he was a young man in Queens. He now makes documentary films and wrote to tell me he will never forget my father's kindness. Neither will I.

8:15 A.M. My first phone call comes in, from Paul Spengler of Pebble Beach. It's 5:15 in the morning in California, and he's already up and at it. My kind of guy!

Norma comes in to tell me of her meeting with Random House about the three-book gift set being planned for the Christmas holidays. We have to think ahead these days.

Richard LeFrak comes in to view the construction on his building from my office, which directly faces it. The curtain wall he is erecting now looks perfect. He's another guy I like doing business with, and our meetings are always lively and fun. Richard mentions that my office seems a little cluttered, so I show him Norma's office and our small conference room, both of which are completely covered with bins of fan mail, proposals, and letters that we haven't been able to get to yet. We've been receiving up to twenty bins of mail a day, and we've had to hire six people just to sort it all. So I start a little earlier each day, as do a lot of us here. In showing Richard our offices and what's been happening here, I notice most people are already here, and our day doesn't officially start until 9 A.M. We're all trying to keep up.

8:45 A.M. I go downstairs with Richard to show him the set and living quarters of *The Apprentice*. The new *Apprentice* candidates are due to arrive in under a week, and it's looking good.

9:15 A.M. The calls have begun, so I begin to return them. Jerry Schraeger, Tom Bennison, Lee Rinker. Lee is the golf pro at Trump International Golf Club in Palm Beach, and I enjoy talking about the game with him. He's explaining how a winner's strategy will include losing, and the greats will have a contingency plan close at hand. There's a reason golf is known as a brain game.

9:45 A.M.   Rhona comes in to remind me that I have a lunch with Steve Florio at the Four Seasons today. Seldom do I go out to lunch, but Steve is a friend and the former president and CEO of Condé Nast publications (and I like the guy a lot). Going to the Four Seasons with Steve is always fun and interesting. We cover a lot of territory when we get together, from cross-promoting to publishing to fragrances. Steve is up on everything and has worked with one of the most interesting and brilliant men in business today, S. I. Newhouse.

Jim Dowd of NBC calls to chat. After the media blitz of the past few weeks, we feel like we are having a mini-vacation from each other. Jim is one of those people who is extremely efficient yet easy to work with. An ideal business associate.

Matthew Calamari and his brother Mike come in for a meeting, and I ask Andy Weiss and Don, Jr., to join us. We are still fine-tuning Trump Park Avenue. Putting up the front entrance canopy is a big deal if you're on Park Avenue, and we are using a steel reinforced structure. A work of beauty deserves our total attention, and this building, which has turned out to be a great success, gets it.

10:30 A.M.   Melania calls to see if we are still on for the Broadway opening of *Bombay Dreams* coming up in a couple of weeks. We are, and we've decided to go to Da Silvano, a great Italian restaurant in the Village, afterward for dinner. We try to plan ahead as much as possible.

Jason Binn, the publisher of *Gotham,* calls, and we discuss what's happening on both coasts. Then I read a thank-you note from Mark Cuban regarding his show *The Benefactor.* This note was published on the Web. He mentions that "our encounters proved to be a reality check for me" because he realized he would never want to be like me. But then, I ask myself, why did he buy an apartment in one of my buildings with my name on it? I think it's strange that he's trying to take me on just to get some publicity for his show, but he's actually a nice guy and I hope his show will be more successful than his basketball team. Besides, he has no chance of beating *The Apprentice*.

Kevin Harris comes in for a meeting about my schedule during the second season of *The Apprentice*. I have another week "off," and then it all begins again. I tell Kevin he's a real pain in the ass but I've gotten used to him. He's also gotten used to me, so I can tell him that. He laughs and leaves.

11:15 A.M. Jeff McConney comes in to go over some license issues, followed by Eric Sacher, who updates me on the financials of Trump Model Management. Then I ask Bernie Diamond to come in to review a list of projects, followed by Nathan Nelson, who gives me the latest on our commercial leasing. These guys stay on top of things and are fast at giving me what I need to know. Allen Weisselberg, chief financial officer, comes in to go over sales and acquisition of properties, and we do a general overview. Allen has been with me for thirty years and knows how to get things done. Then Jason Greenblatt briefs me on *The Apprentice*. Six important meetings in forty-five minutes isn't a record, but it's a good indication of how we operate here.

12:00 noon. I call Mark Burnett and we go over a few things. Just because we had one successful season doesn't mean we can take it easy. We are talking about the dynamics of the boardroom scenes, which were the highlight of our episodes so far. We are wondering whether we should expand them or keep them tight and fast like last season. We decide to see how they play out naturally, and take it from there. It's a realistic approach. Mark is an amazing guy, a good friend, and a true visionary. He said my first book, *The Art of the Deal*, had a great influence on him, and here I am, writing a book sixteen years later and mentioning him—the American Dream!

Anyway, back to our boardroom scenes: Sometimes I schedule an hour for a meeting and find it takes no more than ten minutes. Or just the opposite, it will take two hours instead of one. Some things can't be predicted, and as the show is unscripted, that's part of the excitement. Mark's a busy guy, too, and we connect quickly on every issue. He keeps his momentum going, much like I do, which I think is a common denominator in successful people.

Jeff Zucker calls in and we discuss the ratings. This year, ABC had the Academy Awards, CBS had the Super Bowl, and NBC had *The Apprentice*. It is still hard to believe that *The Apprentice* is one of the most successful shows in television history.

I take a call regarding the announcement of my syndicated radio show on Clear Channel, which is to begin in the fall. I've always enjoyed radio programs and have been almost a regular on Howard Stern's and Don Imus's shows over the years. This will be something new and another challenge. I'm looking forward to it. To find time in my schedule, Clear Channel has agreed to record my programs in my office on a weekly basis. I read so many papers and magazines each week that I will never be at a loss for topics, and I will choose to talk about whatever interests me that week. It will be a form of public speaking without the hassle of travel. The sixty-to-ninety-second daily pieces will soon turn out to be the biggest launch of a new show in the history of radio—which is really cool.

12:30 P.M.   I decide to go over to Trump Place on the Hudson River. New York City can be so spectacular in the spring. I can't think of a more beautiful place than this today. Even the river is sparkling. Paul

Davis escorts me around, and the work is going terrifically. Waiting for twenty years to see something come to fruition definitely adds an aura to a project.

1:45 P.M. Back in the office, I begin returning calls and ask for lunch from the new Trump Grill, which is fast becoming one of the best and most popular restaurants in New York. Norma comes in to go over some upcoming events and business proposals. One lady has written in to ask that I pay for her breast implants, to go along with my credo to "think big." Just when you think you've heard them all!

2:15 P.M. I have a meeting with architect Andrew Tesoro and Andy Weiss regarding the new clubhouse I am building at Trump National Golf Club at Briarcliff Manor. We call Carolyn Kepcher to discuss a few things.

2:45 P.M. Steve Wynn of Las Vegas calls. He'll be in New York next week, and we will catch up. He's been interested in *The Apprentice,* so I tell him a bit about the new season.

Then Regis calls. I will be doing a phone interview on *Live with Regis and Kelly* tomorrow morning about some big news that I have. Right now it's a secret.

I take a call from Tony Senecal, my fantastic butler and historian at Mar-a-Lago. Melania and I will be going down to Florida next weekend.

Billy Bush, from *Access Hollywood,* calls, so I talk to him for a while. We all thought there might be a slight media break after the final episode of *The Apprentice,* but we were wrong. Not that I mind, as I like a lot of the media people we deal with very much—Billy, for example. But their interest in the show still surprises me.

I haven't really adjusted to being a TV star yet. For example, one day when I was going to NBC to rehearse *Saturday Night Live,* I walked into the building with Brian, and there were lines of people behind ropes waiting for the NBC tour. Our page was not there to guide us to the elevators yet, so I was face-to-face with about two hundred people who were surprised to see me just standing there. They stared at me in silence, and then our page arrived to direct us to the correct elevator. The silence continued until I got into the elevator, and as the doors were closing, a lady yelled out, "Hi, Mr. Trump! You're fired!"—and everyone else started to scream wildly. I managed to wave back before the doors shut. A funny moment.

Since *The Apprentice* started airing, I am often greeted with a friendly "You're fired!" by people who see me on the street or in a restaurant. Who would have ever believed that phrase would be a replacement for "Hi, how ya doing?"

3:15 P.M.   Don, Jr., and Charlie Reiss come in for a meeting, during which I take a call from my daughter Ivanka. Someday she'll be in on these meetings, too.

Norma comes in to go over requests for speaking engagements. I'll be doing one for Patti Giles in June but have to keep these at a minimum for a while.

4:00 P.M.   Don Thomas is here for a visit. It's always nice to see him. Then I sit in on a meeting in the large conference room with Jill Cremer, Russell Flicker, Don, Jr., and Charlie Reiss. My boardroom is really beautiful. It's an elegant room with perfect lighting. I think people function and think clearly just as well in a well-appointed room as in an overlit and badly decorated one. Businesspeople should think about interiors when they design their offices. Some that I've visited were so dreadful that the only thing I could think of was how to get out of them as soon as possible, and I can imagine their employees may have felt the same way.

4:30 P.M.   I call Melania, and we confirm dinner plans with Regis and Joy at Jean Georges for tonight.

Rhona comes in with some faxes, and I begin to return calls that came in during the meeting. One of the contractors has called back several times, but I just won't deal with him yet. There's a difference between "can't deal with" and "won't deal with." Contractors definitely get the latter until they shape up. As for the good ones, I adore them and treat them the best.

5:15 P.M.   I review documents and reports and ask that my calls be held, except for urgent ones. George Ross comes in, and we review a few things together.

6:00 P.M.   I ask Robin for my calls and return them, and take a call from Kevin Cook of *Golf Magazine*. We'll be playing a round of golf together next month at Trump National/Briarcliff Manor, a course that *Golf Magazine* really likes.

6:30 P.M.   I say good night to Norma and Robin and notice that seven or eight more bins of mail have arrived from the afternoon sorting. We'll have to figure this out. Tomorrow.

THURSDAY

8:30 A.M.   I have a meeting with Bernie Diamond, general counsel, regarding Trump: The Game, being developed with Big Monster Toys and Hasbro. We have a productive meeting for about half an hour, and then I return a call to Jean-Pierre Trebot, the executive director of the

New York Friars Club. I'll be the guest of honor for their celebrity roast in October, and we discuss a few matters.

9:00 A.M. I have a phone interview with Regis, announcing my engagement to my girlfriend of five years, Melania Knauss. We are both extremely happy being together, and I am fortunate to have her in my life.

9:30 A.M. I do a video in the small conference room for my casino in Indiana.

I return calls to Bob Dowling, Sandy Morehouse, and Vinnie Stellio, who is in charge of many of my projects and is doing a great job. I also talk to Richard LeFrak. Richard has the kind of eye that notices everything.

Some people come in to discuss the leather-bound editions of my books, which are in the works now. I also go over my travel plans for the next few weeks, which have to be worked out around my schedule for *The Apprentice*.

I take a call about my new hotel/condominium tower going up in Chicago. Considering that it is scheduled to open in 2007 and it's sixty percent sold already, I'd say we've received a warm welcome from the Windy City. Chicago's a great place.

10:30 A.M. I take a call from Alfons Schmitt of Palm Beach, and then Chris Devine, chef at Trump Tower Grill and Trump Tower Food Court, comes in for a meeting. I will tell you one of the best-kept secrets in New York City: His DT Burger is the best hamburger in town. It has portobello mushrooms, grilled onions, and Swiss cheese. Try one at the

Trump Tower Grill, and you'll agree. Everything else is great, too, but the burger is my favorite item. I'll be having one for lunch tomorrow. The atrium with the waterfall is also a terrific backdrop for a midtown meal. Check it out once, and you'll be back for more.

Mohamed Al Fayed calls in, so I take his call. It's a pleasure to talk to him. He's calling to congratulate me and Melania on our engagement. Stewart Rahr calls in to tell me he's having lunch delivered for my entire staff today as an engagement celebration because now they'll have an even happier boss. He's right.

11:00 A.M. I leave to go up to Trump National Golf Club in Briarcliff Manor to check out the course and clubhouse. We are ready for the new season, so I want to make a property check myself. Carolyn Kepcher and Vinnie Stellio will meet us. It's another wonderful spring day, and these kinds of trips are one of the many pleasurable aspects of my job.

11:45 A.M. Why not? I'll play a round of golf with John Spitalny and in doing so, do a thorough property check. This course is a beauty all the way. My game is getting there, too. I take it as seriously as I can, considering my schedule. I notice a few things on the property that need to be improved. Notes are taken, and I'm sure things will be taken care of promptly. This is a good operation. I have a chat with Cary Stephan, our golf pro, and then it's time to go.

4:00 P.M. I'm back in the office at Trump Tower, where I return some calls. I speak to the very talented Richard Johnson of the *New York Post* and Shawn McCabe, a young man who has been with me for a long time and is doing a superb job of maintaining and building additions to Mar-a-Lago.

5:00 P.M.   Kevin Harris shows up with yet another monster schedule for me to review. I try to keep the "don't kill the messenger" proverb in my mind as I go over it with him. This guy doesn't stop. He must've been trained by Mark Burnett. Good thing I'm such an easygoing guy.

Someone tells me David Letterman said on his show, "Donald Trump is the biggest star in America, and he won't do my show, but I like him anyway." David's a good guy, always has been, always will be. He's just on the wrong network, that's all. But I'm going to do his show anyway.

I call Melania to see what we're doing this evening, and it looks like it will be Le Cirque. I call in Charlie Reiss to go over some development ideas. Charlie can be blunt—just ask Amy of *The Apprentice*—so we get along just fine. He never wastes my time. I appreciate Charlie's ability to quickly size things up and deliver the goods.

7:00 P.M.   I check in with Matt Calamari and some others, who are still working, and go upstairs.

FRIDAY

8:15 A.M.   Norma and I have a meeting about how to handle the huge amounts of mail we have been receiving. Now I know how publishers or movie companies must feel about submissions, and why they have rules about it. We can hardly walk through our offices anymore, and she shows me where an extra ten or twelve bins have been stored.

8:45 A.M.   I take a call from Bernd Lembke about being in Palm Beach for Mother's Day. That marks the end of the season there for us, and it's always a big day. I'm not big on melancholy, but it's a day for fond memories of my mother, and it deserves a celebration.

I call my sister Maryanne to see if her offer for a home-cooked meal tonight is still on. It is. Not only is she smart, she is a great cook.

9:00 A.M. I have a meeting with Tom Kaufman, Allen Weisselberg, and George Ross; we cover a lot of territory in under thirty minutes.

9:30 A.M. I speak to Bill Fioravanti, who is Paul Anka's tailor. Paul has offered to have a tailored suit made for me—a nice gesture from a nice guy. The suit is great!

I talk to Paula Shugart and Tony Santomauro about the upcoming Miss Universe pageant in Ecuador. The buzz is huge there. I'll be flying down for the event, in between my *Apprentice* assignments.

Speaking of which, here are Jay Bienstock and Kevin Harris at my door. Why did Mark have to hire such efficient guys? At least they know how to give efficient meetings, and we're through in fifteen minutes.

10:00 A.M. I call Sean Compton, vice president and national program coordinator for Clear Channel, regarding my radio program, and Rhona comes in to advise me of an upcoming photo shoot with Scott Duncan. Not my favorite thing, but I like Scott a lot, so it shouldn't be too painful.

I read a few letters. There's one from a young lady in Arizona, who writes: "Finally! A reality show that is as captivating as it is compelling. Maybe it's because I have a degree in business and a law degree . . . or maybe it's because of your no-nonsense approach to dealing with people. Thank you for allowing the viewing public to be a part of this experience." I'm glad to know people are enjoying the show as much as I am.

I make a call to Paul Chapman and ask for a Diet Pepsi. Norma comes in to remind me of the Damon Runyon Cancer Breakfast at the Rainbow Room later this month, honoring the great Bob Wright of NBC, and a few other engagements.

10:30 A.M.   I have a meeting with Bernie Diamond, general counsel, and then Costas Kondylis arrives for a meeting. I ask Don, Jr., to come in, and we have a discussion about contractors, so I call one, and sure enough, he's at least $100,000 over the amount that is necessary to do the job. After I finish talking to him, he's down to a reasonable price, $100,000 less than he had originally figured. Need I say more?

10:45 A.M.   I take a call from John Stark of Stark Carpet and talk to Bernd Lembke regarding the weekend at the Mar-a-Lago Club. I'm happy to report that work on this incredible place will never end. I am now building what will soon become the finest ballroom facility in the United States. I call Tony Senecal to go over a few things.

I take a call from David Hochman of *Playboy* about an interview in May, and have a meeting in the large conference room with my development team to go over plans and to see what's in the works. Part of being a good builder is planning into the future, which is one reason I enjoy these meetings so much. A room with blueprints equals a room with a lot of action in the works.

11:45 A.M.   I go down with a group of Wall Street bankers to show them the new suite for the eighteen new *Apprentice* applicants. They agree that it looks great, and I realize I'm looking forward to having another group of enthusiastic young people to work with. The boardroom looks ready for another dynamic season. We go down to the atrium level. A few people wave and say, "You're fired!"

I take a tour through the beautiful new space occupied by Asprey, the famed jewelers, which covers three floors in the front of Trump Tower. When you see the British flag flying next to the American flag on Fifty-sixth and Fifth Avenue, it's because of Asprey. They are the jewelers to the royal family and many other people of discerning taste.

As I pass through reception back to my office, I stop to ask Georgette how she's doing in her first week back at work. Very well. She's a trouper.

12:15 P.M. I return the calls that have come in and call Tiffany in California for an update. George Ross comes in for a meeting, and we discuss a few things pertinent to the new season of *The Apprentice,* as well as business issues. Andy Weiss, Bernie Diamond, and Allen Weisselberg also come in for meetings.

I take a call from Rudy Giuliani regarding a dinner together, and I talk to Random House about a sales conference where I will appear. I told Random House that I wanted to give readers everything needed to be successful in life in fewer than three hundred pages. That's a challenge, and I like to challenge myself as much as possible. But my books aren't strictly educational; they might become less interesting if they were one-dimensional.

Robin comes in to remind me of the Police Athletic League Board of Directors meeting next week, and we discuss some invitations and business proposals that have come up. Here's someone who wants to build a tower on top of Trump Tower with me, after hearing the idea on *Saturday Night Live.* I seriously doubt if this guy knows that *SNL* is a comedy show, and he's decided he's my new partner because he also likes chicken wings. We couldn't make these things up if we tried. In fact, if the *Saturday Night Live* writing team ever runs out of ideas, they should come over here for a day or so and read my mail.

1:00 P.M.   I take a call from Wagner College in Staten Island. I will be receiving an honorary doctorate degree in May—certainly an honor. "Dr. Trump" sounds good to me.

It's surprising what a few days of honest reflection and number crunching can do, because one of the contractors from earlier this week calls back and finds he can do the job "easily" for $150,000 less than he'd originally thought. I figured as much, and that's why I finally took the call.

I take a call from Vinnie Stellio, who is checking out the golf course development and construction at Trump National/Los Angeles. We are building a truly great course there.

I make a call to my brother Robert to see what's up. He'll be going to London next week.

I tell Bobby "Hollywood," one of my bodyguards, that I want to take a walk over to Trump Park Avenue. These days that can be quite an adventure, but he's up to it.

1:45 P.M.   I arrive at Trump Park Avenue. The lobby looks great, but I want the doormen to be wearing white gloves. After all, this is Park Avenue. I notice some of the woodwork is off-kilter in one of the elevators; I ask that it be fixed immediately and that they take the elevator out of service until it is. I have an eye for little things, which can either amaze people or irritate them, depending on the circumstances. I do a property check, and it's looking good overall, although not perfect, so we go over a few things that need attention. I always pretend that I'm a tenant in all of my buildings. What things would bother me if I were? First of all, everything has to shine, otherwise it just looks lousy. The lobby and the halls have to be in mint condition at all times, all the fixtures should be polished and lit, and the carpeting has to look brand-new, always. Run-down anything looks run-down, and run-down is not acceptable—ever! Most landlords wouldn't want a tenant like me, but that's why most tenants want a landlord like me: Being a perfectionist works to their benefit.

3:00 P.M. Robin has my messages waiting, so I return ten or twelve calls that have come in and review notes from a meeting regarding 40 Wall Street, my jewel of a building in the Financial District. Downtown has made a good rebound. As I told the *New York Post:* "Even 9/11 couldn't put a permanent dent in that place."

Carolyn Kepcher calls in. We go over some notes I made yesterday about Trump National/Briarcliff during my round of golf and afternoon on the grounds. Once the season at Palm Beach winds down, I'm on the course a lot in Westchester, and we are constantly fine-tuning everything.

3:30 P.M. I have a meeting with Charlie Reiss and Bill Rancic concerning the Chicago tower. We go over some brochures for the building. We discuss the Las Vegas tower being planned. I will be building a luxury condominium/mixed-use tower there with Phil Ruffin, one of the greatest guys I know, so I'll be flying out there for a quick visit within the next couple of weeks. You can see why having a jet is a necessity in my life.

I call Katie Couric to congratulate her on the great job she did for the colon cancer benefit on the *Queen Mary 2*. She raised $5 million for this important cause, and she's a great lady, even if she did have Harry Connick, Jr., "fire" me after my duet with him. I'll try to forgive her, but only because I like her so much.

4:00 P.M.   Norma comes in with a stack of letters and proposals to go over. She says I cringe when I see her come in. She's become "the homework queen" in my eyes, and she knows it.

Random House calls to tell me they've sold the rights to *How to Get Rich* to publishers in twenty-one foreign countries. A friend of mine told me his son of sixteen read it three times and wants to run his own organization as a result. Now he even reads financial magazines and papers every day, his favorite being *The Wall Street Journal.* I liked what I was hearing.

I call my son Eric to see what he's got planned for the weekend. He says "studying," but somehow I think otherwise. Not that he isn't a good student (he definitely is), but he's an outdoor type and has a lot of activities that interest him. All of my children are very well balanced as far as being hard workers, and they are disciplined people, so I never have to worry about them too much.

4:45 P.M.   Rhona comes in to give me my latest faxes and messages. I call Steve Wynn and tell him I'll be visiting soon, and I call John Myers, then Mark Brown. Mike van der Goes calls in from California, and Paula Shugart calls in about an interview for a magazine in Ecuador. And of course, another one of those contractors from earlier in the week calls in, with radically altered prices for his services. Why are certain things so predictable? Anyway, it's nice when they become so agreeable—another word for "reasonable" in this case.

5:30 P.M.   I sign a few books to be sent out to friends and colleagues, make a few final calls, and Allen Weisselberg stops by for a few minutes on his way out. It's been a good week, in fact a milestone week for me, and we're all looking forward to the weekend.

6:30 P.M. I turn out my lights and head upstairs. I'm looking forward to some golf this weekend, as we'll be staying in town. We need a weekend just to relax, which means we may visit Atlantic City tomorrow night by helicopter, check out the course in Bedminster, New Jersey, on Sunday, and have dinner at the '21' Club tonight. This weekend will be relatively quiet for us. Trump Tower is a great home base.

PART V

Inside The Apprentice

The Final Episode
of <u>The Apprentice</u>

The final episode of the first *Apprentice* series, filmed live at NBC in the *Saturday Night Live* studios, felt for me like a bit of a homecoming. I'd spent a few days there just a couple of weeks before. I knew where the canteen was, I knew where the pretzels were, I knew the wardrobe people, and I knew my way around the set.

Jeff Zucker, Bob and Suzanne Wright, and Darrell Hammond came to visit me, and we even had the same stage managers, Gena and Chris, so it seemed like the continuation of a terrific event. I also noticed that my photograph had joined the *SNL* greats on the hall-of-fame photo gallery that lines the walls as you walk to the set. I was ready for another new adventure.

At 3 P.M. I had an interview with Pat O'Brien, then of *Access Hollywood,* followed by a conference with Mark Burnett to go over the live broadcast. Then we had a lighting rehearsal on the set, where they had constructed a boardroom to emulate the one in Trump Tower. Carolyn Kepcher and George Ross joined me.

I had my old dressing room from *Saturday Night Live,* and the sixteen original *Apprentice* candidates had their dressing rooms one floor up. There was definitely a celebratory feel to the backstage area, a reunion for everyone of a truly great success.

I wondered what property the winner would pick. After all, it's my business, literally, so I was trying to assess the outcome of both possibilities. I had a terrific guy running Trump National Golf Club at Palos Verdes, Mike van der Goes, and I didn't want to lose him or put him into a different position. The tower in Chicago was more open to someone new coming in, because it is still in development, so I was hoping the winner might pick Chicago. But I had two sincere offers out to the winner, and it would be his choice. I'd have to deal with whatever he dealt me.

After the lighting rehearsal, I had another meeting in my dressing room with Mark Burnett and his producers, Jay Bienstock and Kevin Harris. We reviewed the impact of the show and how certain members had been perceived. Two of the contestants in particular had received a lot of attention: Omarosa seemed to emerge as the villain, while Troy emerged as the hero. Recently, someone asked me if I'd give Omarosa a job reference. My answer: I'd give her a good reference for a soap opera.

We also discussed how the group might interact during the live show and whether we might encounter any difficulties. We tried not to leave ourselves too open to any possible blowups or problems, but a live show is always a bit of a gamble. I sent signed copies of my book *How to Get Rich* up to the sixteen while they waited for the show to begin. George Steinbrenner called in to wish me well and said his entire family would be watching. George was behind the show before anyone else.

I went back to visit the friendly and helpful wardrobe team, where I spoke to Dale Richards, who has been with wardrobe at *Saturday Night Live* for eighteen years. He told me there was a buzz in the air, even a bit of nervousness among the *SNL* veterans, because whereas *SNL* has been operating for twenty-nine years, *The Apprentice* was only a few months old at that point. It was new territory for them. They couldn't just relax and expect things to go as usual, because this show was *not* usual. But he said considering my performance on live TV already, they were not concerned about me. They knew I could handle it, and I felt very confident.

What's great about NBC is that they do things professionally and with pizzazz as well. It wasn't necessary, but they had a live band for the final episode, with members of the *SNL* band, which added to the excitement. Just to hear them warming up gave the place the air of a great event about to happen.

As it turned out, it was. Mark Burnett, Melania, and I watched the taped portion of the final episode in my dressing room, and then I went out for the final boardroom scene with Carolyn and George, and Kwame and Bill. We also had the other fourteen candidates on the set, and we gave updates on several of them to the television audience.

It probably helped that I didn't know how huge the TV audience was during those final minutes, but I pretended this show was just another deal for me, so I wasn't too nervous. In a way, it was business as usual, and my choice of Bill to be my apprentice felt right to me. I've never been a histrionic person, so even with an audience watching, I knew what would be the best decision for the Trump Organization. Experience just kicked in and took over.

But I will admit that it was exciting. The culmination of all those weeks of ups and downs—the many assignments, personal problems, infighting, the deviousness as well as the camaraderie—happened incredibly quickly. And, lucky for me, Bill chose the Chicago Trump Tower for his assignment. It seemed to be over so suddenly.

Or so I thought. We had an aftershow party at Trump Tower for everyone involved with the program, and I have never experienced that amount of media in my life. It was a media extravaganza. Fifth Avenue was blockaded, and there were thousands of people there just to see who went in. It took Melania and me over an hour to walk the red carpet from the front door to the elevators, probably a distance less than one hundred feet. It was a crush from every side, but the mood was jubilant, and I can't complain. It was terrific.

NBC, Mark Burnett, and everyone else involved with *The Apprentice* worked so hard, and I had a great experience—one I will never forget. I'm looking forward to the new season.

The Apprentice II

With the worldwide excitement surrounding the first season, the incredible ratings success, and four Emmy nominations, Mark Burnett, NBC, and I knew that we would have to deliver an even better show for the second season of *The Apprentice*. It's going to be incredible, and here is a blow-by-blow of the making of the first four episodes.

MONDAY, MAY 10

Monday, May 10, marked the opening day of filming the new season. Mark Burnett and his team came to my offices to show me the tape to introduce me to the eighteen new apprentice candidates. I would soon be face-to-face with these men and women in the boardroom downstairs.

They looked like a dynamic and energetic group. Type A personalities all the way. Not only do they look good, but their backgrounds include West Point, Princeton, Harvard, and Wharton. Not bad.

At 11 A.M. we all went to the fourth-floor suite, which had been beautifully redesigned by Kelly Van Patter. She did the first season's suite, too, and this one was even better. Jim Dowd of NBC met us there, along with Craig Plestis, senior vice president of alternative programs and development at NBC, and Lee Strauss, vice president of business affairs at NBC, also known as the reality-show "deal maker." I got quite a welcome, and it made me think that maybe I matter to this network, which is a great feeling. As business partners go, NBC is the best.

Carolyn Kepcher, George Ross, and Robin Himmler from my staff were there and ready to go into our second season as regulars, as is Scott Duncan, a photographer with great-looking dreadlocks and talent to match, who is also the brother of Tim Duncan, of the San Antonio Spurs. Mark introduced me to his beautiful girlfriend, the television star Roma Downey, and we gave her a tour of the infamous boardroom. Then it was time to meet the eighteen new candidates in person.

Sitting before the new contestants, I noticed that George was looking especially dapper. I think TV stardom agrees with him. However, I clued in the new eighteen that while both George and Carolyn can be tough and nasty, to watch out—George actually *is* nasty. They laughed. I don't think they believed me.

All of the candidates introduced themselves. They were obviously and understandably nervous, but I could tell that the anticipation level was completely positive. That energy gave me a great first impression of them, and I told them that taking a shot at this show deserves some self-congratulation. They have drive.

I also mentioned that Bill Rancic is doing very well as the winner of the first season, but all the other candidates from that show are certainly on their way as well. There were no losers in this new lineup before me.

Carolyn mentioned to them that only eighteen out of one million applicants were chosen. That should give them a lot of confidence going into the challenges that await them. George, trying to be polite for a change, told them that they were all highly qualified and that he expected them to do a good job.

I also told the men and women that they would be divided into two groups according to gender. I took a lot of heat for that the last time, but that's too bad. I'm not running for office, and it's my decision. They would soon be put through the wringer, and they would feel every emotion—both positive and negative—in the process. But someone would emerge as my apprentice, with another terrific opportunity waiting for him or her at the finish line. It might be a nasty race, but it will also be fun.

With that, they were off to the suite, which had been furnished with plenty of champagne, caviar, and other indicators of their good fortune just to be here today. I think they all felt that way, just as we did.

I found myself wondering whether we had another Sam Solovey in this group. Sam is odd but talented. Some of his quirky behavior didn't make it to the television show. For example, he actually dressed up in an evening gown (not really a pretty sight) for a commercial promoting my Miss USA pageant. Not many people would have done that; I have to give him credit. And the $250,000 that Sam supposedly gave me? It wasn't $250,000 at all, but about $1,100 with lots of newspapers tucked under it. But that's Sam—he's tricky, he's smart, and he'll be just fine.

I had the advantage of introductions to the eighteen new candidates, so here's a brief bio of each of them for you.

Kevin *(Chicago, Illinois), law student*
Kevin, 29, grew up in Silver Spring, Maryland, and then went on to attend the Wharton School of Business. He gave up his pursuit of a professional football career when his brother was diagnosed with leukemia. He later received an M.B.A. in M&A and finance from Emory. He is currently working toward earning his law degree at the University of Chicago. He and his brother have founded their own software company.

Raj *(Vail, Colorado/Philadelphia, Pennsylvania), real estate developer*
Raj, 28, received his secondary education at the Hill School, a boarding school outside Philadelphia, and later earned degrees in both economics and history from Boston College. Moving on from a successful stint in investment banking at the firm of Violy & Co. in New York City, Raj founded Automovia Technology Partners at the age of 23. The company worked closely with some of the largest and most respected firms in the automotive industry to develop custom-built cutting-edge technology related to the valuation and distribution of pre-owned automobiles. After this time in the technology sector, Raj turned his focus to real estate and created Vanquish Enterprises. This led to the acquisition of a hotel, retail, and condominium project in Vail, Colorado. Through an extensive renovation and repositioning of this asset, the project is on track to increase revenue by 300 percent.

Maria *(Virginia Beach, Virginia), marketing executive*
Maria, 31, grew up in Tallahassee, Florida. Her primary residence is in Virginia Beach, where her husband is an FA-18 pilot in the United States Navy. Maria has a B.S. in business and completed her M.B.A. with a specialty track in entrepreneurial marketing. In 2002, Maria was named the youngest vice president in the history of her publicly traded company. She is currently the vice president of marketing for a real estate investment trust company headquartered in Richmond, Virginia, and has ten years of experience in the fields of marketing/branding, sales, business management, and advertising.

Bradford *(Fort Lauderdale, Florida), attorney*
Bradford, 32, hails from a small town in Massachusetts. He later settled in South Florida, where he obtained his J.D. from Nova Southeastern Law School. In addition to being a successful lawyer and handling several high-profile cases, he is also a real estate investor and owns several pieces of commercial and residential property in south

Florida. He can be seen daily, commuting to the courthouse or inspecting his properties in his customized gas-powered golf cart, complete with monster-truck tires.

Jennifer C. *(New York, New York), real estate agent*
Jennifer, 31, graduated with honors and a B.F.A. degree from Syracuse University, and immediately went on to become one of the youngest photo editors hired at a leading international entertainment magazine. Jennifer quickly rose through the ranks, working at many of the country's top-selling publications, producing shoots for some of the world's most famous celebrities. Jennifer soon made a lucrative career change into real estate and was offered a desk at one of the most prestigious firms in New York City, Prudential Douglas Elliman. Though told by her managers that it could take well over six months to close a deal and earn an income, Jennifer went into multiple contracts within her first six weeks in business, impressing even the most seasoned veterans. Jennifer is now successfully selling multimillion-dollar, high-end residential real estate. As her competitive career mirrors, Jennifer also excels as an accomplished award-winning equestrian.

Pamela *(San Francisco, California), investment firm partner*
Pamela, 32, is an accomplished and well-trained business executive who has founded two successful companies from the ground up. She holds an undergraduate degree in economics from the University of Pennsylvania and an M.B.A. from Harvard Business School. During the 1990s, she worked as an investment banker on Wall Street, underwriting IPOs and doing M&A advisory work for two top-tier investment banks. In 2000, Pamela founded Blazent, Inc., from her loft in San Francisco. Blazent has grown to become a successful enterprise-software company, now with offices all across the country. After two years as the company's CEO, Pamela left Blazent to form Crimson Holdings, a private investment firm focused on real estate investments

and equity hedge strategies. The Crimson Funds, including Crimson Advisors and Crimson BridgePoint Funds, have performed exceptionally well, and the Crimson family of funds is quickly becoming a leader in the management of alternative investments.

Sandy *(Rockville, Maryland), bridal shop owner*
Sandy, 28, was born and raised in a Portuguese home in the Washington, D.C., area. By the age of 21, she was the youngest bridal-store owner in the country. Since then, Sandy has evolved to become an exclusive wedding and event planner in the metropolitan D.C. area. Her clientele has included heirs to the Tiffany & Co. family and elite politicians. Sandy's entrepreneurial enthusiasm has also led her into real estate ventures and investments. Presently, Sandy keeps busy growing her award-winning bridal business and wedding-and-event-planning company.

Rob *(Frisco, Texas), corporate branding salesman*
Rob, 32, grew up in Plano, Texas, and later earned a football scholarship to Northeast Missouri State University, where he started four years in the linebacker position. After graduating with a bachelor of science degree from the University of Texas, he and his wife founded Flanagan Enterprises, Inc., and grew it into a multimillion-dollar business, selling corporate-branded items and custom solution-packaging products worldwide. In November 2003 Rob partnered with HotLink, Inc., an industry leader utilizing marketing automation, based in Austin, Texas, where he is VP of Dallas Sales. Along with raising his two young children, Rob enjoys golf, scuba diving, playing his guitar, and fishing.

Elizabeth *(Marina Del Ray, California), marketing consultant*
Elizabeth, 31, has more than thirty Fortune 500 companies and over forty multimillion-dollar brands relying on her to help them develop

creative ideas to build their businesses. Elizabeth currently owns and runs Pulse40, a successful consulting firm, where she pioneered a unique interviewing process. With products ranging from laundry detergent to movies, you might recognize much of her work on TV today. Elizabeth graduated with a 4.0 from the University of Michigan Business School, where she was recognized as an Angell Scholar, received the Branstrom Prize, and was ranked in the top one percent of the nation for academic excellence and leadership. Elizabeth's professional foundation began when she was hired by Procter & Gamble Brand Management and very quickly became a highly successful brand manager. Fun facts most people don't know about Elizabeth are: she's a published poet, state champion basketball player, avid Salsa dancer, motivational speaker, and an award-winning short-film director.

Stacie J. *(New York, New York), sandwich shop owner*
Stacie, 29, grew up in Colorado. She has a B.A. from Emory University and an M.B.A. from Mercer University, both of which are located in Atlanta, Georgia. She is a professional model with Ford Model Management, based in New York City, and Elite Model Management, with offices in Los Angeles, Atlanta, Miami, and Chicago. She currently owns a successful Subway sandwich shop franchise in Harlem, New York.

Andy *(Boca Raton, Florida), recent Harvard graduate*
Andy, 23, was born and raised in south Florida, where he recognized early on what it would take to succeed in business. At the age of 13, Andy co-founded a concert package company that focused on both corporate and individual clients. As the youngest of four boys, Andy learned to use his speaking skills to defend himself at an early age. In 1999, he utilized those verbal skills to win the U.S. National Debate Championship in Commentary Speaking. Andy is a recent graduate of Harvard University, where he was a founding member of an organiza-

tion dedicated to fighting infectious diseases in developing countries. A competitive tennis player, Andy is looking forward to continued success both in and out of the Boardroom.

Ivana *(Boston, Massachusetts), venture capitalist*

Ivana, 28, earned her B.S. from the McIntire School of Commerce at the University of Virginia, with a concentration in finance. She has spent the past five years in the venture-capital industry, investing in technology companies. Ivana enjoys running and cycling, and recently raised five thousand dollars for the Leukemia and Lymphoma Society by completing a one-hundred-mile ride around Lake Tahoe. She lives in Boston with her fiancé, Brian, who attends Harvard Business School.

Jennifer M. *(San Francisco, California), attorney*

Jennifer, 29, received her undergraduate degree in English from Princeton and her law degree from Harvard. She graduated magna cum laude and Phi Beta Kappa from Princeton, and was nominated for the Pyne Prize, Princeton's highest honor. She is currently a securities litigator for a law firm in San Francisco and has worked with management teams from start-ups to Fortune 500 companies. Jennifer lives in San Francisco with her husband, Aron.

Wes *(Atlanta, Georgia), private wealth manager*

Wes, 27, grew up the son of a veterinarian and the eldest of four rambunctious siblings, learning responsibility and leadership at a very young age. Wes hails from Atlanta, Georgia, where he lives with his wife, Lynne. He holds an economics degree from the University of North Carolina at Chapel Hill. Postgraduation he moved to Atlanta, and within five years he became a vice president with one of the world's largest global-investment firms. Wes leads a large team specializing in investment management for wealthy individuals, families, and large corporations. He is in his sixth year as a financial adviser and one of the nation's youngest certified financial planner practitioners. He also serves as an instructor at Emory University's prestigious High Net Worth Institute in Atlanta, Georgia.

Kelly *(Carlsbad, California), software executive*
Kelly, 37, earned a B.S. degree in national security and public affairs from the United States Military Academy at West Point. He earned an M.B.A. from the Anderson School at UCLA and a J.D. from the UCLA School of Law simultaneously. After graduating from West Point, Kelly completed Ranger school and served two years as a military intelligence officer in the United States Army. Kelly raised over $5 million in equity financing for three start-up companies, and as the acting president led the sale of one of those start-ups (eteamz.com: the largest amateur-sports portal on the web at the time) for eight figures to a company that has since filed for an IPO. He is the co-founder and chairman of a motor-enthusiast community website called motorpride. com and is currently the president of CoreObjects, an outsourced software development company based in Los Angeles.

Stacy R. *(New York, New York), attorney*
Stacy, 26, is a native New Yorker who received her B.A. in art history from Columbia University, where she graduated with honors. Stacy received her J.D. from Brooklyn Law School, and she currently practices corporate law at a top law firm in New York. Stacy has worked in the legal departments of both Sotheby's Auction House and the Metropolitan Museum of Art in New York. Stacy loves to travel; she has studied abroad in Paris and speaks French. She is an active member of various bar associations and charitable organizations in New York.

Chris *(Long Island, New York), stockbroker*
Chris, 30, was raised in New York, and has been an entrepreneur since he was 11. He started with a candy business, which was followed by a

landscaping business by age 14. He sold flowers every holiday, and Christmas trees in the winter. After being a stockbroker for seven years, he opened his own firm. In fewer than five months he was ranked thirteenth in a field of over a thousand brokers, and his branch was eighth out of 171. Perhaps most impressively, Chris has achieved all this with only a high school degree.

John *(San Francisco, California), marketing/real estate director*
John, 24, has lived for the majority of his life in the San Francisco Bay area. He attended the University of California at Berkeley, where he graduated in 2003. While at Cal, John won three division-one national titles in the sport of rugby. After graduation, John submitted a business plan to an automotive magazine, *The Rodder's Journal,* where he was then hired as marketing director. John also co-founded a real-estate-development company in San Francisco, and is currently in the midst of a number of projects. When not at the office, John spends the majority of his free time pursuing his other passion, auto racing.

These are the candidates I met that first day, and I could already tell that it was going to be a fantastic season. Maybe even better than the first.

After saying goodbye to the candidates, I went back to my office to do some business for a couple of hours, and then it was off to NBC studios to shoot the promos for the NBC Primetime Preview 2004/2005, known as the Upfronts, coming up next week at Radio City Music Hall. This is a huge, two-hour sales presentation that takes place once a year and generates $2 billion in ad sales. This is Jeff Zucker's forte, and I've learned it's a very important industry event.

I was talking to Craig Plestis, a vice president at NBC, on the way over to the studio, and he mentioned Jeff Zucker's reaction to the first episode he saw of *The Apprentice,* when I was still considered a gamble in their eyes. He said Zucker, who was seeing raw footage without music or any embellishments, became mesmerized by what he was watching and said he knew that it was special right then. By the time he saw the boardroom scene, he knew they had a hit on their hands.

The boardroom was the clincher because it seemed "so real." That's because it *was* real. People don't always understand this, or maybe they forget: I am a businessman, and my instincts are finely honed as a businessman. I can't act my way out of that, ever, and that's what comes across. Jeff Zucker and Mark Burnett recognized this trait in me, and that's why *The Apprentice* has been such a big hit!

The Upfronts would be promoting the second season of *The Apprentice* in a scene set in a small boardroom in an NBC studio. The scene would be a spoof of our boardroom scenes on *The Apprentice,* only we would have five actual NBC executives playing prospective employees. I got to fire them all. George got to slug one, which he did in one take. He didn't need any practice or warm-up shots. Even Sam Solovey, from our first season, did a guest appearance, announcing his big new job at a rival network, which is very good news for *our* network. My secret nickname for him was Sam So-long-now, which is particularly funny to me now, since it seems he's always around—even more so than if I'd hired him. However, I think Sam is enormously talented, and I guarantee that he will be a huge success.

Then, just when I thought my TV day was over—wrong again. We went outside to Rockefeller Plaza to do some shots, and we caused a pedestrian and tour bus jam in the process. I was standing on the back of a truck for everyone to see. How do I get myself into these things? I don't know. But everyone was fast and professional, and we were done in ten minutes. Day One was a wrap. I ducked into my limousine to return to my office and make phone calls.

TUESDAY, MAY 11

The day of the teams' first assignment. We met the film crew and the new eighteen at Toys "R" Us in Times Square. This space is the largest toy store in the world, and it really is incredible. The first assignment always has a certain edge to it, as it marks the true beginning of the show's plot and dynamics. The streets were quiet, since it was 8 A.M., and the store was open just for us. I couldn't help thinking what the new candidates must have been thinking: Last time we started at the New York Stock Exchange on Wall Street, and this time we were at a toy store? But here's a fact: Toys are big business—big to the tune of $20 billion a year. So this was *not* a small-fry assignment.

The group informed me of the two team names and that both the designated leaders are of the opposite sex from the teams they will lead. This could be a good idea, to keep the score a little more balanced than it was the last time, when the women trounced the men for a while. That showed me that maybe they'd learned something from watching the show.

Along with Carolyn, George, and me, several executives from the Mattel toy company—Richard Weintraub, Evelyn Viohl, and Mark Sullivan—were present. They would be in charge of this assignment, which was to develop the prototype for a new commercially viable toy. The target market? A raucous group of children, from six to eight years old. Believe me, that's a tough market.

I told them to get busy and do a good job, and they proceeded to Mattel headquarters in Chelsea to continue their work. I would check on their progress tomorrow. Meanwhile, I returned to the office to get back to work myself.

WEDNESDAY, MAY 12

At 6 P.M., in the midst of an ominous thunderstorm, we drove down to Mattel headquarters for the task resolution. I was looking forward to seeing the results and what the two teams had come up with, even though I prefer grown-up-size toys such as helicopters and airplanes. I remember wishing that we could use my helicopter right then. The traffic was terrible.

We finally arrived in Chelsea, a thriving, bustling area. Mattel occupies a beautiful building with a seven-floor skylit atrium.

As I was descending the stairs into the Mattel conference room, an eight-year-old boy going up the stairs saw me and wasted no time in pointing at me and telling me I was fired, and in no uncertain terms. Fortunately, he was smiling, so it wasn't too scary.

As we waited for the room to be ready for the resolution scene, Richard Devinki, a producer with Mark Burnett's team, mentioned that he had seen *Candide,* an opera by Leonard Bernstein that had recently been revived at Lincoln Center with Patti LuPone. The judge in the opera was dressed to look like me, hair and all, and in one scene he told the exiled Candide, "You're fired!" I couldn't believe I actually made it into an opera, and one by Leonard Bernstein at that. I don't think he'd mind. Bernstein loved New York, too, so I'm in good company.

The eighteen candidates arrived, and Carolyn, George, and I entered the room, which was filled with an amazing assortment of toys. We got right down to business and asked the Mattel executives how the two teams had performed.

They both did well, but it seemed that Apex, the women's team headed by Brad, edged out the men's team. I asked Richard Weintraub of Mattel why he had chosen them, and he said the children in the focus group responded more favorably to their toy. He added that children like action-packed toys, with crashes, energy, and speed—a slam-dunk toy, in other words. The executives also thought their idea had more commercial viability.

I asked him whether there was a chance of ever seeing this new toy in stores, and he said to look for it early next year. It was good enough to develop and market, which is the mark of an effective and imaginative team. It looked like we were off to a fantastic start.

I informed the losing team that I would be seeing them in the boardroom tomorrow, where one of them would be fired. I informed the winning team that the prize for their work would be to have dinner with me in my penthouse apartment that night, along with Melania. Last time, the winning team got to see my apartment and to meet Melania. This time they got to have a filet mignon dinner with us at twilight. I think that's an improvement.

I spent a few minutes talking with Megan Left of Mark Burnett's location crew. While some New York City locations can be a breeze (particularly if I own them), other locations can present an enormous challenge. For example, the shots at the Statue of Liberty required contact with the New York Police Department, the Coast Guard, the U.S. Navy, and Bernadette Castro, the amazing woman who is the commissioner of the New York State Office of Parks, Recreation and Historic Preservation.

Megan told me that finding locations is less of a problem in New York City when I'm involved because they've found that people think I've done a lot for the city and willingly try to be helpful. Several people mentioned to her that *The Apprentice* is like a postcard for NYC. I have to agree.

THURSDAY, MAY 13

The first boardroom scene of the new season took place at 5 P.M. It almost seemed like a reunion to be back there all together again. Aptitude is an interesting thing. I have it for business and making money, and sometimes it's just as clear as day to see when other people don't have it. My first firing wasn't terribly difficult, although I always feel bad for the first person to go because he or she will miss out on so much.

We finished the boardroom scene, and I left immediately to attend a cocktail party for the Metropolitan Golf Association. I went with Carolyn Kepcher and met Rudy Giuliani there. Never a dull moment with Rudy around. We had a great time. The speaker was David Fay of the United States Golf Association, who has done a brilliant job of watching over golf and the game's integrity. He is also a wonderful guy.

FRIDAY, MAY 14

We met in the atrium of Trump Tower at nine in the morning to give the second assignment, which was to create an ice cream flavor and sell it, in tandem with Ciao Bella Gelato. I'm building an ice cream parlor in Trump Tower. Since Starbucks went into the mezzanine level last year, the company now has one of its most lucrative stores anywhere. We are thrilled to have them on the premises.

SATURDAY, MAY 15

At 6 P.M., we met for task resolution in the boardroom. I spent a few minutes talking to Paul Ahern of the art department about what he does, and he described how they covered the mirrors at Petrossian, the restaurant where that night's winning team would indulge in the most expensive caviar in the world. The screen to cover the mirrors is called Hampshire Frost, a translucent plastic that blurs or diffuses any reflection, which is essential for filming there. The details are myriad in shooting a TV series.

It turned out that vanilla was by far the most popular ice cream flavor, and the winning team, Mosaic, capitalized on that consumer preference by coming up with a vanilla-based flavor. This choice, to me, was common sense, and they won because of it. Off they went to Petrossian, and Melania and I went off to Atlantic City for an event at the Taj Mahal.

While being greeted by hundreds of fans waiting outside Trump Tower, I asked them how they liked *The Apprentice*. I was reassured that we would have a strong audience waiting for the new series in the fall.

SUNDAY, MAY 16

A big day for me. My eldest daughter, Ivanka, was graduating from the Wharton School in Philadelphia. She did, as expected, incredibly well. We all went to the ceremony and luncheon at Wharton. It was a beautiful day. On the way back, we stopped at my golf course in Bedminster, New Jersey, and checked things out with Ashley Cooper, who has done an incredible job of making this club such an outstanding success.

We arrived back in New York in time for the second boardroom scene, in which someone from the losing team, Apex, would be fired. This scene was rollicking and very complicated, considering that the teams were doing something as simple as selling ice cream. I couldn't remember a more compelling boardroom scene than this one, even including the firing of Sam and Omarosa.

After being told that the winning team (the men) had dressed for the part in bow ties, I told the losing team that being dressed for the role is an important factor in business. In fact, it's a part of business whether you like it or not. The losing team made no effort to come up with a dress motif that would set them apart. That was just one factor that contributed to their loss, but it was an important one.

We all felt a bit wiped out after this long encounter in the boardroom, but there was just enough time to get to Radio City Music Hall for a dress rehearsal for the big Upfront show. I rehearsed the opening with Darrell Hammond, who played me perfectly, as usual, and Jeff Zucker. I got to fire Darrell, but I was hired by Jeff Zucker and NBC, since I'm a "ratings machine." Not a bad transaction. I told Darrell that I had always wanted to play Radio City Music Hall, and from that stage, it truly is a wondrous place.

MONDAY, MAY 17

We had planned to do the third task assignment on the roof of Trump Tower that morning, but as it was foggy out, we would end up doing it in the lobby. The film crews had to reset, so I went up to my office to meet with Bill Rancic, who was reporting for his first day of work. We also had some people from *Dateline* to interview Bill, and Carolyn and George came in for a meeting.

Jim Dowd from NBC arrived, and we discussed the article in *The*

New York Times business section today on the NBC lineup for next fall; Jeff Zucker's promotion to run the entire television entertainment operation of the new media conglomerate, NBC Universal; and the success of *The Apprentice*. The article was comprehensive and well written by Bill Carter, a writer I admire. I may have my tiffs with *The New York Times,* but they've got some terrific people, including Maureen Dowd, Herbert Muschamp, and David Dunlap.

I noticed Jay Bienstock had a new haircut, and he told me that he'll be getting married in two weeks, so by then it would be just the way he likes it to look. Who says men don't plan ahead for important events? I congratulated him on a big decision, and we got to work discussing the task assignment for that day. Jay has already won one Emmy Award, and I suspect there's a lot more to come for him.

I made a call to Ed Molloy, took a call from Regis Philbin, and reviewed a few faxes that came in. Then it was time to go downstairs for the task assignment. We took the elevators to the mezzanine level, surprised a few Starbucks patrons as I walked by, and met Diane Dietz and Matt Barresi, general managers at Procter & Gamble, who would be judges for the outcome of the next task, which was to create and implement a highly visible promotional campaign for a new Crest vanilla mint toothpaste in New York City.

We descended to the lobby on the escalator and greeted the two teams. Each team would work with DeVries Public Relations on its campaign. The team that created the most effective buzz about Crest Vanilla Mint toothpaste, as judged by Procter & Gamble, would win. Each team would have $50,000 in seed money and until the next day at 4 P.M.

I went back up to my office to return calls to Regis Philbin and Phil Riordan of GE. Then I had a meeting with a group from Costas Kondylis's office about furniture for the golf clubhouse in Bedminster, New Jersey. I also had a quick meeting with Allen Weisselberg and Bernie Diamond.

After these meetings, Brian came in to tell me that my limousine was ready, so Melania and I were off to the red-carpet media extravaganza at Radio City for the NBC Upfronts. It took us close to an hour to get into the building because of the media and the crowds. Carolyn, George, and Bill Rancic also received a lot of attention. I saw Sly Stallone, Jeffrey Katzenberg, Matt LeBlanc, and some other friendly faces as we inched our way to the entrance.

Once inside, I was whisked away to my dressing room, where I had five minutes or so to prepare to open the show. Actually, Darrell Hammond opened the show as me, and then I appeared to set things straight. Darrell won me no brownie points by referring to Jeff Zucker as "Jake Zuckerman" and "Jack Zuckerstein," and referring to my hair as "the onion loaf hairstyle," which "I" intend to implement into the dress code when "I" eventually take over NBC.

Then I made my appearance, told Darrell he might have been funny the first few times, that I even enjoyed doing *Saturday Night Live* with him, but that he's just got to go. I had to admit that firing Darrell not only felt good but was a lot of fun. I was relieved when Jeff Zucker appeared onstage to hire *me*. NBC isn't stupid. Jeff then stated that "Jennifer Aniston has better hair than Donald, but Donald has better ratings."

I let Jeff Zucker take over the stage. Watching Jeff in action made me realize that NBC has a true dynamo in residence, the kind of partner I like to have. He noted that twelve of the top twenty shows were unscripted, so reality shows were no passing fancy. He also explained that for twenty years, Thursday nights on NBC have never been surpassed in ratings. In addition, since *The Apprentice* emerged, NBC now has a twenty-eight percent upscale viewer advantage over all other networks. *The Apprentice* was the phenomenon of the season—not only the highest-rated but *the* most upscale show on all of television.

The show continued with an overview of new programs to be

HOW ARISTIDE WAS REALLY DEPOSED:

introduced next season. The lineup included another reality show by Mark Burnett and Jeffrey Katzenberg called *The Contender*, which will star Sylvester Stallone and Sugar Ray Leonard. We also saw previews of another Jeffrey Katzenberg show, *Father of the Pride*, which will feature Siegfried and Roy and their white lions in animated form. We saw a taped interview from Hamburg with both Siegfried and Roy speaking about the new show. Roy has made a partial recovery, and everyone was happy to see him. This interview marked his first public appearance since the accident.

We also saw a preview of *Joey*, Matt LeBlanc's new series; Tom Brokaw appeared; and then Kevin Reilly, the incoming president of NBC Entertainment, closed the show. The Upfronts were intense, and I was impressed with NBC, its lineup, and the terrific presentation. Mark Burnett and I were very pleased with the statistics on *The Apprentice*, and we couldn't help but congratulate each other. Our anticipation for the new season had already been high, and by then it was even higher. Jeff Zucker pulled off a huge event with flying colors, and everyone had a lot of fun. All in all, it was a great afternoon.

But it wasn't over yet. We (meaning several thousand people) went over to Rockefeller Center for a cocktail reception and a photo session, followed by a dinner party for key people.

TUESDAY, MAY 18

We had the task resolution that afternoon for the third assignment, so I could put in close to a full day's work in the office. I returned the many calls I had received the day before, met with Sherman Boxer to go over some advertising campaigns for my properties, and then went over to Trump Park Avenue for a walk-through with John Myers, Phil Riordan, and Don, Jr. I went over my interview commitments, charity events, and review meeting and office updates. Sometimes I feel like I'm in a constant state of catching up, but I'm not complaining. This life's exciting.

I ordered one of those wonderful DT Burgers from the Trump Grill downstairs, and sure enough, Kevin Harris, like clockwork, showed up at my door at the same time as my lunch to brief me on the day's task resolution. He was wearing some kind of shoes that light up when he walks. If he weren't such an effective producer, I'd think he was a space cadet, to use an old but apt term. He ogled my hamburger, so I ordered one for him.

By the time we had finished our lunch, it was time to go down to DeVries Public Relations agency, where the task resolution was to be held. Both Procter & Gamble and DeVries were impressed with the ideas the teams had come up with. That said, the women's team was able to get the Mets' Mike Piazza to brush his teeth in Union Square on behalf of the product. They far outperformed the men's team. But performance isn't everything, and the women were disqualified due to a late budget. The next day's boardroom scene would not be a pleasant one.

WEDNESDAY, MAY 19

That morning I returned to my office to have a meeting with George Ross, where we discussed the events of yesterday's tumultuous task resolution. Minutes and seconds count, whether you're in the Olympics or in business. George mentioned the day's *New York Times* article on my Brazilian partner, Ricardo Bellino, in which Ricardo mentions how I gave him exactly three minutes to sell his idea to me in January 2003. We've been in business together ever since, and he may be bringing *The Apprentice* to Brazil in the near future. He's a good example for these aspiring apprentices of the value of time.

My *Playboy* interview with David Hochman was about to start, followed by a photo shoot. Richard Devinki of Mark Burnett's team stopped by for a minute to brief me on the day's schedule. He wanted to prepare me for the possibility of a long boardroom scene, considering the events of the day before. Richard is in charge of a crew of 275, and he is always calm, unassuming, and professional. I've noticed that Mark Burnett has a knack for finding the best people in the business.

After David Hochman was settled in my office, he began by telling me an interesting fact. In preparing for the interview, he had been given a stack of interviews and articles about me that was several feet high. He was stunned. It was more information than he had for Julia Roberts or Bruce Willis, or anyone else that he has ever interviewed.

We were interrupted a few times during the interview by calls and visits from my staff, but David is a pro and he took it professionally. I enjoyed talking with him. He's informed and easygoing. I told him that an odd thing to me is that it seems my overall image is better since *The Apprentice* started. People see another side of me, and even though I fire people every week on the show, they don't seem to mind. Maybe they can see that I make an effort to be fair. Who knows? It's still a mystery to me. I've always been the same.

After the interview, I ducked down to the fourth floor and met Carolyn and George to prepare for the third boardroom scene. I checked on the crew in the monitor room, and everyone was ready to go. If you've never been behind the scenes of a television show, you'd be surprised at how much goes into it and all the details we as viewers tend to take for granted.

I decided to check out the snack table to see what they had. Production crews have long hours, so nourishment is provided at all times. I don't know what a nutritionist would think of this layout, but it looked healthy enough to me. I even opened the refrigerator, which I was pleased to see was well stocked with Trump Ice water.

Then I spoke with Robin Himmler, from my staff, and asked her how these candidates differed from those from the first season, and she mentioned that they seemed much louder this time around. She could hear a lot of commotion coming from the boardroom. I also noticed that some of the male candidates had put their cards and phone numbers in her prop Rolodex on the set, which was nothing new. It happened last time, too, but she's good-natured and handles the attention well.

Jay Bienstock soon arrived, and we were ready to roll. This boardroom scene could become historic for its histrionics. It was a cross between a soap opera and a court of law. How could something so seemingly simple—a team that went over budget by about ten percent and disqualified itself for being late for a deadline—turn into such chaos?

The scene took a while. After I dismissed the team, except for three of the members, I learned that one of those three had alienated her team to a point where they felt they could not continue to work with her. I had no choice but to find out from the entire team what had actually transpired, so all the dismissed women were called back into the boardroom immediately.

We spent a lot of time talking about the events that were bothering the women and whether or not this person should be given another chance. Given the unanimous feelings of the rest of the team, I saw that I had to act decisively for the good of the show. The decision was serious and important. And difficult, but she had to go.

Afterward, Mark Burnett, Craig Plestis, and I discussed the intensity and length of the last two boardroom scenes, each of which had taken close to two hours. They were riveting to shoot, and the monitor room thought they were great television, so we decided there could be a Saturday-night episode that would feature the boardroom scene in its entirety. We left the set after a long night and set a meeting to discuss this idea further.

THURSDAY, MAY 20

At 9 A.M. I went downstairs to meet the Mark Burnett crew; we were going to meet the candidates at Jean Georges, the restaurant in the

Trump International Hotel and Tower, for the fourth task assignment. It was a perfect spring day in New York. We traveled over to the West Side and saw the seemingly never-ending construction at Columbus Circle. I'm not the only one who thinks the construction is endless: Regis did a comedy segment on his show about how this entire area had been in scaffolding and under demolition and construction for so long that when the scaffolding finally came down, people couldn't figure out what was different about their neighborhood, though they knew something was.

It has looked like a disaster zone for years. The traffic jams have been unbelievable, too, and we're talking years, not months. It's getting there, but it's been an ordeal for everyone. Fortunately, the Trump International Hotel & Tower has been spared this mess by its location, which is directly across from Central Park on Central Park itself, not on Broadway and Columbus Circle, like the Time Warner building. I still wonder whether the new tenants there are enjoying their view of my building. Location isn't always the most important consideration, but in instances like this, it can be.

Mark Burnett and I greeted Jean-Georges inside his restaurant as the apprentice candidates entered the formal dining room to await their next task assignment. This room is beautifully serene—so much so that everyone seemed uncharacteristically calm. Someone mentioned that the room is very much like a Milton Avery painting, which we agreed was a good observation.

Bill Rancic was also with us today. We decided it was fitting, the return of the original apprentice to the second season of the show. Bill mentioned that he cannot walk down the streets in Chicago without being mobbed. He is a big celebrity there, as it's his hometown. Apparently he has also been named the most eligible bachelor of the year. If any of this attention has gone to his head, we've seen no indication of it whatsoever.

Carolyn, Bill, and I entered the dining room, and I explained that since George Ross was away on business, Bill would be replacing him for this week. I also explained that they were standing in the highest-rated restaurant in New York City, which also happens to be in the highest-rated hotel. I also told them that Tim Zagat is a friend of mine, a great guy as well as a talented one, and his Zagat guides to restaurants are considered the bibles in the restaurant business. The name is just that powerful.

The Zagat guides include ratings by customers, and the editors compile all the information they receive, in addition to their own scouting, to come up with fair and insightful reviews that combine comments on food, service, decor, and ambiance. It's updated every year, so restaurants stay on top of their game.

Then we got to their task. We had two empty spaces that were to be made into restaurants. If the two teams couldn't decide who got which space, they would flip a coin. By the next night they would have to be serving food and bringing customers in from the street. In addition, someone from Zagat would be there, incognito, to review their work. I wished them well and gave the floor to Carolyn and Bill.

Both Carolyn and Bill mentioned that the two teams look "too well rested," and Bill informed them that it would only get worse from there on out—especially with this particular task assignment. Anyone who thinks running a restaurant looks like fun hasn't ever been in the restaurant business. The margin of failure is wide.

I went back into the front dining room and talked with Jean-Georges and Mark for a while. The other breakfast customers had adjusted to us by then and just carried on with their newspapers and conversations. It's amazing how quickly New Yorkers can adapt to anything. I headed back to my office.

A bit later, Kevin Harris arrived to take us out to my jet at La Guardia Airport for an inside shoot. When we arrived, it was hard not to miss it, with "TRUMP" printed on it in twenty-four-carat gold. Twenty-four-carat gold cannot be duplicated. It looks great, and if you're ever at La Guardia, be sure to keep an eye out for it—you can't miss it.

My pilot, Mike Donovan, greeted us, even though we wouldn't be flying anywhere that day. We went inside the aircraft to film a few scenes and shots, and while we waited for everyone to set up, Mike and I reminisced about the first time we met, ten years ago. He gave me permission to tell this story, in case it helps those people who have interview nerves.

Ten years ago, when I was looking to hire a pilot, Mike was invited to my office in Trump Tower to meet me. He bought a new suit, stopped at St. Patrick's Cathedral for good graces, and showed up at my office. We had been chatting a bit when suddenly Mike somersaulted off his chair and onto the floor. He just fell off his chair and disappeared from view. That made quite an impression; in fact, no one before or since has topped that performance. But Mike was sure that was the last time he'd ever see me. Needless to say, he was wrong. He was the right guy—just a little nervous. He's kept my jet on balance for ten straight years.

Once the crew had set up, we did a few takes in the jet. It didn't take too long, but it was about eighty degrees out that day and we had to turn off the air-conditioning because of the noise level. Additionally, every time another jet took off or landed, we had to stop and wait for the noise to subside. We finally finished and did a few shots outside. Then it was back into the limousine.

I was accompanied by Matthew John, the director of photography, who was nominated for an Emmy for his camera work the first season. He's been with Mark Burnett for eight years and is a quiet and professional guy. I asked him which was easier, the first season of *The Apprentice* or this time around. He said the first show was easier in the sense that we had a certain anonymity that's not possible now. On the other hand, we can perform bigger tasks, since we are a proven entity. Trying to carry things out incognito is not as easy now, because people know the show to be a hit. But we have the biggest companies wanting to be a part of it, whereas before it was a risk for them. Matthew also explained that there was a minimum of fourteen camera crews working a twenty-four-hour staggered schedule every day for forty-six days to cover the action involved with the show.

I asked him about the inevitable spin-offs and mentioned that I'd seen Richard Branson on television talking about his show. I like Richard Branson a lot, and his show looks interesting and not too similar. Then we got on the subject of Mark Cuban. I have to say that right after he lost in the play-offs, I felt bad for him. But nobody's going to beat *The Apprentice*.

Before long, we were back at Trump Tower, and I told Matthew I was sure to see him again soon. There was a crowd in front of Trump Tower, so I ducked out of the limousine and made a run for it to the door.

FRIDAY, MAY 21

Believe it or not, I had a day off from *The Apprentice*. This time off would be a rare occasion in our forty-six-day shoot schedule. In the morning I gave the commencement address at Wagner College on Staten Island and received an honorary doctorate.

I told the graduates that they already have what it takes to succeed. They have achieved, and they've been given, the tools necessary for success. All they have to do is apply themselves one hundred percent every single day to their endeavors and remain tenacious until they're 102 years old, if necessary. There's something exciting about graduations, and I enjoyed this one in particular.

After tending to some business in my office, I prepared myself to introduce Jessica Simpson at Madison Square Garden later that night. It was a pleasure. Melania accompanied me.

SATURDAY, MAY 22

We had a 9 A.M. call in Trump Tower for the resolution of the restaurant assignment. I took the elevator down and met Carolyn Kepcher and Bill Rancic. We were looking forward to seeing what had been accomplished by the two teams.

The women's team earned a combined Zagat rating of fifty-seven, while the men received a rating of sixty-one. They were rated in three categories: food, decor, and service. The descriptive portion of the ratings said the women appeared to be "uptight stewardesses," while the men were "hot eye-candy waiters," plus they scored higher in decor and service than the women. For once it appears that the men beat out the women in sex appeal, and once again the men's team won. Their prize was a great one: They would get to go over to Rudy Giuliani's new office at Times Square and have a discussion with the man himself.

Ducking the crowds outside of Trump Tower proved to be another highlight of a busy morning, but we were beginning to get used to it. I even rolled down my window and waved. Noel, my driver, is all business, however, and he cut the episode short. We took off down Fifth Avenue.

After the article came out describing me as the Elvis of Business, my security team took to saying "Elvis is leaving the building" whenever I was on my way out. I was sure Noel was behind that, so I asked him to put the word out to stop those announcements. They did. Now they say "Mr. Trump is leaving the building" instead.

We arrived at Rudy's offices high above Times Square, an area that is now thriving due to Rudy's vigilance and foresight, and we were met by Rudy and his lovely wife, Judith. I made a brief introduction and then left the rest to Rudy. True to form, he generously gave over an hour of his undivided attention to the candidates and their questions, and then gave them a tour of the mementos in his office, such as the Wilkinson sword given to him by Queen Elizabeth II when he was knighted, and a painting of St. Paul's Chapel, near the World Trade Center, which served as a refuge for the rescue workers and remained miraculously unscathed during the terrorist attack in 2001.

After hearing about the candidates' restaurant assignment, Rudy told them that the toughest job he's ever had was being a waiter; that as a young man, he had wanted to be either a priest or a doctor; that he was initially a poor public speaker, which he finally remedied by backing away from the podium and his notes and just talking to the audience; that he sees business leadership and political leadership as being the same; that he has a sign on his desk that reads "I'm Responsible"; and that he thinks leaders are made, not born, but, of course, you have to be born first.

His advice to the candidates was to find a good role model, a great example in life. For him, Joe DiMaggio was one, because he led by example. So was Winston Churchill, whom he used as a model when he was a student and also when he was mayor, for the simple reason that Churchill knew how to focus and would concentrate on the *solution* of a problem rather than the problem itself. Rudy also believes you can train yourself to be an optimist.

Pamela asked about women leaders he has admired, and Rudy mentioned Margaret Thatcher and Golda Meir. He also advised the group to find out what's really important to them first, to know their own core, and to get on top of every day before it gets on top of them. Being mayor of New York City taught him that one. If one inch of snow fell, he would receive calls because the plows weren't out yet. You can't plow one inch of snow, but don't try to tell New Yorkers that.

After the discussion, all the candidates asked him questions, and he signed books for them and walked them to the elevator. What a memorable morning they had with one of the great men of our time. We thank Rudy for that.

We had a break until 6 P.M., so I decided to drive up to Trump National Golf Club in Briarcliff Manor to check things out and get in a round of golf. It was a humid day, but the course was looking lush and inviting. I love having my own golf courses to play on.

By 6 P.M. we were back for the boardroom scene, featuring the women's team, who lost in the Zagat rating. Bill, Carolyn, and I talked about our afternoon, and then it was back to business as usual. Funny how doing a television show about business has actually become business to us.

I began by mentioning how Rudy Giuliani spoke about leadership to the men's team, and how that seems to be lacking among the women. Even the women admitted the men's team exhibited solidarity and camaraderie lacking among themselves. This particular boardroom scene was an easy call because the leader did not display leadership qualities, and she refused to call into the boardroom the person who had lost $2,000 for the team. A bad call on her part, and even Carolyn had to say that this group of women made her embarrassed as a businesswoman. During the boardroom scene, I remember thinking that I hoped they could pull it together, and soon.

We were finished by 8 P.M., and Melania was making dinner tonight, so we headed upstairs for a relaxing evening at home. Tomorrow, after the task assignment, I would be the grand marshal in the Salute to Israel Parade on Fifth Avenue, so it would be a busy and exciting day. I would be walking in the parade with Howard Lorber and the New York Board of Rabbis. I've always enjoyed parades, and this parade would be a special one.

I have to sign off on *The Apprentice* coverage now, as I don't want to ruin the show by giving you too much information prior to airing. I hope you've enjoyed the background information, and I hope you will tune in and watch for yourself these amazing episodes. As much as I like to write, I can't imagine writing a script for drama like this. Just seeing it unfold every day is as surprising as it is entertaining, and I hope I've given you an idea of what it's like behind the scenes. Enjoy the show, and stay tuned. I can guarantee you'll learn a few things.

Acknowledgments

Like my previous book, *How to Get Rich,* this book never would have happened without the hard work and help of Meredith McIver. Also, Norma Foerderer, who manages my schedule, kept this project on schedule.

Thanks to the people at Random House, particularly editor Ben Loehnen, who did a terrific job under deadline pressure and has the mind of a first-rate capitalist; editor in chief Jonathan Karp and publisher Gina Centrello, who made sure Random House paid me an even bigger fortune for this book and provided valuable editorial direction; associate publishers Anthony Ziccardi and Elizabeth McGuire; executive director of publicity Carol Schneider; director of publicity Thomas Perry; associate director of publicity Elizabeth Fogarty; associate editor Jonathan Jao; art director Gene Mydlowski; managing editor Benjamin Dreyer; production chief Lisa Feuer; design director Carole Lowenstein; production manager Richard Elman; production editor Janet Wygal; copy editor Ginny Carroll; advertising director Magee Finn; rights directors Claire Tisne and Rachel Bernstein; and everyone in the Random House sales force, which remains the best in the business. Special thanks to Donald M. Karp, of Independence Community Bank, and Sean Compton, of Clear Channel.

At the Trump Organization, I am surrounded by professionals: Matthew Calamari, Allen Weisselberg, George Ross, Bernie Diamond, Jason Greenblatt, Rhona Graff, Tony Morace, Andy Weiss, Don, Jr., Jeff, Eric, Robin, and many more.

Meredith McIver would like to thank Richard Casares, Steve Palitz, Tassos of Patmos, Chris Papanikolas, her family, Mark Burnett's team, and the members of the Trump Organization, especially Rhona Graff, Robin Himmler, and Renee St. Jean. A very special thank-you to Norma Foerderer for her generosity, to Melania Knauss for her kind assistance, and, as always, to Donald Trump for being himself.

Behind the Scenes
at The Trump Organization

ABOUT THE AUTHORS

DONALD J. TRUMP is the very definition of the American success story, continually setting standards of excellence while expanding his interests in real estate, gaming, sports, and entertainment. In 2003, he partnered with NBC and executive producer Mark Burnett on *The Apprentice,* which became a smash hit, the highest-rated debut of the season. He and the network are also partners in the ownership and broadcast rights for the three largest beauty competitions in the world.

In New York City, the Trump signature is synonymous with the most prestigious addresses, including the renowned Trump Tower, the Trump International Hotel & Tower, and the soon-to-be converted Delmonico Hotel at Park Avenue and Fifty-ninth Street (Trump Park Avenue). In the gaming arena, The Trump Organization is one of the world's largest operators of hotels and casinos, most notably in Atlantic City, New Jersey, as well as Trump National Golf Club in Briarcliff Manor, New York, and other great courses throughout the United States.

Mr. Trump is the number one *New York Times* bestselling author of *The Art of the Deal, Surviving at the Top,* and *The Art of the Comeback,* as well as *The America We Deserve.* All told, these books have sold millions of copies.

An ardent philanthropist, Mr. Trump is involved with numerous civic and charitable organizations. In June 2000, he received his greatest honor, the Hotel and Real Estate Visionary of the Century award, given by the UJA Federation.

For more information on Donald Trump and The Trump Organization, go to www.trumponline.com.

MEREDITH MCIVER was a Ford Foundation scholar and is a graduate of the University of Utah. She lives on the Upper West Side of Manhattan and is a member of The Trump Organization.

ABOUT THE TYPE

This book was set in Galliard, a typeface designed by Matthew Carter for the Mergenthaler Linotype Company in 1978. Galliard is based on the sixteenth-century typefaces of Robert Granjon.